D1321155

Abberline

THE MAN WHO HUNTED
JACK THE RIPPER

PETER THURGOOD

The
History
Press

First published 2013

The History Press
The Mill, Brimscombe Port
Stroud, Gloucestershire, GL5 2QG
www.thehistorypress.co.uk

British Library Cataloguing in Publication Data.
A catalogue record for this book is available from the British Library.

ISBN 978 0 7524 8810 3
Typesetting and origination by The History Press
Printed in Great Britain

Contents

Foreword

The name Frederick George Abberline, later to become Detective Inspector Abberline, has become synonymous with the Whitechapel murders, particularly those attributed to 'Jack the Ripper'.

Indeed, the murders have been shrouded by controversy from day one. We have been led to believe that Jack's reign of terror spread like wildfire through the streets of London; that the population were too scared to leave their houses at night. *The Star* newspaper wrote an editorial in September 1888, stating the following:

> London lies today under the spell of a great terror. A nameless reprobate – half beast, half man – is at large. The ghoul-like creature who stalks through the streets of London, staking [sic] down his victim like a Pawnee Indian, is simply drunk with blood and he will have more.

At the time of *The Star*'s editorial being published, the second murder attributed to the Ripper had only just taken place, and considering that murders were not exactly scarce in London at this time, these two did not score as being very significant to London's crime figures, apart from the fact of their ferociousness. We need to bear in mind here that this 'ghoul-like creature' who was said to be 'stalking the streets of London' and casting his spell of terror upon ordinary Londoners had, in fact, only been in existence for just over one week.

The press at this time intimated that women were not safe in the streets, that people were hiding in their homes, too afraid to venture out after dark, and that bodies were being found scattered throughout the streets of London. The truth, however, was much simpler; two women had been murdered in the Whitechapel area of London, thus causing some panic, if any, in that area alone, and certainly not causing people to lock themselves in their homes.

From 31 August 1888, when the first victim, Mary Ann 'Polly' Nichols, was discovered, to 9 November that same year, when the body of Marie Jeanette

Kelly was found in her room, a total of just five Ripper murders had taken place, over a period of ten weeks. All five Ripper victims were mutilated and dispatched with a grizzly precision, their throats slit and their entrails removed and displayed, almost in a sacrificial manner by someone with what has since been described as a considerable amount of anatomical knowledge.

If we are to believe this more reasoned version of the series of events that became known as the Jack the Ripper murders, then we must also discount the sensationalist reports of the press at the time, who much like their counterparts of today, would do almost anything to sell their newspapers. Their reports of a crazed madman terrorising a whole city and haphazardly butchering women on the streets is pure sensationalism carried out by journalists in order to make money.

Within hours of the first murder, letters started pouring into the press offices, and by the time of the last murder, more than 250 of them had arrived in the in-trays of the popular press, and all purporting to have come from the killer. It was in a letter received by the Central News Agency on 27 September 1888 that the name Jack the Ripper was first used. This letter was originally believed to be just another hoax, but three days later, the double murders of Stride and Eddowes made the police reconsider, especially once they learned a portion of Eddowes' earlobe was found cut off from the body, eerily reminiscent of a promise made within the letter. The police deemed the 'Dear Boss' letter important enough to reproduce in newspapers and post-bills of the time, hoping someone would recognise the handwriting.

The image that was being popularised by the press was one of a blood-thirsty killer stalking women at random through the dimly lit streets of the East End, before ripping them to pieces for no apparent reason other than to satisfy his blood lust. From the letters that arrived on the editors' desks, however, it is clear that although a few of them must have come from isolated cranks intent on generating a lurid terror in those that read them, many more were written by genuinely concerned members of the public. The character of Jack the Ripper nevertheless remains a paradox. His letters purport to come from a rough-and-ready 'working-class man' who had learned his writing skills in a 'national school', but their contents are cleverly headline-seeking, and the astuteness with which they were targeted, suggest that the senders came from a different stratum of society. As George R. Sims, the successful author and playwright, wrote in *The Sunday Referee* newspaper, in October 1888:

> How many among you, my dear readers, would have hit upon the idea of 'The Central News' as a receptacle for your confidence? You might have sent your joke to the Telegraph, The Times, any morning or evening paper, but I will lay long odds that it would never have occurred to you to communicate with

a Press agency. Curious, is it not, that this maniac makes his communication to an agency which serves the entire press?

Sims was by no means alone in suspecting that the authors of many of the letters, certainly of those purporting to come from the Ripper himself, were in all probability educated and worldly men who were fostering a reign of terror to underline their own political agenda.

From the first body found, there were rumours that the highest in the land were involved in the killings. As *The Star* wrote in November 1888:

> We have heard the wildest stories ... it is believed by people who pass among their neighbours as sensible folk that the Government do not want the murderer to be convicted, that they are interested in concealing his identity.

Could this be true? Inspector Abberline certainly didn't think so. He was appointed to the case on 1 September 1888, which was the day after Polly Nichols' disembowelled body had been found on 31 August 1888 lying on the ground in front of a gated stable entrance in Buck's Row, Whitechapel.

Abberline worked on the Ripper case during its entirety, though unfortunately never procuring a conviction. It is this case that people know him for, but during the course of his career he did head up other investigations that resulted in much better outcomes than the Ripper case did.

1

The Cleveland Street Scandal

July 1889 was one of the hottest Julys on record. Office staff at the City of London Police headquarters at 26 Old Jewry had been given special dispensation, allowing them to work in their shirt sleeves; probably a first for this period in time, but not something carried forward to uniformed police officers. Even though Sir James Fraser was the Commissioner of the City of London Police, he did not receive any different treatment on this particular ruling than his uniformed officers. Sir James wasn't an easy man to get on with at the best of times: an ex-military man who was used to issuing commands and having them obeyed without question, something that didn't quite work in the same way in the city police force. He was also used to having his every comfort taken care of by his own personal batman; again, something sorely missing in his new post.

It came then as no surprise to his subordinates when he went absolutely berserk, after opening a letter addressed personally to him from Scotland Yard telling him to deal with a case regarding a series of alleged thefts from the London Central Telegraph Office, in St Martin's le Grand. 'Who the hell do these people think they are dealing with?' he bellowed. 'This is nothing more than a case of petty theft, I am the Commissioner, God damn it.' He threw the letter across the room to the sergeant who had just delivered it, and told him to deal with it. The sergeant had seen Sir James in one of his moods before on several occasions, and knew instinctively when not to say anything; he just scooped the letter up, mumbled a brief 'yes sir' and left the room.

Police Constable Luke Hanks was on desk duty when the sergeant approached him and gave him his orders to go to the London Central Telegraph Office, where he was to be in charge of this investigation. The amounts of money, the sergeant told him, were believed to be mainly small sums, but added together they could become a considerable amount. 'If you handle this correctly,' the sergeant said, 'it could lead to promotion, so get over there and be thorough in your investigation.'

PC Hanks couldn't wait to get out of the heat of the office, and the thought of being in charge of his own case, with possible promotion at the end of it, prompted him to move quicker than he had done for years.

One hour later, Hanks, with his note pad and pencil at the ready, was at the London Central Telegraph Office being shown into a room, which had been allocated to him to work and take statements. The room was not much bigger than a broom cupboard, with a tiny desk, two upright wooden chairs and one small window, set so high on the wall behind him that he could not see out of it, let alone reach it in order to open it. Hanks nevertheless entered into his work with gusto, and by midday he had interviewed and taken statements from at least twenty workers. Not only did Hanks carry out his work with verve and vigour, but he also stuck strictly to the rules regarding police dress code, meaning that he kept his heavy serge tunic buttoned to the neck and his large and cumbersome helmet on his head the whole time he was conducting the interviews. By the afternoon, however, the heat generated by the close proximity of the interviewees and PC Hanks, in such a small room, became more than he could bear. He was not, after all, a very young man: fast approaching 50, and with a little more body weight to carry around than he was prepared to admit.

No one from his station was likely to turn up, so at 4 p.m., Hanks decided to take a chance and take off both his tunic and helmet, along with a few pounds in weight which he had possibly shed as well. The heat, however, was still unbearable, even though he was working in his shirtsleeves, so while waiting for the next interviewee, he climbed up on to the desktop and wrestled with the catch on the small window, finally managing to ease it open slightly. The first draft of air that drifted through the open space was wonderful, cooling him down almost immediately, but along with the air, came something else: a smell so foul it almost caused him to vomit; for what he hadn't known was that immediately outside this room was the stabling yard for the Telegraph Office's horses. No wonder the window had been set high into the wall and kept closed. Needless to say, Hanks closed the window immediately, and preferred to sweat it out rather than try to open it again.

Weather-wise, the second day wasn't very different from the first, and as there was no way he was going to have the window open again, Hanks decided to try to speed things up a little. Instead of just taking formal statements, which was very slow and laborious, he insisted on each staff member supplying a written statement, which would include all their personal details, as well as all monetary transactions they had dealt with in the last two weeks. Each interviewee then had to empty their pockets out on to the desk, where Hanks would make a note of the exact amount each person had on them. Younger members of staff, who were employed as telegraph boys, were strictly forbidden to carry any personal money on them in the course of their duties, purely to prevent any confusion as to whether such money could be classed as their own or the customer's. This, of course, helped Hanks out a lot, especially when he called the next boy, Charles Thomas Swinscow, into the room, and asked him to empty his pockets on to the desk. Hanks was more than surprised to see the princely sum of 14s, which was approximately four weeks' wages at that time, or around £400 today.

A look of satisfaction spread over Hanks' face, as he stood up and started putting his tunic and helmet back on, which had been hanging on a hook behind the door. He felt that, at long last, he was getting somewhere with his investigation, and there was no better way to impress the young, and the gullible, than to confront them with authority; the overall look of his complete uniform would, he was sure, do exactly that.

'How would you feel about spending the next ten years of your life locked up in a prison cell?' he asked the young lad. Within minutes, the boy had broken down and was pleading with PC Hanks not to imprison him. He hadn't stolen this money at all, he had earned it, he said. Hanks, however, begged to differ, pointing out that he would have had to work for a whole month to get such a large amount as this. He gave the lad an ultimatum: either say where the money had really come from or he would place him under arrest and charge him with theft.

Charles Swinscow was still in his early teens, and was almost at breaking point. The very thought of imprisonment would probably kill his mother, he said, let alone what it would do to him. He begged PC Hanks for mercy, saying he would tell him all he knew, if he promised not to gaol him. Hanks told the boy to calm down; if he started talking, he would do everything he could to help him.

Swinscow blurted out how he came by the money: he hadn't stolen it, but had earned it from a man named Charles Hammond, for supplying services at his premises at 19 Cleveland Street, in neighbouring Fitzrovia. 'Services,' said Hanks, 'is a very vague word, would you care to elaborate?' The young Swinscow squirmed in his chair, his face starting to redden, and his voice lowered a tone as he explained that the 'services' he had provided were in the form of male prostitution for clients that Charles Hammond provided at his premises. He went on to say that he was introduced to Hammond by 18-year-old Henry Newlove, who worked as a General Post Office clerk. In addition to this, he named two 17-year-old telegraph boys, George Alma Wright and Charles Ernest Thickbroom, who also rented out their services to Hammond.

PC Hanks quickly realised that he was on to something much bigger here than petty theft from the Central Telegraph Office; for at this period in time, all homosexual acts between men, as well as procurement or attempted procurement of such acts, were strictly against the law, and punishable by varying terms of imprisonment. With this in mind, Hanks obtained corroborating statements from both Wright and Thickbroom. Once armed with these, it was much easier to squeeze a confession out of Newlove, which included him dropping several well-known names into the equation, probably in the hope of being seen as someone who was willing to help the police in every way he could. Amongst those named were Lord Arthur Somerset, who was the head of the Prince of Wales' stables; Henry FitzRoy, Earl of Euston; and an army colonel by the name of Jervois. Newlove agreed that all these men were regular visitors to the Cleveland Street address, but said it was more than his life was worth to state this in writing.

PC Hanks began to realise that what he had stumbled upon here was probably a matter of great, maybe even national, importance, for these men were connected to royalty. When his superiors saw his report they would undoubtedly recognise the excellent manner in which he had handled the case so far, and hand him the much-wanted promotion that he so desired. This was what PC Hanks hoped for, and indeed expected when he presented his findings, along with the statements and confessions that he had obtained from the boys. But instead of the recognition that he craved for, all he received was an obligatory nod and a smile, coupled with 'Well done Constable Hanks'. His superiors deemed the case far too important for them to handle on their own, and immediately passed it over to Scotland Yard, thus ending PC Hanks' dream of obtaining promotion and the possible fame and money that went with it. He was immediately detailed to forget about the Cleveland Street scandal, as it became known, and to continue his work, in the miserable little office backing on to the stables, regarding the alleged thefts at the Central Telegraph Office.

Sir James Monro, was greatly worried by the names listed in Hanks' original report, which were allegedly connected to the Cleveland Street case. There was no doubt in his mind that the case needed thorough investigation, but at the same time, he also felt that it needed to be handled in a very restrained manner. He feared if the press discovered such people as Lord Somerset, with his royal connections, might be involved, as well as the other names and their political implications, it could bring down not just the government, but possibly the royal family as well.

Monro knew that he had to tread very carefully indeed with this case; he needed a top officer in charge, but not one who would bring too much publicity along with him. The obvious first choice was Melville Macnaghten, whom he had great faith in, and whom he had earlier offered the post of first chief constable in the Metropolitan Police. This appointment, however, never came to fruition, as it was opposed by Charles Warren, who at this time, was London's Commissioner of Police. It seemed that Warren and Monro had never had a great affinity to each other, which only succeeded in Warren's rejection of Macnaghten, or probably anyone who Monro suggested.

With this ongoing rift between Monro and Warren, Monro decided to go for what some say he saw as a soft option: a name that everyone would recognise, but without any of the controversies attached that a more senior officer such as Macnaghten would possibly bring to the case with him. He announced, without delay, the appointment of Inspector First Class Frederick George Abberline to the case. Abberline had previously worked at Scotland Yard for almost a year, until September 1888, when he, along with several other officers, were drafted into H Division, Whitechapel, East London, working on the infamous Jack the Ripper case. Abberline's move to East London came just after the disembowelled body of Mary Ann Nichols was discovered lying in the gutter of Buck's Row, Whitechapel. Nichols was allegedly the first Jack the Ripper victim. I use the word 'allegedly' as there were eleven separate murders dating from 3 April 1888 to 13 February 1891, all of which were included in the London Metropolitan Police Service investigation. They were known collectively in the police files as the 'Whitechapel murders'.

Only five of these murders, however, are counted today as definitive Jack the Ripper murders. The other six were kept separate, thus making a clear distinction between those of Jack the Ripper and those committed by a person or persons unknown. The murders were considered far too complex for the local Whitechapel H Division CID, headed by Detective Inspector Edmund Reid, to handle alone; which is why Scotland Yard were drafted in, and the name of Inspector Frederick Abberline became forever synonymous with that of Jack the Ripper.

Frederick George Abberline was 46 years old at this time, and had been in the police force for twenty-six years. Described as medium height and build, with dark brown, thinning hair and a friendly disposition, he sometimes walked with a slight limp, especially during the summer months, due to a varicose vein on his left leg.

Inspector Abberline wasted no time in organising the team appointed to him by Sir James Monro. He was determined to bring this case to a speedy conclusion. Armed with all the evidence acquired by PC Hanks, he quickly obtained two arrest warrants, the first being for the arrest of Charles Hammond, the owner of the brothel on Cleveland Street, and the second being for the arrest of 18-year-old Henry Newlove, who acted as a procurer for Hammond. The crimes they were to be charged with were for the violation of Section 11 of the Criminal Law Amendment Act 1885. The law made all homosexual acts between men, as well as procurement or attempted procurement of such acts, punishable by up to two years, imprisonment with or without hard labour.

Abberline and two of his officers arrived at 19 Cleveland Street, at precisely 6 a.m. the following day, a time when most people were still in bed and an easy arrest almost a certainty. Abberline grasped the huge iron door knocker and banged it repeatedly as loudly as he could against the door. The two officers beside him stood with their truncheons drawn, ready to charge into the house the moment the door was opened, but unfortunately it never was; the occupants had long since flown the coop.

Had someone tipped the occupants off? With so many high-profile names involved, this theory certainly couldn't be ruled out. Abberline's priority at this time was to get into the house and carry out a thorough search to see if any clues had been left. In order to do this, however, he either needed someone to actually let him in or, failing that, he needed a search warrant, which would probably take another twenty-four hours to obtain. Applying for a search warrant would not only delay his investigation, it might also warn his opponents, if they didn't already know, as to exactly what he was up to. He made his decision, and rightly or wrongly, told his officers to put their shoulders to the door and smash it down if necessary.

A few minutes later, Abberline and his men were inside the house, which looked very much as if the previous occupants had left in quite a hurry, with books scattered the floor, small pieces of furniture overturned, and vases and crockery smashed and broken. The larger pieces of furniture, such as beds, bookcases and armchairs, had been left, but little else. The lounge, which was elaborately decorated with red velvet flock wallpaper, a crystal chandelier and two plush day beds, was also bereft of any personal effects. After about an hour searching from room to room and not finding anything that might possibly give him a lead, Inspector Abberline decided to leave the premises. He paused for a moment by the street door, where he noticed a side table with a vase standing on it. The vase had a Chinese pattern and square base, and was exactly the same as one his parents had when he was a boy. Underneath the base, however, was something else. He discovered it to be a small black book, and a quick glance through showed it to contain addresses, which might prove valuable to his investigation. He didn't have time to look at it in detail, so he stuffed it into his pocket and left.

Abberline knew that if he was to succeed in this case, he needed to make an arrest very quickly, as someone seemed to be one step ahead of him and relaying his moves before he made them. Leaving one officer to secure and guard the premises, Abberline hailed a hansom cab and hurried off with the second officer to Camden Town. He knew from the witnesses' statements that

Newlove's mother lived here, and Henry Newlove sometimes stayed there when he was not with Hammond at the Cleveland Street house.

The driver stopped his cab at the end of a narrow alley, explaining that this was the address but it was too narrow for him to drive down. Camden Town at this time was known for its slums, and this alley, which didn't even have a name exhibited anywhere, was certainly no exception. The tiny, two-up, two-down houses, many of which had broken windows and doors that looked like they were hanging off their hinges, didn't look fit to house animals, let alone human beings. Abberline recognised Mrs Newlove's house by the number 9, which had been drawn in chalk upon the brickwork beside the door.

From another house, somewhere along the street, he could hear the sound of a baby crying, but there wasn't any sound coming from Newlove's house. One of the officers peered in through the small window beside the door, and told Abberline that it looked like someone was still asleep in a bed. By now it was 8.45 a.m., a time when most people would be out at work. However, in this particular area of London, work wasn't a word that rolled easily off the average citizen's tongue.

A few loud knocks at the door usually did the trick, and got even the deepest of sleepers out of bed. As there was no knocker on this door, Abberline did his best to wake the house by pounding and kicking at it, only to find that it swung open of its own volition, having no lock as well as no knocker.

Abberline pushed the door open and called into the house, asking if anyone was there. A door to his right opened and Mrs Newlove appeared, holding a piece of grubby-looking material around her, probably one of the bed sheets. 'Who are you?' she screamed. 'What do you want here?' Abberline told her he was a police officer and he wanted to question her son. Mrs Newlove quickly moved in front of him, barring his way to the stairs, as she told him her son wasn't there. Not exactly the best way of convincing a detective not to look on the upper floor. Abberline shook his head in disbelief as he told one officer to stay by the door and the other to follow him up the stairs, pushing Mrs Newlove aside as they did so.

There were two doors at the top of the stairs, both leading to tiny rooms with beds in each of them. The first room looked like it was also used as some sort of storeroom, piled high with what looked like second-hand clothes or rags. The second room contained just a bed and a wardrobe. The bed was unmade, but still warm to the touch, meaning they had found the right room and Henry Newlove had only just vacated it. A quick glance around also showed the most likely place for young Newlove to be hiding. Abberline nodded to his officer, who quickly drew his truncheon, as Abberline flung the wardrobe door open to reveal a very frightened youth, standing naked and trying to hide his dignity behind an old overcoat, the only item of clothing in there. Abberline pulled the bedclothes off the bed to see Newlove's trousers and shirt that he had tried to hide. Throwing the clothes at Newlove, he told him to get dressed, and that he was under arrest.

Newlove was taken back to Scotland Yard, where he was formally charged and further questioned. During his questioning, he admitted that that he had warned Hammond, who had immediately locked up the Cleveland Street house and fled the scene to somewhere on the continent. This, he said, was after the initial police investigation into the missing money at the Central Telegraph Office, and the subsequent details of the Cleveland Street affair coming out.

When asked why he had warned Hammond, Newlove replied that his father had left him and his mother when he was just a child, and that Hammond had been like a father to him. Abberline didn't answer Newlove on this, as he did feel sorry for anyone brought up in such circumstances, but as he later discussed with a work colleague, 'Fathers don't sleep with their sons, or sell their bodies to other men either'.

Whatever Abberline's real feelings, he was still furious that his main witness had managed to escape so easily in this manner. If he could lose Hammond like this, it was possible other participants in this case could also escape the net, and he would be made to look a complete fool. As much as he didn't like threatening witnesses, especially young and vulnerable lads of Newlove's age, he didn't see that he had any alternative. He threatened the young Newlove with practically everything he could think of, from life in prison to whipping, and even hanging, if he did not start co-operating and naming names. Unorthodox it may have been, but within hours, Newlove had made a fresh statement with a list of names that filled up nearly four pages. Most of the names were of unknown members of the public, but amongst them were some that stood out like proverbial sore thumbs, including Lord Arthur Somerset and the Earl of Euston, who were without a doubt no ordinary members of the public. Lord Somerset was the third son of the Eighth Duke of Beaufort, a much-decorated major in the Royal Horse Guards, and equerry to the Prince of Wales and superintendent of his stables. The Earl of Euston was the eldest son of the Seventh Duke of Grafton and a prominent Freemason.

The naming of Somerset and the Earl of Euston by Newlove was exactly what Abberline needed; there could be no case worth proceeding without such names. Even though the Cleveland Street house was now closed, he was sure that there would be some customers who were unaware of this. His next step was to post surveillance teams of undercover officers to watch the Cleveland Street address, and take notes and descriptions of everyone who tried to gain access there. During the next few weeks, Abberline's team noted the comings and goings of a great number of potential customers to the address, as well as their descriptions, times of arrival and departure etc. They also noted, with some glee, many of the visitors' visible disappointment when they found the premises closed.

Inspector Abberline was still smarting from the fact that he had not managed to solve the Jack the Ripper murders just a few months earlier. It was probably this fact, more than anything else, that drove him relentlessly to do his best to bring swift justice to the Cleveland Street case.

Detectives in those days, just as today, worked very closely with their informants, and within days a reliable source came up with some very important information regarding Hammond's whereabouts. Hammond was now living quite openly in Paris.

Armed with yet another arrest warrant, a very determined Inspector Abberline boarded the next steamer to France and made his way to Paris, where he contacted the French Sûreté, in the hope of securing their co-operation in extraditing Hammond. The one thing that Abberline had overlooked, however, was that he knew absolutely no French at all. Like most people at that time, and probably more now, he expected them to speak English. Whether the officials he met in Paris could or could not speak his chosen language is open to debate, but whatever it was, they certainly were not prepared to co-operate with the English detective.

During the two days he was there, the only development he made was by way of a severe case of gastroenteritis, which he put down to the 'horrible foreign food' he was forced to eat. What he didn't know at the time, however, was that Hammond had left Paris the very night that he had arrived, and had made his way to Belgium, from where he then escaped to America. In other words, 'someone' must have tipped him off that Abberline was hot on his trail. Who this someone was, we will probably never know!

A very angry and frustrated Inspector Abberline returned to London, refusing point blank to speak to reporters, who by this time had started to get a whiff that something important was going on, as by now, his team at Scotland Yard had arrested several other telegraph boys and were holding them for questioning. Any reporter worth his salt knew, without a doubt, that they would not do this if it were just in connection with petty theft from the Central Telegraph Office. Unbeknown to the reporters, and it seems everyone else apart from the investigating team, more of those arrested had now also made statements, and named Somerset as a regular visitor to 19 Cleveland Street.

Abberline was getting fed up with chasing suspects, who were, in his eyes, obviously being tipped off by some mysterious third party, so he decided to proceed with the prosecutions on the evidence that he and his team had collected thus far. Two days later he presented his case to Sir James Monro against Hammond, the telegraph boys who acted as his willing accomplices, and a variety of gentlemen whom the boys had named. Monro seemed more than happy with the prospective prosecution, which had done exactly what he wanted, taking the case forward whilst excluding the really big names. Monro was sure that this would ingratiate him with his superiors, or so he thought, because when he decided to go ahead with the prosecution, he was suddenly faced with a solid wall of resistance.

The Home Secretary demanded to see the notes on the investigation and within hours, threw them back at Monro, telling him that the case was very weak indeed, and in his opinion should be dropped forthwith. When Monro and Abberline both appealed against this, the Home Secretary was joined by the Attorney General and the Lord Chancellor, and if that wasn't enough, the Prime Minister, Lord Salisbury himself, also joined in the chorus of disapproval.

When Inspector Abberline was informed of this decision, he was absolutely furious and suggested to Monro that they should ignore these dissenters and go ahead with their case against Somerset and his cohorts; they had a strong case as far as he was concerned, with witness statements to back it up. Monro, however, had already been warned of the political implications right from the start, and even though he felt as strongly as Abberline on the issue, he also knew that his job could possibly be in jeopardy if he did not toe the line on this case.

During the following few weeks, friction mounted even more, as Abberline allegedly threatened to resign from the police force if the case was going to be swept under the political carpet, as he put it. One of the main reasons that Monro had inducted Abberline into the Cleveland Street case, apart from him being an excellent detective, was because he thought he was going to be an easy ride, a yes-man, who would do exactly as he was told. By this time, however, Monro was discovering a completely different side to Inspector Abberline, a rebellious side that he never knew existed.

While all this was continuing, the telegraph boys were still being questioned, and by 19 August, another new name had been thrown into the arena. This was George Veck, who had at one time also worked for the Telegraph Office, but had been fired from his job for improper conduct with some of the telegraph boys. Veck had never been charged with any offence regarding this, but after leaving the Telegraph Office, he became a close acquaintance of Hammond, allegedly procuring more young boys whilst posing as a vicar.

Abberline immediately issued an arrest warrant for Veck, and along with four officers from his team, made a dawn swoop on Veck's London lodgings. The only person there when they arrived was a 17-year-old youth, who they found in a large double bed on the first floor. The youth told them that Veck was away in Portsmouth and would be returning that morning, via Waterloo Railway station.

Inspector Abberline and his team wasted no time in rushing to the station, where they arrested Veck as he alighted from the Portsmouth train. They took him directly to Scotland Yard, where he was questioned and searched. Among his possessions, they found several letters, two of which were from someone named Algernon Allies, whom, according to the letters, had been very 'close' to Somerset. Allies was interviewed at his parents' home in Sudbury, Suffolk, where he admitted to having a sexual relationship with Somerset and receiving money from him. He also admitted working at Cleveland Street for Hammond.

Now armed with this extra evidence, Abberline decided he was not going to allow himself to be intimidated by his superiors any longer, and to take matters into his own hands. On 22 August, he called, unannounced, at Lord Somerset's home, where he proceeded to interview him again. But Somerset proved more than a match for the detective, and refused to answer any more questions until he had his solicitor present. Abberline could do nothing but agree, and gave him twenty-four hours to attend his office at Scotland Yard, along with his solicitor. Somerset, however, never did go to the Scotland Yard meeting, and left that same day for Bad Homburg vor der Höhe, in Germany, where the Prince of Wales was then holidaying.

While Somerset moved around Germany, from Bad Homburg to Hanover, apparently purchasing horses for the Prince of Wales, the trial in England was getting ready to begin. Monro was relatively happy that no big names were firmly attached at this point, and Abberline saw the case as foolproof; one that he was sure would re-endorse his reputation and if he was lucky, ones that he might even be able to surreptitiously bring a name or two into before he was stopped again.

Finally, on 11 September, Newlove and Veck, alongside a number of the telegraph boys, were committed for trial. The big surprise of the day, especially for Abberline, was that Lord Somerset's solicitor, Arthur Newton, suddenly announced that his firm, who was being paid by Somerset, would be handling Newlove and Veck's defence. If that on its own wasn't enough to prove Somerset's involvement, then nothing was, but still the message came down the line that his name was not to be pursued in this case.

On 18 September, Newlove and Veck pleaded guilty to indecency. Newlove was sentenced to four months' hard labour, and Veck to nine months. The judge in the trial was Sir Thomas Chambers, a former Liberal Member of Parliament who had a reputation for leniency, but it was never expected by anyone that even he would dish out such lenient sentences as this. The telegraph boys were also handed out sentences that were considered by both the police and the general public to be far too mild. Even the assistant public prosecutor, Hamilton Cuffe, said that the trial was a travesty of justice, but when asked to elaborate on his comments outside the court, he declined, as he 'Didn't want to miss the 6.15 p.m. train from Waterloo'.

Charles Hammond, meanwhile, still lounged somewhere, either on the continent, or in America. Abberline was still eager to bring him back to face trial, but the Prime Minister, Lord Salisbury, made it absolutely clear that no extradition proceedings should be instigated against him, and the case against Charles Hammond was quietly dropped.

After the trial had ended, and presumably thinking that he was now safe, Somerset returned to Britain on 30 September, apparently to attend horse sales at Newmarket. As soon as Abberline got wind of this, he had him followed night and day, wherever he went. Abberline ordered the surveillance to be purposefully open; he wanted Somerset to be fully aware at all times that he was being watched. Why Abberline used this method of surveillance, no one seems to know. One theory was that Abberline thought by doing it this way, he would break Somerset down, and hopefully induce him to confess to his role in the scandal. Others alleged that, by this time, Abberline personally hated Somerset so much for escaping justice in this case that he simply decided to harass him in every way he could.

On 18 October, Lord Salisbury, whilst on his way back from France, received a telegram from Sir Dighton Probyn VC, the Prince of Wales' comptroller and treasurer, asking him to meet him urgently. Lord Salisbury said later that, thinking the meeting to be about Foreign Office business connected with the Prince of Wales, he agreed to meet Probyn for a few minutes in a private waiting room at the Great Northern Railway station, where he would be waiting for his 7 p.m. connection home.

It was at this meeting that Probyn warned Lord Salisbury that Lord Arthur Somerset, extra equerry to the Prince of Wales' eldest son, Prince Albert Victor, Duke of Clarence, was about to be arrested for gross indecency at a male brothel at 19 Cleveland Street, London. The day following this meeting, Somerset fled the country to France. Did Newton warn Somerset that his arrest was imminent? This was denied by Lord Salisbury and the Attorney General, Sir Richard Webster. The Prince of Wales wrote to Lord Salisbury expressing satisfaction that Somerset had been allowed to leave the country, and asked that if Somerset should ever show his face in England again, he would remain unmolested by the authorities; however, Lord Salisbury was also being pressured by the police to prosecute Somerset. On 12 November, a warrant for Somerset's arrest was finally issued. By this time, Somerset was already safely abroad and the warrant caught little public attention.

This now left the question open as to Arthur Newton's relationship with Lord Salisbury. Had the Prime Minister himself passed this privileged information on to Newton, for the express purpose of it then being relayed to Lord Somerset? After all, it was Newton who had supplied the money that Charles Hammond used to escape to Belgium and America, and it was Lord Salisbury who had said that he did not consider it appropriate for an official application to be made for Hammond's extradition.

Arthur Newton was subsequently tried for conspiracy to pervert the course of justice, after he was caught attempting to pay off the telegraph boys to go abroad before they could testify. He was found guilty and sentenced to just six weeks' imprisonment; another ridiculously lenient sentence!

As more names and rumours started to emerge, the young editor of the *North London Press*, Ernest Parke, decided to publish the names of Somerset and Henry FitzRoy, Earl of Euston, hinting that 'They had been allowed to leave the country and thus defeat the course of justice, because their prosecution would disclose the fact that a far more distinguished and higher placed personage than themselves was involved in these "disgusting crimes".

Parke wasn't any different to most newspaper editors: he saw a good story and decided to cash in on it. These names and the rumours surrounding them were being widely spread in Britain, whilst on the continent they went even further and printed allegations in their newspapers that Prince Albert Victor, the heir to the throne, had been a regular visitor to the Cleveland Street brothel.

The Earl of Euston, however, wasted no time in taking legal action against Parke, suing him for libel. He admitted that he had been to the premises, but not for the purpose that Parke had alleged. He claimed that his reason for visiting the Cleveland Street house was because he had been misinformed that the house was a sort of 'theatre', where one could see naked women posing motionless – all very arty and not at all against any law. As the case continued, both sides tried their best to implicate the other, calling long lists of witnesses. At the same time, the rumours about Prince Albert Victor's involvement intensified. Whether this actually worried the prince or not is difficult to judge accurately, for he left the country just about the same time as the trial started, for a royal wedding in Greece and an extended tour of India, which would last the best part of seven months.

Parke called every witness he could muster to try to prove his allegations against the Earl of Euston, but found the odds stacked against him with hardly a word he was saying being believed. He constantly mentioned other evidence which would prove his allegations without a doubt, but when pressed he said he could not divulge this without betraying his source. As everybody knows, rumours and unfounded allegations are not enough to convict anyone in a courtroom it was now a case of 'put up or shut up'. The name that was then being bandied about was none other than Inspector Abberline. Could it have possibly been him? Whoever it was, it certainly didn't help Parke, for he was found guilty and sentenced to a year in prison for libel.

The Cleveland Street scandal, as it had come to be known, ended with minnows, such as Newlove and Veck, a handful of telegraph boys and Lord

Somerset's solicitor, Arthur Newton, all being found guilty of somewhat minor infringements of the law and handed miniscule and ridiculous sentences. Then there was, of course, the newspaper editor, Ernest Parke, who received the largest sentence of them all, for his terrible crime of daring to name names. As for the names themselves, as we now know, none were ever brought to trial.

In February the following year, Henry Labouchère, the Radical MP for Northampton, took an interest in the case, and began to investigate Salisbury's role in helping Somerset escape justice, suggesting that Lord Salisbury and several others should still be prosecuted.

Labouchère made a long speech in the Commons, accusing Salisbury of a criminal conspiracy to defeat the ends of justice. The house settled back in awed silence, as Labouchère continued his devastating and largely accurate account of what had happened, and ended with stating that in his opinion, 'The government wish to hush this matter up'. Labouchère refused to accept the Attorney General's defence of Salisbury, saying that he didn't believe either him or the Prime Minister. The speaker of the house warned Labouchère on two occasions, and finally rose and called Labouchère to order, suspending him from the Commons for a week. Labouchère's resolution for an inquiry was meanwhile defeated by 206 votes to 66. At the end of the vote, Labouchère rose again and pointed to his fellow Northampton MP, the atheist Charles Bradlaugh. 'My honourable friend was suspended for disbelieving in God,' he joked, 'and I am suspended for disbelieving in Man.'

Lord Salisbury continued his career with complete disregard to Labouchère's accusations. Somerset, meanwhile, searched for employment in Turkey, Austria and Hungary, and then went off to live quietly in self-imposed and comfortable exile in the south of France with a companion, until his death in 1926.

The other, and certainly the most famous name, to be bandied about with regard to the Cleveland Street scandal was Prince Albert Victor, the Duke of Clarence. He was away in India during the trials, and only returned to Great Britain in May 1890, but that, of course, would not have prevented him from visiting the Cleveland Street brothel during the previous years.

There were plenty of rumours and innuendo, but there was absolutely no conclusive evidence ever found that placed the Prince at the Cleveland Street address. Somerset was said to have hinted on several occasions that he had letters which would place the Prince in a very embarrassing situation, with regard to the Cleveland Street brothel, and that he would make such letters public if ever he was forced to appear in court. In all probability, Somerset was using the threat of exposing such letters, if indeed he did have them to begin with, in the hope that it would keep him out of the dock.

The fact that such letters never came to light did not do much to enhance Somerset's reputation, and neither did it do any harm to the Prince, as statements made in such circumstances would never be considered by a court, and would be classed as hearsay, which is defined in law as 'Evidence that does not derive its value solely from the credit of the witness, but rests mainly on the veracity and competency of other persons'.

Needless to say, Abberline was furious and frustrated to say the least. After what he saw as his failure to solve the Jack the Ripper investigations, he had put everything he had into this case, even to the point of ignoring the advice of both his boss, Sir James Monro, and the Prime Minister not to go ahead with the case. He knew he had a watertight case, and he was sure that if he was left unhindered, he could bring all the guilty parties to justice, but it seemed that the odds were stacked against him whichever way he turned.

The book, which he had found at the Cleveland Street house, was to be his *pièce de résistance*. It was a sort of guest book that Charles Hammond had kept as a record, listing every visitor to the house during the last eighteen months. Abberline knew that when this book was produced in court, it would bolster his case up and bring not just a few minnows to justice but the real predators along with them. No name in the book was safe from justice.

About a week before the trial was about to begin, Abberline received a message from the Prime Minister, requesting to see all the evidence that was going to be produced in court. This was a very unusual request, and one which Abberline was not too sure of its legality. He consulted Sir James Monro, and was told in no uncertain terms that if the Prime Minister had requested such documents, then he had no option other than to supply them to him.

Inspector Abberline knew how important the book was to his case, and had kept it under lock and key, in the safe of his office at Scotland Yard, since he had first found it. He took the book out of the safe and placed it in a box, along with other written evidence referring to the case. The box was then tied and secured with sealing wax, and sent by special courier to the Prime Minister at 10 Downing Street. After waiting several days, Abberline started to become impatient and sent a message, asking what the Prime Minister thought of the documents. He was told that in the Prime Minister's opinion, the documents, without any form of back up, were inconclusive, and that the case should be dropped. Abberline could not believe his ears; what on earth was the Prime Minister talking about, hadn't he even bothered to look at the book? He reported the Prime Minister's findings to his boss, Sir James Monro, who was, firstly, very angry with Abberline for contacting the Prime Minister without his approval, and secondly, for not mentioning this book to him in the first place.

Sir James Monro, nevertheless, did contact the Prime Minister, and reported back to Abberline exactly what he had been told. He reported that there was absolutely no record anywhere of a book ever having been received by the Prime Minister. All he had received, he said, were a number of different documents pertaining to the case, which he had now sent back to Scotland Yard, along with the recommendation to drop the case. The book, Abberline's main piece of evidence, had somehow managed to disappear en route from Scotland Yard to 10 Downing Street.

Was it any wonder then, why the case floundered, why no further names were brought to book and why those tried received such minor sentences? It seems an obvious conclusion, therefore, that there was indeed a cover-up of the scandal, but proving such action is another matter. There was certainly intervention by the government, much to the chagrin of Abberline, Monro and the Metropolitan Police in general. Did the authorities try to delay action and thwart justice, just because the prince might possibly have been involved?

Sir James Monro was reported to be so angry at the way he perceived himself to have been treated that he resigned from the force in June 1890, and went to live in India. The official explanation for his resignation was given that he was not happy with the new police pensions scheme. When Inspector Abberline heard of his boss' intention to resign, he told fellow officers that if Monro went, then he would follow. One of Abberline's great misgivings was his inability not to speak his mind, which certainly seemed to have upset his superiors, and was probably why Abberline was deciding to leave before he was pushed.

It was whispered that behind Monro's tough exterior, he had a great respect for Abberline, and that just before leaving he took Abberline to one side and told him to stick it out a little longer, as promotion was most definitely on the cards for him. Abberline took the advice of his superior and settled back into his job, with the hope that another case might possibly come his way which would help him to finally redeem himself.

Several months elapsed with no significant cases arising and no sign either of the promotion that Monro had assured him of. Despondency, once again, started to set in, and he was just about to offer his resignation when, on 22 December 1890, he was promoted to chief inspector. He was elated when he told his wife, Emma, about the promotion, claiming it was the best Christmas present he could have wished for.

The elation he felt, however, quickly changed to one of deflation, when he learned that his new position as chief inspector had a serious setback: he had been taken off the street and re-assigned to desk duties at the yard. This wasn't why he had become a policeman; his sole mission in life was to solve crime, and he did not consider being stuck behind a desk an ideal place from which to do this. He held the job down, at the insistence of his wife, for nearly two years, but eventually couldn't take it any longer and retired on a full pension in 1892. He had served twenty-nine years in the force and was just 49 years old.

2

Early Life – Undercover Work and Marriage

wenty years is not exactly a long time in the career of a policeman; some would argue that it is incredibly short for someone such as Abberline, who became a prominent name in two of England's most famous criminal cases. Those who study British criminal history will undoubtedly know of the Cleveland Street scandal, but one doesn't need to be a historian to know of his other famous case; in fact, there cannot be hardly a person alive in the world who hasn't heard of the Jack the Ripper murders. There have been hundreds of books and articles written about this case over the past 123 years (at the time of writing). There have also been films, television plays and documentaries, nearly all of which feature the character of Inspector Abberline.

So where and how did it all start? Frederick George Abberline was born on 8 January 1843 in Blandford, a pretty little village on the River Stour, in Dorset. His father, Edward Abberline, was a saddlemaker and minor local government official, who unfortunately died in 1859, leaving Frederick's mother, Hannah, to raise Frederick and his three slightly older siblings, Emily, Harriet and Edward.

Frederick George Abberline was just 16 when he took up work as an apprentice clockmaker, in order to help support his mother. He had to get up at 5 a.m. every day and walk nearly 3 miles to the clockmaker's shop. Walking home by the same route every evening meant that he sometimes didn't get home until almost 10 p.m. He worked at the shop for four years, with the intention of opening a clock shop of his own one day. However, the apprenticeship wage was so poor that by the time he had payed his mother for food, he hardly had anything left for personal items, let alone saving to open his own shop.

Having little or no money left, Abberline didn't get to attend dances or meet girls, like other boys of his age did. Instead he spent most evenings, when he wasn't too tired, reading 'Penny Dreadfuls', which a neighbour would supply him with. It was probably these magazines that gave Abberline his first insight into the world of police work and detection, which he obviously took to with great relish. By 1863, aged 20, he decided to leave home, move to London, and join the Metropolitan Police. With a meagre £2 in his pocket, he found himself at the Metropolitan Police Recruiting Office at Scotland Yard, where after a short test he was accepted immediately, as constable number 43519. He was appointed to N Division, Islington, and given a uniform and living accommodation above the station.

Investigating crime, however, did not seem to be a part of Abberline's duties. 'Just make yourself visible on the streets,' he was told by his sergeant. Crime figures at that time were shown to be falling in the Metropolitan area, but, as Abberline soon discovered, this was due to statistics being manipulated to show favourable figures for the police force.

During his second week on the force, Abberline was sent out with another officer to investigate an alleged theft of several items of jewellery from a house near Upper Street, Islington. There was no doubt in Abberline's mind that this was a straight forward case of burglary, as a back door had been forced open from the outside and the thieves had left two sets of muddy footprints coming into the house from the backyard. Abberline couldn't believe his eyes, however, when he later saw his fellow officer's report on the case, which made no mention of a burglary, but instead noted that they had been called to a disturbance at the house. The stolen jewellery was listed as lost property. In other words, no crime had been reported.

Abberline soon discovered that this wasn't just an isolated incident: the more reports he saw, the more cover-ups of crimes he discovered. He also found that local residents had such little faith in or respect for the police that a large percentage of them did not bother to report offences such as theft or pickpocketing anyway.

How could he, as an aspiring police officer, account for and deal with crimes that were either swept under the carpet or never reported? His superiors turned a blind eye to his observations and requests; as far as they were concerned, crime statistics were looking very positive. Abberline didn't want just to patrol the streets at the regulation 2½mph, which he was assured by his superiors would deter offenders; he wanted to be a part of it by mixing with the locals and becoming accepted by them.

At this time, detective policing, especially by those working in plain clothes, was seen as symptomatic of an intrusive system. Continental police forces might have worked like that, especially the French with their undercover spies and surveillance, but not us, not the British! For the time being then, Abberline's plans and ambitions had to be put on hold.

About this period in time, a relatively new crime became prevalent on the streets of London. Today we know it as 'mugging', but during the mid-1800s it became known as 'garrotting', for the simple reason that the would be muggers/thieves would sneak up on their victim from behind and throttle them, either with a scarf or piece of rope, or with just their hands and arms, and then rob them of their valuables. So prevalent did this form of robbery become that shops started selling anti-garrotting collars which were advertised as 'Patent Antigarotte Collar, which enables Gentlemen to walk the streets of London in perfect safety at all hours of the day or night'. The collar consisted of a leather strap worn around the neck, with metal spikes sticking out of it to deter would be garrotters.

While the police insisted that the crime rate was in decline, the general public were being whipped up by the press into a state of panic regarding this relatively new phenomenon. Members of the public were even expressing their views and experiences by writing to the newspapers, as this letter, which was published in *The Times*, shows:

Sir, I trust you will kindly afford me your valuable assistance towards placing that portion of the public residing in the suburban districts of London on their guard, and also enable me to call the attention of the Commissioners of Police to the fact, that highway robbery, with violence to the person, is in this year 1851, likely to be as common, and, in consequence of the mode of effecting it more easy and free from detection that it ever has been within the present century.

On Saturday, the 1st inst., when returning home at night, and as usual walking quick, I was, without any warning, suddenly seized from behind by some one, who, placing the bend of his arm to my throat, and then clasping his right wrist with his left-hand, thereby forming a powerful lever, succeeded in effectually strangling me for a time, and rendering me incapable of moving or even calling for assistance, although there was plenty at hand, whilst a second man easily rifled me of all he could find. I was then violently thrown on the ground, or rather I found myself lying there when I came to my senses. Two passengers, one a neighbour, raised me up, when we were immediately joined by a policeman, and by two more in less than a minute; but as I could not express myself coherently at first, the men had plenty of time to escape, and pursuit was impossible.

I believe the approach of these persons disturbed the men, for they did not get all I had about me, and I escaped the finishing rap on the head usual in these cases. I could give no description of the thieves, as I saw neither distinctly. Now, this robbery was committed on one of the most frequented highways out of London, viz., Hampstead-road, within a few yards of Haverstock turnpike, and within three miles of Temple-bar, in sight of two other passengers, the gatekeepers, and within hearing and almost within sight of three policemen. But the worst is that I have been obliged to call in medical assistance, and am still under medical treatment, for this violence brought on a return of an old complaint with tendency to an effusion of blood on the brain, besides giving a great shock to the entire nervous system; and I am convinced that an application of this human garrotte to an elderly person, or any one in a bad state of health, might very easily occasion death.

There are many men in this very district, and others who occasionally visit their friends here, who are in the habit of walking home after dark, hitherto without a thought of danger. In a case like this carrying firearms or a life-preserver, &c., is useless, for the attack and strangulation are too sudden.

Therefore, I think, Sir, it is not too much to ask whether the police authorities ought not to render us more security for life and property in what may now be fairly termed part of London itself; for since this most cowardly and atrocious system of Thuggee has prevailed, we have no more protection, if so much, than our forefathers had on Hounslow-heath a hundred years ago

In conclusion, I wish to say that the present police force apparently keep as good watch as they can over this neighbourhood.

I am, Sir, your obedient servant,
Middle Temple, Feb. 11. JAMES BROOKSBANK

It wasn't until an MP was robbed by garrotters, on his way home from a late-night sitting of parliament, that the police were forced to take action. Parliament had responded with such indignation that one of their members had been attacked in the street, in full view of the public at large, that they quickly brought in legislation providing that such offenders were to be flogged, as well as imprisoned. The press picked up on the story, and needless to say, the police were ordered, in no uncertain terms, to crack down on all street crime.

This new initiative was exactly what Abberline had been waiting for: no more plodding the streets at 2½ mph just to make himself seen; this was his chance to get out there, mix with the locals and become accepted by them. His biggest problem, however, was his uniform; no ordinary PC was allowed to carry out his police duties unless he was wearing a uniform or had special dispensation to work in plain clothes. Abberline had tried this route on a number of occasions, but had been turned down every time; he had also tried befriending the locals while still wearing his uniform, but apart from the odd old lady here and there, he had no luck whatsoever in gaining their confidence.

Most offenders, however, were young males not too dissimilar in age to Abberline himself, and most offences committed were petty thefts; but there also lurked another type of criminal, known in police parlance as 'the dangerous classes', and they were said to lurk in the slums waiting for the opportunity for disorder and plunder.

Like all police officers, Abberline did have the occasional day's leave from his duties. It was during these periods that he would go out onto the streets and into the pubs, in his ordinary clothes, and make 'friends' with the locals. He was breaking no police rules in doing this, as the streets and pubs were not off limits to police officers, and the way he saw it, if he could gain a little useful information at the same time, then so be it. It is often said that drink loosens a man's tongue, and this metaphor certainly worked for Abberline. With the inside knowledge he was starting to gain, he soon started solving more crimes and making more arrests than any other officer in his station.

His superiors, however, were not too happy with his lack of record in arresting women, in comparison with the number of males he arrested. There were plenty of women committing crimes in his area, so why, they asked, was Abberline seemingly ignoring them? As far as Abberline was concerned, the most common offences committed by women during this time were linked to prostitution, with the occasional petty theft or being drunk and disorderly – not exactly crimes of the first magnitude!

Abberline also seemed to find women in general not as easy to get on with as men. There was no hint of homosexuality in his behaviour, but probably more of an inbred feeling of shyness with women. Bear in mind, he was in his early twenties at this time, and as far as we know, had never had any sort of close relationship with a woman, other than in his family.

There seemed to be a general perception at this time that women should be seen as the upholders of true womanhood, and that if a woman was seen to transgress such a viewpoint by committing a crime, not only should she be treated harshly, but she should be treated more harshly than men. This, of course, did not seem to fit in with Abberline's point of view, hence his almost complete abstention in the arrest of females.

By the time Abberline had been at N Division, Islington, for just two years, his superiors had no option other than to offer him promotion to sergeant. He had, after all, made more arrests and solved more crimes than any other PC at his station. It was also possible that his superiors thought a change in environment might be beneficial, not just to Abberline, but to them too. Abberline took up his new post as sergeant in November 1865 and moved to Y Division, Highgate.

The distance between his old beat in Islington and his new beat in Highgate was approximately 3 miles, which meant that many of his old contacts were still relatively close to hand. This, of course, was good news for Abberline, and also for his new superiors, who were more than pleased with the way in which he was fitting in and working closely with his new colleagues.

Highgate at this time had a considerable number of Irish immigrants living within its boundaries, as did Islington to a somewhat lesser extent, so Abberline was quite au fait with the Irish accent and customs. It was just before he moved to Highgate that British agents had uncovered a Fenian plot to increase their activities in Great Britain, and especially London. The Fenians were nineteenth-century Irish Nationalists, organised in 1858 as the Irish Republican Brotherhood. The name 'Fenian' derives from the Old Irish word 'Fianna', who were legendary Irish warriors. Over the years 'Fenian' became an Irish derivative for soldier.

As even more news involving the Fenians started to seep into British Secret Service agents' hands, it was decided that an undercover squad of police officers was needed to try to infiltrate the Irish community and investigate any possible Fenian activities in London. As Abberline was a natural choice for this operation, with his history of plain-clothes work, he was, in 1867, assigned to special plain-clothes duties, with orders to do whatever was necessary to infiltrate and report back any anti-British activities within his area.

Abberline's natural accent was a soft, south country one, but after working in North London for a couple of years, he had quickly picked up quite a reasonable Cockney accent, which was enough to fool most people and one of the reasons he had managed to gain the confidence of the criminal element in his area. The Irish accent, however, was something new to him; it didn't come naturally as the London Cockney accent had done, but to give him his due, he did try.

There were a number of Irish pubs along the Holloway Road, so dressed in what he thought was suitable attire, Abberline chose a Saturday night to visit as many as he could, in the hope of picking up some hints on the Irish accent, and maybe a word here and there regarding the Fenians.

Most pubs at this time were what is known as 'spit and sawdust' pubs, a term relating to the sawdust which was liberally scattered over the floor to accommodate the habit of spitting; it also helped, as Abberline soon found out, soak up the blood from the fights which broke out at regular intervals in such establishments. Guinness was the natural drink in these pubs, sometimes used as a chaser after a dram or two of good Irish whiskey. As Abberline wasn't exactly a strong drinker, a pint of ale with his colleagues now and then being his usual limit, he soon found himself the worse for wear, and this was in his first pub!

By the end of that first evening, he had learned what to drink, if not how to actually drink it. He had also picked up a few Irish phrases, which were mostly obscenities or profanities, but he had heard no mention of any anti-British or Fenian activity. Not one to give up easily, Abberline continued his quest the following Saturday, and the Saturday after that; this was due mainly to the fact that he had leave on those particular days. He did have permission to carry out this type of undercover work during his normal working week, but he had decided to work alone for the first few weeks, bringing in the rest of his team only when he felt confident enough to show them that he knew the ropes where the Irish contingent were concerned.

After three weeks, the only contact he had managed to make was with a man named Martin, who seemed to like the idea of having an English drinking partner, whom he could brag to about how many people he knew. Not exactly what Abberline had been hoping for, but maybe someone who could be cultivated in the future? He had not heard a mention of the word Fenian, or any other anti-British activity, and as for his hopes of being accepted as an Irishman, that seemed to be completely out of the question, as even his new-found 'friend' Martin referred to him as 'the Brit'.

Abberline decided to change tack. He put several of his team onto surveillance of the Irish pubs, while he decided to disguise himself as a cabdriver. He left his face unshaven for a week or two, wore a cap, polka-dot scarf and an old jacket. Scotland Yard provided the horse-drawn cab, which completed his disguise and allowed him carte blanche to go almost anywhere in London without anyone taking a second glance at him.

It was while waiting at a cab shelter in Kilburn one evening, which was, and still is, a particularly large Irish area of London, that Abberline noticed two young men as they emerged from a house nearby. The men waited on the corner of the street for some time before a third man met them and spoke to them for several minutes. Abberline had thought the men looked suspicious, as it was raining hard yet they did not seek shelter, and the third man wore no hat. After a few minutes, the third man handed one of the men a piece of paper and then left. The two men hurried across the street and asked Abberline to take them to the Horse and Groom pub in Holloway, which was one of the pubs that he had earlier tried to infiltrate.

It was almost impossible to hear what the occupants of the cab were saying, as the noise of the horses hooves, coupled with the heavy patter of the rain, drowned everything out. All Abberline could hear was the constant drone of the men's voices from within the cab, but not what they were actually saying. He had one option, which was to open the trapdoor in the roof slightly, which he did as carefully and quietly as he could, but instead of hearing their conversation, all he heard was a very strong Irish accent shouting at him, with a few expletives thrown in, to shut that door as they were getting soaked.

As the men alighted from the cab outside the Horse and Groom pub, Abberline tried to get a good look at their faces, but from his position, high above them, this was very difficult. The only thing he did notice was that one of them had a large bushy moustache and, from what he could see of it, bright ginger hair. He continued to watch as the men went to go into the pub and had a slight collision with another man, who was coming out at the same time. By pure chance, this other man proved to be Abberline's Irish 'friend' Martin, who noticed Abberline straight away and leaned up towards him to shake his hand. 'I didn't know you were a cabbie,' he said. 'If I had the money, I would ask you to take me to the Three Nuns pub.' Abberline saw this as a chance to hopefully find out if Martin knew anything about the two men. He lent down, opened the door of the cab and told Martin to jump in. 'It's on the house,' he said.

As the cab rattled along the well-worn cobbles towards the Three Nuns, Martin didn't seem to mind getting a little wet from the rain, as Abberline opened the trap door and started to talk to him. It turned out that Martin didn't know the two young men personally, but he had seen them in the pub, and from what he had heard, they had only just arrived in London a couple of days earlier, direct from Belfast. He warned Abberline off them, telling him that they were a couple of hotheads who couldn't hold their drink and liked to fight.

This snippet of information didn't sound like much, but to Abberline, coupled with the fact that the two men had come out of a house that he had marked down as a possible safe house, it was enough to make him feel that it might just provide a lead to possible Fenian movement within the city.

Unbeknown to Abberline at this time, an undercover British spy in Belfast, who used the name Ray O'Mara, had managed to infiltrate a gang of robbers who were blowing bank safes in order to fund the Fenian movement in Ireland. O'Mara's contacts within the gang led him to meet some of the Fenians' top brass, from whom he found out that they were planning outrages in Great Britain and were eager to buy arms and explosives with the money coming in from the bank raids.

O'Mara knew that he needed to get this information back to his superiors in Great Britain, in strictest privacy and without delay. The telephone had not yet been invented at this time, so it left him with two options: the first to send a colleague to deliver the message by hand, which would take approximately twenty-four hours, travelling by horse and carriage, boat, and then horse and carriage once in Great Britain. The second, which would be the quickest method, was to send a telegram, but this involved writing out his message and passing it to a worker at the post office, who would read it and then transmit it, using international Morse code.

The telegram was obviously the better option, but how safe would it be? O'Mara talked it over quickly with one of his fellow operatives, and between them, they decided that they had no option but to send it by telegram. No secret codes had been agreed between O'Mara and his superiors in Great Britain, so he had to spell out the whole message, just leaving out obvious names and locations, and pass it to the telegraph operator.

No telegram was ever received by O'Mara's superiors, and O'Mara himself was never seen again. The body of a man, with bruising around his neck, was found floating in the sea just off Carrickfergus. The man was never identified, but it was thought to be Ray O'Mara. In the meantime, however, O'Mara's fellow operative had decided to get back to England as quickly as possible and relay to his superiors what he knew, and what O'Mara had told him.

By the time this news got through to Abberline and his team he had already followed up his first lead and raided the house from which the two young men had emerged from. Unfortunately the men were not caught in this raid, but they did manage to detain several other suspects, from whom information was extracted, resulting in a number of houses around London also being raided with several arrests.

The Clerkenwell House of Detention, which was just a very short distance away from Abberline's patch, had housed many felons over the years, including at one time the notorious highwayman Jack Shepperd. Prisoners came and went at this prison, some detained for many years, others hanged and some, from time to time, released. People could be imprisoned during this time for the pettiest of offences, from stealing a handkerchief to begging on the street for food.

In November this same year (1867), Richard O'Sullivan-Burke was remanded in custody alongside a compatriot, Joseph Casey, at the Clerkenwell House of Detention. The two men had been charged with planning the outrageous escape of a well-known Fenian member from a prison van in Manchester a few months earlier.

Scotland Yard, alongside the British Intelligence Services, seemed to have completely overlooked the fact that Richard O'Sullivan-Burke, one of the Fenian chief armaments officers, and his second-in-command, Joseph Casey, were incarcerated in the middle of London. The very city which, as reliable sources had informed them, was about to become the target of more Fenian atrocities.

While all eyes in Great Britain were focused upon finding possible Fenian groups here, with special emphasis being placed upon the capital, it was still business as usual back in Belfast. Orders were being issued from Fenian High Command in Ireland that Richard O'Sullivan-Burke and Joseph Casey should be sprung from the Clerkenwell House of Detention as soon as possible, as their expertise was sorely needed.

Two weeks passed without any further arrests being made in London. Abberline and his men had started to relax and were beginning to think that the whole Fenian threat had been called off. In fact, far from being called off, it was just about to erupt.

Just before 4 p.m. on 13 December, a horse and carriage drew to a halt at the end of St James's Walk in Clerkenwell. One side of the street consisted of a tall wall which enclosed part of the Clerkenwell House of Detention; the other side of the road consisted of a grimy row of tenement houses, whose windows were bereft of any light due to the closeness of the prison wall, and being December, the sun had also started to set.

Two young men emerged from the carriage and started to manhandle a large object, which turned out to be a barrel, out of the door and onto the pavement. The horse and carriage drove off, leaving the two men to move the barrel by turning it onto one edge and wheeling it along the street. St James's Walk was quite busy with people going about their work and doing their everyday shopping, as the young men wheeled the barrel past them. No one seemed to take any notice at all as the two young men reached the corner of the wall, turned the barrel up straight, and placed it against it; no one, that is, apart from a small boy about 6 years old, who was sitting on his doorstep opposite. He watched as one of the men pulled a short fuse from the side of the barrel and then lit it. As the fuse started to spit and crackle, the two men ran away as quickly as they could. The young boy, however, being curious as children of his age are, crossed the street to get a closer look at the sparkling fuse. Seconds later, the fuse ignited the gunpowder, which the barrel was packed with. The explosion was tremendous, instantly killing the young boy and blowing an enormous hole in the prison wall, sending bricks and debris flying in all directions.

The explosion was heard for miles around, and it knocked down nearby tenement houses across the street in Corporation Lane (now Row). Four people were killed instantly, including the young boy, and eight died later of their wounds with at least another 120 injured, including many children. The bombers' idea had been to detonate the explosives while their comrades inside the prison were exercising in the yard, thus blowing a big enough hole in the wall for them to climb through and escape.

The two young bombers, however, were complete amateurs and had no idea of how much gunpowder they needed to use, and how much damage they were going to cause. Luckily for their comrades, and all the other prisoners inside, the two amateurs had chosen the wrong wall, and no prisoners were exercising on the other side of it. If they had been, they would surely have been killed.

There was public outrage at the incident. The press demanded to know why two very important people within the Fenian movement were kept in a London prison with no visible police presence, when it was common knowledge within the police that a Fenian plot to bomb London was at hand. Calls were made for a shake up within the police service and for a permanent solution to the Irish problem. So vociferous did the press become on this issue that it became an urgent priority for the incoming Liberal government. Abberline's team was quietly and quickly disbanded, and the government authorised the foundation of a new specialist department which was to be known as the Secret Service Department.

To say Abberline was dispirited was an understatement to say the least. He felt that he had accomplished a great deal in the short while he had been working on this particular case, and that it was not the Fenians who had caused this massive incident, but a pair of amateurs trying to make a name for themselves within the Fenian movement. His suspicions were confirmed when he paid another visit to the Horse and Groom pub and made contact with his 'friend' Martin again. He told Abberline that the two young tearaways he had warned him off earlier had entered the pub about an hour after the bombing, both looking quite dishevelled and one of them had a large burn on his hand. Abberline was sure in his mind that it was this pair that had caused the bombing, but by this time they had completely disappeared from the London scene. He passed the information on to his superiors, who seemed to ignore him completely.

Some months later, the newly formed Secret Service Department arrested a man named Michael Barrett, and charged him with the Clerkenwell bombing. Months earlier, before the Clerkenwell incident, Michael Barrett had been arrested in Glasgow for illegally discharging a firearm. The prosecution alleged that Barrett had told another man, an Irishman named Patrick Mullany, that he had carried out the Clerkenwell bombing with an accomplice by the name of Murphy.

In court, Barrett produced a list of witnesses who testified he had been in Scotland on the date of the bombing, but the court was more inclined to believe Mullany, who had a criminal record and had been found guilty of giving false testimony to a court on a previous occasion. After two hours' deliberation the jury pronounced Michael Barrett guilty. He was subsequently hanged, and was the last man to be publicly hanged in England. Patrick Mullany was rewarded with a free passage to Australia.

While all this was going on, Abberline's team was disbanded and he found himself back in uniform once again, demoted to normal everyday duties including mundane activities like arresting street drunks, pickpockets, rowdy children and even rounding up stray dogs – something the police took very seriously at the time, as they were often used by local thugs as weapons.

Abberline felt despondent and demoralised. He had gained important information on one of the most dangerous organisations in Great Britain; he had made numerous arrests, which in all probability had stopped other atrocities being carried out; and he had also offered yet more information on the identity of the real bombers. His reward for all this work had been his demotion, and in his opinion, an innocent man had been sent to the gallows.

At this point in time, the shine had diminished somewhat from his police work, and Abberline found that, to take his mind off the mundane work he was being allocated, he started to socialise more by going to pubs and spending the occasional night at the theatre. One Saturday evening he was invited to dinner at a colleague's house, where he was introduced to a lovely 25-year-old girl, Martha Mackness, who was a friend of his colleague's wife. It seems that the purpose of inviting both himself and Martha Mackness was to hopefully pair them off. It certainly worked, for Frederick George Abberline, who under normal circumstances was not very comfortable around women, pulled his chair closer to hers and chatted constantly to her, almost ignoring his hosts throughout the whole evening.

Abberline wasted no time in arranging to see Martha again and picked her up from her rented accommodation in Islington the following morning. Abberline was certainly a God-fearing man, but not exactly an avid church-goer, but being a Sunday, and probably in the hope of impressing her, he took her along to his local church which was only a very short distance from his police lodgings. After the service they walked over Highbury Fields and, even though there was snow on the ground and the air was freezing, Abberline felt warmth and comfort with Martha.

The couple saw more and more of each other throughout the following weeks, and within six weeks they had decided to get married. Abberline told Martha about his early life in the pretty little village on the River Stour, in Dorset, and of his early ambitions to open a clock-making shop there. By this time, Abberline felt totally despondent with the police force and was seriously thinking of giving it all up and moving back to Dorset. Martha was a little more realistic than Abberline and talked him into waiting for a while; after all, she explained, he was still relatively young, had his own flat and was earning a decent wage by the standards of the day.

Abberline took notice of Martha, and they married in Islington, in March 1868. She moved into his flat where they planned to stay for a while, until they found a larger place where they could hopefully start a family.

Life was idyllic for the first few weeks, with Abberline and his new wife still acting like a young courting couple. At weekends they would go for walks in the park during the day and sometimes the theatre during the evening. Martha was a wonderful cook and would always have a meal ready and waiting for

Abberline when he got home from work in the evenings. Just five weeks after they were married, Abberline returned home from work to find Martha lying in bed. She was terribly pale and couldn't stop coughing; she said that she felt very weak, and couldn't bring herself to eat anything.

Thinking that it was probably nothing more than a bad winter cold or chest infection, which would normally clear up within a few days or so, Abberline did not take it too seriously. By the end of the week, though, her condition had deteriorated; she now had a very high temperature and was coughing up blood. Abberline rushed to the nearest doctor and told him of Martha's symptoms. The doctor wasted no time and returned to Abberline's flat with him, where he diagnosed Martha with tuberculosis. Within two weeks Martha was dead. They had been married just eight weeks.

Needless to say, Abberline was devastated. He had Martha's body taken back to Oundle, Northamptonshire, where her family originally came from, and she was buried in the local churchyard. He stayed in the area for nearly two weeks, contemplating his future, which he found hard to perceive without his beloved Martha. Friends and family eventually talked him into returning to London and continuing with his career in the police force, which he eventually did. There was only one thing for it, in his mind, and that was to throw himself into his work with renewed vigour, in the hope of overcoming his distress. He couldn't bear to move back into his old flat, which was filled with memories of his life there with Martha, so he put in a request for a change of accommodation and was quickly given a new place in Kentish Town Road police station.

He worked day and night, refusing even to take a Sunday off. His sole purpose in his private life was to try to forget Martha, which he never really did, but he did manage to turn his life around regarding his police work. Within a few months he had been promoted to police sergeant, which was a great achievement, especially at such a catastrophic time in his life. Although his promotion gave him more money and prestige, it still didn't offer him exactly what he had always been looking for, which was more detective work. He had a taste of it while he was investigating the Fenians but had been demoted from it – something he was still smarting from. Now, however, his promotion would hopefully lead to another chance, but for the time being his duties consisted of him patrolling his North London beat, exactly as he had done as a constable.

As unexciting as this period in his life was, it did help him to an extent to take his mind off his great loss. It was probably the sheer quantity of cases he had to handle, rather than any real interesting facts they might possibly throw up, that helped in this instance. Most cases he had to deal with were very mundane: cases such as drunks charged with assault, a man charged with stealing a purse, another with forging a cheque, and yet another charged with stealing 5s. In 1872, probably one of his more interesting cases was the arrest of three women, Elizabeth Sullivan, Maria Sullivan and Jane Adams, all three charged with disorderly conduct for the 'heinous' crime of dressing in male attire. If this law still applied in Britain today, probably 60 per cent of the female population would have to be arrested and charged with wearing trousers and masculine-looking shirts and jackets.

Another interesting case was that of Thomas Ross, who was charged with unlawful gaming; this involved two men or more playing a game of pitch and toss, where they toss up a coin and call 'heads or tails'. Not exactly organised crime by any standards, but together with more petty larceny, and drunk and disorderly charges, Abberline somehow managed to fill his days and nights, and take his mind off the terrible loss of his wife. Another case, which is worth mentioning, was one that involved the Great Eastern Railway Company, which was charged with obstructing the public thoroughfare. It isn't very clear just how a railway company managed to obstruct a public thoroughfare: not with a locomotive engine surely?

Abberline's diligence, and his often very boring work, managed to get him through his bad period, although it didn't happen overnight. The days progressed into weeks, the weeks into months, and the months into years, until finally, on 10 March 1873, he was promoted again, this time to inspector, and transferred to H Division, Whitechapel.

This was just what he had been waiting for: real promotion and a completely different setting. Whitechapel had long been known as a hotbed of crime, which would presumably be something he could really sink his teeth into.

There was more to Whitechapel than the newly promoted Inspector Abberline could ever have dreamt of. There were certain streets where police officers wouldn't patrol, unless in pairs. Before leaving the office, the outgoing superintendent in charge of H Division stated that assaults on police officers were more frequent in H Division than any other part of the country. This was an area where the inhabitants fought with each other using knives, knuckledusters and coshes. The intended victim, who was usually a drunk emerging from a pub, would be mugged, in the hope that he or she might provide the mugger with their beer money for the evening. Apart from shopkeepers, many of whom employed personal minders, no respectable person, man or woman, would walk through many of these streets, especially at night.

It didn't take Abberline long to find out most of these facts; and far from putting him off, they made him more determined than ever to make the streets of Whitechapel safe again for ordinary people. He was probably one of the first police officers in Great Britain to install amongst his officers what we call today a zero-tolerance policy.

Just a couple of weeks after becoming installed at H Division, a case was brought to his attention which involved a Jewish shopkeeper named

Abraham Kikal, who had apparently attacked two men with an axe. One of the men lost two fingers in the attack and the other one suffered multiple cuts and bruises.

Abberline went down to the cells where Kikal was being held. He wanted to see for himself what sort of monster could commit such a crime on an open street in broad daylight. He interviewed Kikal for nearly an hour before returning to his office, where he summoned the arresting officers. Abberline was furious as he paced up and down his office, shouting at the officers at the top of his voice. 'How long have you two worked in Whitechapel?' he asked them. 'Did either of you take a good look at this man, or ask him his age?' he demanded. Kikal, it seemed, was in his mid-seventies, and had never been in trouble with the police since he had come to Great Britain some thirty years earlier. The two officers were dumbfounded; they were under the impression that they needed to come down heavily on any wrongdoer, especially one who committed such a violent attack as this.

'This man,' yelled Abberline, 'was the victim in this affair, not the aggressor.' He explained to his men that all Kikal had done was try to protect his business, and possibly his life, from a local gang of thugs known as the Bessarabians, who were demanding protection money from local shopkeepers, stallholders and publicans.

The Bessarabians were a forty-strong gang, who owed their curious name to a region of southern Russia, located on the Romanian border. They specialised in terrorising mainly Russian Jewish immigrants, who had an ingrained terror of authority and the police in general. In almost every case involving the Bessarabians, the victim refused to give evidence against them and consequently the majority of cases had to be dropped through lack of evidence.

When local people heard about Kikal, and the way he had stood up to the gang, they decided to organise themselves and take an example from the old man's books. They set up a vigilante group for their mutual protection, but within a few weeks, the vigilantes, who termed themselves the Odessians, had seen the huge profits that were made by offering protection, and they also started demanding money with menaces.

Instead of bettering the situation, it grew worse, with shopkeepers now being attacked and beaten up just for paying off the wrong gang. Meanwhile, the Bessarabians and the Odessians fought each other openly on the streets, in a battle for control of the Whitechapel area. At one point, the Odessians lured a leading Bessarabian named Perkoff into an alley and sliced off one of his ears. In revenge, the Bessarabians smashed up a coffee stall which was supposedly under the protection of the Odessians.

Abberline worked ceaselessly with his team to combat the gangs, but on the rare occasions that the police did manage to get either of the gangs into court, the case would invariably collapse, with witnesses intimidated into silence. The climax eventually came when the two gangs held a meeting, which was to supposedly sort out their differences. The meeting took place in a hall over the York Minster public house in Philpot Street. Needless to say, neither gang would give ground to the other, and within thirty minutes, the 200 gang members present erupted into violence. One man, known as Kid McCoy, who, despite his name, was a Jewish boxer, killed one of his rivals and the police were called in. This time, the evidence was there before them and people started to come forward to add their testimony. A case was brought not just against Kid McCoy, but against the leaders of the gangs as well. The case ended up in court and both gangs were eventually smashed.

Smashing the Bessarabians and the Odessians did not, however, solve the overall problem of protection gangs in the East End, for no sooner had these gangs been sent off to prison, than others were jumping eagerly into their shoes. The Strutton Ground Boys were one such gang, who decided to take over the stallholders and shopkeepers of Petticoat Lane market.

The Strutton Ground Boys were a motley collection of youths, with no real experience of organised crime. They had heard of the demise of the Bessarabians and the Odessians, and had decided to take over where they had left off. All six of them swaggered into Petticoat Lane market one Sunday morning and started throwing their weight around, demanding protection money from the street's traders. The traders were not quite as hapless, however, as the Strutton Ground Boys thought they would be, and told this motley bunch of would-be gangsters, in no uncertain terms, to clear off or face the consequences.

This wasn't quite what the gang had in mind, and so they took to their heels, running as fast as they could through the crowded market street, overturning stalls, throwing goods into the gutters and shoving the traders over wherever they could. As they departed they shouted that they would return the following week, and if their demands were not met, then the traders could expect more of what they had just received.

Unbeknown to the gang, the street traders were so incensed at the way they had been treated that they called a meeting that same day after the market had finished. One of the traders had recognised one of the youths as coming from an area close to Westminster, where Strutton Ground was, and where the gang had got their name from. The traders were not prepared to wait until the following week and lay themselves open to attack again, so they decided there and then to take the battle direct to the gang. They armed themselves with clubs, sticks, rocks and any other weapon they could lay their hands on, and proceeded to Strutton Ground, where they located the homes of the youths in the gang and duly started wrecking them. The Strutton Ground Boys got wind of what was going on and hurriedly returned to their homes to find the market traders still in action, smashing their properties to pieces. A fierce fight developed and the local police were called, who eventually arrested all concerned, including the market traders. However, when the facts were established the traders were released and the gang members were charged and imprisoned, ending yet another attempted gangland coup in the East End.

Petticoat Lane, however, was still not devoid of its criminal groups. A twenty-strong group of pickpockets, called the Blind Beggar Gang, after the famous or now infamous pub of that same name, were happily plying their trade there in broad daylight. This was until undercover police officers, using Abberline's plain-clothes techniques, finally busted them.

Abberline's persistence and dogged determination were starting to pay off. Whitechapel was beginning to get an air of normality about it. This is not to say that crime no longer existed there, as it most certainly did, but people were starting to feel safer, even the women, many of whom would now walk down streets where they would not have dreamt of walking a few months earlier. Abberline became a well-known face and name on the streets of Whitechapel, as a desk-bound office job wasn't for him and he never felt better than when he was out there, meeting and talking to the local inhabitants. 'How else,' he would say, 'are we going to get to know them, and find out what is happening on the streets?' Even his colleagues in the force were now starting to accept him as a leading expert on the area, and many of these were men who had lived in the Whitechapel area all their lives.

However, even the most dedicated policemen need to take some time off for recreation now and then, and Abberline was no exception; in fact, he was very pleased indeed when members of his team decided to treat him and another senior officer to a night out at the Hoxton Varieties Music Hall, in Pitfield Street, Hoxton. On the night, however, the other officer backed out because of a severe case of influenza and Abberline was forced to go alone.

Nevertheless, it seemed that fate had different plans for Abberline, for as he arrived at the theatre he found his way blocked by three young women who were engaged in some sort of dispute at the entrance. One of the young ladies had lost or mislaid her ticket and was being refused entry. Being the gentleman that he was, Abberline offered his spare ticket to the young lady, which not only solved her problem, but also allowed him to get in before the show actually started.

Once inside the theatre, Abberline quickly took his seat in the second row from the front, as the lights began to dim for the start of the performance. The orchestra began to play, the curtains swung open and a troupe of acrobats came bounding onto the stage. At this point he heard voices to his left, and glancing round, he saw the young lady making her way past the other members of the audience towards the seat next to his. He had let the three young ladies go before him, how come she was late taking her seat and disrupting the show, he thought. 'Sorry,' she whispered, as she finally took her seat. He noticed that even one of the acrobats took a slight tumble as he took his eye off the others in the troupe for a moment, to look at the young lady.

Did the acrobat falter because of her interruption to his show, or was it because of her beauty, Abberline wondered. He shed a brief glance towards the young lady, and sure enough she was very beautiful. As he did so, however, she also glanced towards him. Abberline felt himself blush at being caught in the act of looking at the girl, but she quickly overcame the situation by smiling at him and saying, 'They're very good aren't they?'

True to form, Abberline didn't look in the direction of the young lady for the rest of the performance, and only gave her a very brief look and half smile as the show finished, and she got up to leave. She, in turn, smiled back at him and bade him goodnight.

During this period of time, theatres were not the relatively genteel places that we know today, especially in areas such as the East End, where the audience went to drink as much as they did to see the actual show. There was also plenty of interaction between the audience and the performers, mostly from the direction of the audience, who could not only be very vociferous at times, but also threw bad fruit and vegetables at the performers if they thought they were not performing up to scratch.

Women, as a whole, did not usually attend such places of variety unless accompanied by a man, which was probably another of the deciding factors that encouraged Abberline to give the young lady his spare ticket. Sitting next to him, he thought, would surely offer her some sort of protection, and so it did, while she was inside the theatre.

It had started to rain as Abberline made his way out of the theatre and a crowd was building up under cover of the theatre's awning. Hansom cabs were few and far between on such a night, and especially in weather like this, so Abberline turned his coat collar up, patted his hat down firmly upon his head and stepped out into the pouring rain. He had only just made it across the road when he heard a scream, followed by a lot of shouting. He turned to see a young man pushing and shoving his way through the crowd, and then starting to run. The man was carrying a ladies' purse in his hand, which he had just stolen, and the victim, who was screaming and attempting to run after him, was none other than the young lady Abberline had given his ticket to.

Without hesitation, Abberline took up the chase after the man, who, obviously not knowing who Abberline was, had run across the road, in Abberline's direction. As the man reached a horse-drinking trough, Abberline threw his walking cane at him, catching him between the legs and causing him to stumble. By the time the man had started to pull himself back to his feet, Abberline was upon him, causing the man to stumble back, half falling into the horse trough and enabling Abberline to retrieve the purse and make an arrest.

Cases like this were dealt with very quickly during this period, and within a couple of weeks the man had been tried in court and sentenced to two years' hard labour. During the course of preparing the case, Abberline got to know the young lady victim of the crime: her name was Emma Beament, a 32-year-old daughter of a merchant from Hoxton New Town, Shoreditch.

The criminal case against the man might well have been over, but Abberline's case for Emma Beament was only just beginning. As shy and awkward as he was with women, Abberline made sure not to lose contact with Emma, first calling on her on the pretext of seeing how she was bearing up, to use his own words, after the terrible ordeal she had been through. Her father was very impressed with Abberline, firstly for going to the aid of his daughter and apprehending the criminal, and secondly, for having a man of such distinction visiting his house, even if it was, as he quite rightly suspected, to court the favours of his daughter.

The relationship between Abberline and Emma continued to grow, but after the terrible calamity he had experienced with his first wife, he was adamant that nothing like that would ever happen again, and so it took him nearly three years to pluck up the courage to ask Emma to marry him, which she immediately accepted. They were married on 17 December 1876.

On 8 April 1878, Abberline was promoted yet again, this time to local inspector in charge of H Division's CID. His reputation for hard work was obviously starting to grow, with his name cropping up more and more on various documents and cases. On 26 February 1887 Abberline was transferred to A Division (Whitehall), and then moved to CO Division (Central Office) at Scotland Yard on 19 November 1887.

On 17 December 1887 the *East London Observer* reported on a guest of honour celebration at the Unicorn Tavern, Shoreditch, where Abberline was honoured with promotion to Scotland Yard from H Division:

On the occasion of a dinner and a presentation to Detective Inspector Abberline, late of the H Division of police but now attached to the central office, Great Scotland Yard. The chairman, Mr. George Hay Young said, 'The inhabitants felt they could not let such an officer leave them for another district after being many years in their service without some little souvenir of their esteem and regard, and in recognition and appreciation of his services'.

Turning to Abberline, Mr Young presented him with a beautiful gold keyless hunting watch and a purse full of gold. On the watch was engraved 'Presented together with a purse of gold to Inspector F.G. Abberline by the inhabitants of Spitalfields, Whitechapel etc, on his leaving the district after fourteen years of service as a mark of their esteem and regard'. Abberline, in responding, said he could hardly find the language to express his thanks to the chairman for his too flattering expressions, and to the company present for the honour they did him that evening and for the beautiful and substantial testimonial of their goodwill presented to him by the chairman on their behalf. He assured them that he was deeply indebted to them for the many kindnesses he had received during the fourteen years he was with them. Superintendent Arnold commented that he was very sorry to lose Mr Abberline from the division, for a better officer there could not be, and he was afraid it would be a long time before he could find another to equal him.

The move, however, was not to last, for on 1 September 1888, Abberline was seconded back to Whitechapel to investigate the murder of Mary Ann Nichols.

3

The Whitechapel Murders

*N*ichols was the third woman, who had been working as a prostitute in the area, to have been found murdered and horribly mutilated within the past six months. The first was Emma Elizabeth Smith, a 45-year-old mother of two, a widower and a prostitute. Emma Smith was the only Whitechapel murder victim to live long enough to tell the tale.

On the night of Easter Monday, 3 April 1888, Emma Smith left her lodgings in Limehouse and went out, apparently looking for trade. In the early hours of the following morning, she was seen by a neighbour staggering back towards her lodgings with her face covered in blood and her left ear almost severed. She was clutching her woollen shawl, which was also dripping with blood, tightly between her legs. It was later discovered to be there to try to stem the flow of blood from another terrible injury, which she would later die from.

The neighbour rushed to help her as she tried to hold herself up against the brick wall next to her door, and called for the lodging house manager to come out and help. The lodging house manager brought a chair with her, which they sat Smith down in while the lodging house manager ran off to call a hansom cab. Ignoring Smith's protestations, they managed to get her into the cab when it arrived and rushed her to the London Hospital on Whitechapel Road. George Haslip was the house surgeon on duty and had been working all night, since 3 p.m. the previous day. As tired as Haslip was, he tried everything in his power to save the young woman, but she had already lost so much blood that he knew he was fighting a losing battle. Before she eventually slipped into a coma, she managed to describe her assailants and the details of her assault, which a nurse took down. Smith's wounds were unfortunately too severe for her to survive, and she died four days later having never regained consciousness.

The details of what had happened to her that night, as she reported before her death, were that she was returning home, 'after having a drink or two', when a group of three or four young men started to follow her. She first noticed them as she crossed the road near to Whitechapel church and made her way into Brick Lane. The men stopped her on the corner of Brick Lane and Wentworth Street, where they pushed her into a doorway, and beat, raped and robbed her. If this wasn't bad enough, before leaving the scene, one of them slashed at her face with a knife causing the severing of her ear, while another of the men viciously jabbed a blunt object into her vagina, tearing the perineum.

Emma Smith passed out with the excruciating pain and collapsed in a heap in the doorway. Passers-by ignored her, probably thinking she was just another rough sleeper taking refuge in the doorway, but some twenty minutes later, when she finally regained consciousness, she managed to pull herself to her feet and drag herself back to her lodgings, which were at least 1 mile away.

The murder of Emma Smith was at first attributed to one of the many Whitechapel gangs who were known to patrol the area in which the incident occurred, extorting money from prostitutes in return for their protection. In fact, it wasn't until September 1888 that she was first attributed as a Ripper victim by the press.

Whether or not Emma's death should be attributed to the Ripper is debatable. There is no reason to doubt her story that she was attacked by a group of men, but no other Ripper victim, with the possible exception of Elizabeth Stride, according to witness Israel Schwartz's account, was believed to have been killed by more than one man. Neither was any other Ripper victim raped. These two facts, however, do not necessarily mean that Emma Smith was not a victim of the Ripper, for what if the Ripper had been one of the members of the group that attacked and killed her? This is a possibility, but unfortunately, there is little evidence to back this theory.

The second possible Ripper victim was Martha Tabram, who was found dead in a stairwell in Spitalfields just three weeks prior to Mary Ann Nichols, on 7 August 1888, in what we would now term classical Ripper victim pose.

Martha Tabram had previously been married to Henry Samuel Tabram, but their marriage ended after six years due to Martha's heavy drinking, which seemed to be a common factor in most of these cases. She moved in with another man but that relationship was also affected by Martha's drinking, which left her to fend for herself in the only way she knew: prostitution.

Bank holiday Monday, 6 August, Martha Tabram went out with a friend, Mary Ann Connelly, who was known as Pearly Poll. They visited a number of local pubs during the evening, where witnesses say they were seen with various men, some of whom were soldiers. When questioned by the police later, Pearly Poll said that Martha and her had picked up two guardsmen, a corporal and a private in the Two Brewers public house, and then drank with them in several pubs including the White Swan on Whitechapel High Street.

It was around 11.45 p.m. when the two women left the White Swan. Pearly Poll took her corporal into the nearby Angel Alley, and waved goodbye to Martha as she took the private into George Yard. Both, obviously, for the purpose of having sex. This was the last time Pearly Poll would see Martha Tabram alive.

At 4.45 the following morning, it was just starting to get light as John Reeves, a tenant of George Yard Buildings, left his lodgings and saw the body of a woman lying in a pool of blood on the first-floor landing. Reeves rushed off and found PC Barrett patrolling nearby. The body, although not yet identified, was that of Martha Tabram. She was lying flat on her back, face upward, with her arms and hands outstretched by her sides. Her knees were bent and her legs open in a manner which could suggest intercourse had possibly taken place.

When questioned later on, PC Barrett stated that at about 2 a.m. he had seen a young Grenadier Guardsman in Wentworth Street, close to the northern end of George Yard. PC Barrett questioned the guardsman, asking him what he was doing there, to which the guardsman replied that he was waiting for 'a chum' who had gone off with a girl. This explanation satisfied PC Barrett at the time, but his superiors questioned his immediate acceptance of it later, after the post-mortem revealed that one of the wounds found inflicted on the body was a deep wound to the sternum, which appeared to have been caused by a dagger or bayonet, thereby leading the police to believe that the guardsman PC Barrett saw that night could well have been the murderer. Further inquiries were made, but no further evidence of the guardsman's identity or whereabouts was ever offered up, and for all intents and purpose, the case was put on the back burner, so to speak.

The bayonet wound was not the only injury that the post-mortem revealed. It showed five wounds to the left lung, two to the right lung, one to the heart, five to the liver, two to the spleen and six to the stomach. There were also numerous smaller wounds to various parts of the body, making a total of thirty-nine in all, suggesting a frenzied attack, rather than a straightforward murder, carried out in the anger of the moment.

According to Dr Timothy Killeen, who undertook the post-mortem, the killer focused his attack on the breasts, belly and groin area. In his opinion, all but one of the wounds were inflicted by a right-handed attacker, and all but one seemed to have been the result of an ordinary small knife, or penknife. The one, which was different was the bayonet wound, as already mentioned.

This, then, was the basis of the case that Abberline was now confronted with. Three prostitutes mutilated and murdered, all within a very short distance of each other, and all within a period of less than six months. As intriguing as this might have sounded to Inspector Abberline at the time, nothing could have prepared him for the horrors he was to face in the months that followed.

4

In Charge?

_T_here was no doubt, in most people's minds that Inspector Abberline was the ideal man for this case, due to his extensive experience in the area. He was placed in charge of a team of detectives, who would be investigating what was first known as the Whitechapel murders, but would eventually become known worldwide as the Jack the Ripper murders.

The name of the policeman most people still associate with the Jack the Ripper case is, of course, Inspector Frederick Abberline, but theoretically, the man in overall charge of the investigation into the Ripper murders was Chief Inspector Donald Swanson.

Swanson was placed in overall charge of the investigation into the Whitechapel murders from 1 September 1888. He was freed from all other duties and given his own office at Scotland Yard from which to co-ordinate inquiries. He was given permission to see all the paperwork, reports and documents relating to the investigation. His appointment to the case was one of the few actions taken by his close friend, Deputy Commissioner Robert Anderson, between his sudden appointment to head of the CID that morning and his equally sudden departure on leave to Switzerland later that afternoon.

Swanson, however, was not familiar with Whitechapel at all, which is why Abberline was re-assigned back to H Division in order to co-ordinate operations on the ground. As a result, Abberline ended up doing most of the actual legwork on the case and became the officer most associated with the investigation in the mind of the public.

Abberline relished being put in charge of such a case, for what he had at first perceived to be a sole murder case, was quickly turning into part of a series of murders, and particularly grizzly ones at that, which had caught both the public's and the media's imagination. What he didn't know at this point, however, was that he would be reporting all his findings to Chief Inspector Donald Swanson. Not that there was anything strange in this, for it was completely normal police procedure for someone of Abberline's rank to have to report to a senior officer. What did rankle him, however, was the fact that he hadn't been told that it would be Swanson whom he would be working under. In all probability, Abberline assumed that he would be directly responsible to Deputy Commissioner Robert Anderson himself, and would not need to have to report his every move to someone he classed as just a 'personal friend' of the deputy commissioner.

Abberline's first day in his new office was Saturday 1 September, just a matter of hours after Polly Nichols had been found murdered; he did not have time to settle in, go through the few facts of the case or even organise his team. He instead had to rush straight off to the Whitechapel Working Lad's Institute on Whitechapel Road, next to the present-day Whitechapel Underground Station, where the inquest into Nichols' death was being opened. It was noted that Inspector Frederick Abberline attended on behalf of the CID, but after all the rush to get there, he found that the inquest had now been adjourned until Monday 3 September.

Earlier that Saturday morning, Dr Llewellyn had conducted a post-mortem on the body of Polly Nichols, in which he concluded with the following:

5 teeth missing; slight laceration on tongue; bruise on lower part of right jaw (possibly from a punch or thumb pressure); circular bruise on left side of face (possibly also from finger pressure); left side of neck, 1 inch below jaw, 4 inch incision starting immediately below the left ear; a second throat incision starting 1 inch below and 1 inch in front of the first, running 8 inches in a circular direction around the throat and stopping 3 inches below the right ear, completely severing all tissues down to the spine, including the large vessels of the neck on both sides; no blood found on breast of clothes or of body; on the lower part of abdomen, 2 to 3 inches from the left side ran a very deep, jagged wound, cutting the tissues through; several incisions ran across the abdomen; 3 or 4 similar cuts ran down the right side of the abdomen.

The next morning, Sunday 2 September, Abberline had to break his promise to his wife Emma to accompany her to church. Needless to say, Emma wasn't very happy with this, as they had always attended church together. This was his first full day at his new job, and already he was breaking promises to her. Abberline had no alternative but to attend a meeting with his new team at the Whitechapel office, where he was to instruct them to take witness statements while the facts were still fresh in their minds. Every hour that was allowed to lapse could lose them valuable time, possible evidence and, most certainly, momentum.

From the little they had gleaned so far, the officers in Abberline's team couldn't see his reasoning on this. There were no actual witnesses to the crime, apart from a motley collection of people, neighbours and so on who happened to be on the streets during the hours that Polly Nichols was last seen alive, and the time she was found dead. Abberline was adamant on this, reasoning with them that if they could gain two pieces of identical evidence from the people who had been on the streets that night, they might just add up to one real piece of evidence that could lead to a conviction.

The team obeyed Abberline's instructions and gathered every scrap of information they could, no matter how small or seemingly insignificant. They interviewed three men, Henry Tomkins, Charles Brittain and James Mumford, who all worked as slaughtermen at Barber's Knacker's Yard, Winthrop Street, approximately 150 yards from Buck's Row. Tomkins, Brittain and Mumford left the slaughterhouse at midnight on the 31st, and walked to the end of the street together, none of them seeing anything suspicious at the time.

At 12.30 a.m., an un-named witness said he saw Polly Nichols leaving the Frying Pan pub on the corner of Brick Lane and Thrawl Street, and said that she was alone at the time. Sometime later, although the exact time is unknown, PC Neil passed through Winthrop Street and saw, through an open doorway, Tomkins, Brittain and Mumford hard at work.

At around 1.20 a.m., the house deputy at 18 Thrawl Street, which was the doss house where Polly had been staying, said that she had turned up asking for her room, but he had shown her out as she didn't have any money to pay for it. He stated that she seemed somewhat drunk, or merry, as he put it, and just smiled at him as she left, saying, 'Don't you go worrying about me, I'll soon get my doss money.' Her departing shot to him was, 'See what a jolly bonnet I've got now', referring to her new hat.

Sometime after that, probably around 2 a.m., a huge fire had broken out at Shadwell Dry Docks, and a local woman, Emily Holland, was returning from watching the fire when she stopped for a moment to shelter from the rain, outside a grocer's shop on the corner of Whitechapel Road and Osborn Street. She heard someone cough behind her and turned to see Polly Nichols, whom she was acquainted with, standing in the doorway behind her. She said that she felt sorry for her as she looked very drunk holding on to the wall beside her. Holland told Nichols that it was very late and tried to persuade her to go home to her lodgings in Thrawl Street, but Polly seemed oblivious to what she was telling her and just laughed, saying that she had her doss money several times that night but had drunk it away every time. She then proceeded to show Emily, her new bonnet, saying, in a very slurred voice, not to worry about her, that she would be alright. Polly Nichols then staggered as she pushed past Holland and started to walk away, along Whitechapel Road, in the direction of Buck's Row. That was the last time Emily Holland would ever see Polly Nichols alive.

Sometime between 2 a.m. and 3 a.m., Police Sergeant Kerby passed through Buck's Row and reported all to be quiet. At about 3.30 a.m., Charles Andrew Cross left his home at 22 Doveton Street, Bethnal Green, and started to make his way to work at Pickfords' depot in Broad Street, where he worked as a car-man, or cart driver. As he walked through Buck's Row, Cross said he saw a bundle in front of the stable yard gateway. In the darkness he mistook the bundle for an old abandoned tarpaulin; it was only as he got closer and bent down to look at it that he saw it was the body of a woman.

This is where another witness, Robert Paul, comes into the picture. Paul was on his way to his place of work at Corbett's Court. As he cut through Buck's Row, he saw the figure of a man, slightly bending down, looking at something on the ground in front of him. The figure was that of Charles Cross, who turned towards Paul as he heard his footsteps on the cobbles behind him, and called to him, saying, 'Quick, come over here and look at this, there's a woman lying here'.

Polly Nichols was lying on her back with her skirts lifted almost to her waist. Cross lifted one of her hands and turned again to Paul, saying, 'She's stone cold'. He then turned to Paul, asking him to feel, but Paul declined. He disagreed as well when Cross said they shouldn't leave the woman lying uncovered like she was, and that they should help to cover her up before anyone else saw her.

Paul was very reticent about doing anything like that, and could hardly bear to look at the poor woman, let alone touch her. His immediate thoughts were that they should leave her where she was and go and search for a constable without delay. Cross agreed and the two men hurried away.

Just minutes after Cross and Paul had left the scene in their quest to find a constable, another police officer, PC Neil, happened to enter Buck's Row completely independently, and saw the bundle lying on the pavement. When he shone his lantern upon it he discovered it to be the body of Polly Nichols. In his report, which he wrote later, he described the scene as follows:

The victim was lying lengthwise with her head turned towards the East; her left hand touched the gate; her bonnet was off her head, lying near her right hand; her skirts were rumpled just above her knees; her throat was severely cut; her eyes were wide open and glassy; blood had oozed from her throat wounds; her arms felt warm from the elbows up; her hands were open. The gateway was 9 feet. 10 inches in height and led to some stables; they were closed.

Unlike today, there seemed to be an abundance of police officers on the ground, and within minutes of PC Neil discovering the body, he noticed another constable, PC Thain, further along the road. Neil signalled to him, showed him the body, and told him to 'Run at once for Dr Llewellyn'.

PC Thain did as he was told and immediately left to fetch Doctor Rees Ralph Llewellyn, who had his surgery at 152 Whitechapel Road, just 300 yards from Buck's Row. While he was gone, PC Neil carried out a rudimentary search of the immediate area, apparently finding nothing of any significance.

At roughly the same time, the two men, Cross and Paul, who had first discovered the body, had now found another constable, PC Jonas Mizen, who they informed about their grizzly find. Mizen thanked the men and dismissed them, telling them they should carry on their way to work now as their presence could hamper police procedures.

When PC Mizen arrived at Brown's Stable Yard, PC Neil sent him immediately for an ambulance and reinforcements from J Division, Bethnal Green, as the murder had occurred on their territory. About half an hour later, PC Mizen and another officer arrived back on the scene with the 'ambulance', which was not an ambulance as we know it today, but nothing more than a stretcher on wheels.

By daybreak, the area was teaming with police officers as well as a scattering of nosy neighbours, and the inevitable members of the press, who seem to smell these things out from a radius of 10 miles or more. A very tired and not too happy Dr Llewellyn had also arrived at the scene (direct from his bed) and made a very cursory examination, which he concluded as follows:

Severe injuries to the throat; her hands and wrists were cold, yet her body and legs were still warm; her chest and heart showed life to be extinct, estimating that she died no more than a half hour prior to the examination; very little blood around the neck; no marks of a struggle or of the body being dragged.

One of the detectives from Bethnal Green, who also arrived on the scene, was Inspector Spratling, who immediately gave orders for the nearby premises of Essex Wharf, the Great Eastern Railway, East London Railway and the District Railway as far as Thomas Street to be thoroughly searched. While this was happening, a neighbour came out into the yard with a bucket of water and started washing the blood from the cobblestones. This was obviously not considered important at that time and he was left unchecked by anyone, to wash away the evidence.

Inspector Spratling and PC Thain then went directly to the mortuary where Polly Nichols' body was still lying on the ambulance in the yard. Spratling made notes of her description and what she was wearing. He then recalled

Dr Llewellyn for a further examination. Dr Llewellyn's second cursory examination was noted as follows:

> Throat cut from left to right with 2 distinct cuts being on the left side and with the windpipe, gullet, and spinal cord being cut through; a bruise, possibly from a thumb, on the lower right jaw with another on the left cheek; the abdomen had been cut open from centre of the bottom ribs along the right side; under the pelvis, left of the stomach, was another wound – jagged; the omentum (One of the folds of the peritoneum that connect the stomach with other abdominal organs) was cut in several places; 2 small stabs on the privy parts; the knife used seemed to have been strong-bladed; death almost instantaneous.

This, then, was the 'evidence' that Inspector Abberline was presented with: the body of a prostitute, obviously murdered; a number of witnesses as to where and when the body had been found; and detailed notes of the injuries sustained by the victim, where she was seen directly prior to being murdered and details of what she was wearing. All undoubtedly very important pieces of evidence, but a major piece was missing: was it that there was not one clue or sighting of anyone who could have possibly been the killer? Normally in murder cases, especially where neighbours pop up as witnesses, there is at least one or two names that crop up as possible suspects, but in Polly Nichols' case, as yet, there was no one!

Inspector Abberline attended the second and third days of the Polly Nichols inquest, which were held on 2/3 September respectively, and which, to be perfectly honest, were not exactly illuminating. A number of witnesses were called, including Inspector Spratling, Inspector Helson, PC Mizen, Charles Cross, Dr Llewellyn, PC Thain, plus a number of local people, all of whose statements Abberline had already read, and knew, by this time, almost by heart.

There was one other witness whom he had not heard of at this point, and that was a woman named Mary Ann Monk, who was a former inmate of the Lambeth Workhouse, where she had met Nichols some time previously. She also claimed to have last seen her, recently, in a pub on the New Kent Road, where they drank together. Mary Ann Monk was the first person to positively identify Nichols' body in the mortuary at 7.30 p.m., 31 August 1888.

The third day of the inquest was adjourned until Monday 17 September, to allow for Nichols' funeral, which was held on 6 September. The final day of the inquest was held on Saturday 22 September, when the coroner summed the case up with a verdict of 'Willful murder committed by some person or persons unknown'.

5

Leather Apron

By the time the inquest into Polly Nichols' death had concluded, Inspector Abberline was finding himself becoming deeply involved in what at first he presumed to be a singular murder case. This had quickly escalated into a triple-murder scenario, and had now turned into what the papers were describing as an ongoing series of murders, which today we would describe as serial killings. For during the early hours of Saturday 8 September 1888, yet another grizzly murder had taken place, which was that of Annie Chapman, who also worked as a prostitute in the Spitalfields area.

The local team of officers from Bethnal Green, led by Detective Inspector John Spratling, had no success whatsoever, and to make matters worse, the local press were attributing the Nichols murder, and the two previous murders of Emma Elizabeth Smith and Martha Tabram, to a local gang. *The Star* newspaper, however, took up a completely different line and suggested a single killer was the culprit of all three murders. This in turn led to other newspapers taking up the storyline, with headlines such as 'Maniac Killer at large', and this was before the discovery of Annie Chapman's body.

Abberline found the pressure on him starting to grow; the press was demanding action. They wanted to know why a high-ranking police officer such as him had not come up with one single suspect, after being involved in the case for over three weeks (this was at the time of the Polly Nichols inquest). As the press and the public became more anxious, so too did Abberline's boss at Scotland Yard, Chief Inspector Donald Swanson. What exactly did they expect Abberline to do? Abberline explained to Swanson that he was doing everything possible, including house-to-house searches and questioning literally dozens of witnesses, and possible suspects, all of whom were eventually eliminated from their inquiries after a few days at the most.

The first thing Abberline did do, in regard to the Annie Chapman murder, was to make sure no clues, no matter how small, were overlooked or obliterated, as the bloodstains were in the Polly Nichols case. He ordered a thorough search of the yard where the body was found, as well as the immediate area around Hanbury Street. The search uncovered two clues which were noted down as evidence, as they could possibly be vital to the case; the first was a bloodstained envelope with the crest of the Sussex Regiment embossed upon the front, which was found in the corner of the yard. The second was a leather apron, which was found near a water tap in the yard. There was also something else that Inspector Abberline found at the scene of the crime, and that was two brightly polished farthings, two brass rings and a few assorted coins. At first glance, one might think there is nothing special in these items, but they were not found thrown about haphazardly; they were found neatly laid out around the feet of the corpse, almost as if in a ritualistic fashion.

Unfortunately, the constable accompanying Inspector Abberline at the time, taking notes, failed to realise the possible significance of the order these items were laid out, and the exact location of where they were found, and instead noted them as 'Assorted coins and brass rings close to the body of the deceased'.

Abberline had decided not to release too much detail to the press, as he so rightly said, 'They distort everything'. The press, however, were eager for any bit of news they could lay their hands on, and when one reporter overheard a police officer mention the leather apron that had been found, he decided to run with this as a vital piece of information. Its very name conjures up a picture of a possible morgue attendant; someone who cuts up bodies and is covered with splatterings of blood.

The *Manchester Guardian* reported that: 'Whatever information may be in the possession of the police they deem it necessary to keep it a secret. It is believed their attention is particularly directed to a notorious character known as "Leather Apron".'

No such directive had been issued by Inspector Abberline, or any other member of the constabulary, but that didn't stop the press from printing such. Not only did they report such 'findings' as if they were true, they also exaggerated their 'facts' wildly. John Pizer, a Polish Jew who made leather footwear, was known locally as 'Leather Apron' but he was far from being the notorious character and the crude Jewish stereotype that the press painted him as.

Local feeling nevertheless became so emphatic that something needed to be done. After reading non-stop reports of how the police were ignoring the real suspects for political reasons, the police were forced into making a number of arrests, including that of John Pizer. Inspector Abberline was furious at Pizer's arrest, which had been ordered direct from Scotland Yard; nevertheless, he had to go through the routine, in the knowledge that they had no real evidence to even warrant questioning him, let alone arresting him. Pizer was quickly released after his alibis were confirmed.

The leather apron was later found to belong to John Richardson, a porter from nearby Spitalfields Market; he had given his apron to his mother, who lived at 29 Hanbury Street, to wash. She had washed it and left it in the yard to dry. Abberline suspected Richardson and took him in for questioning, where he did admit to being in the yard in the early hours of that morning, but said that he had only gone there to see how his mother was when on his way to work. Richardson was investigated thoroughly by Abberline and his team, but was eliminated several days later from their inquiries.

The pressure on Abberline was starting to mount. Chief Inspector Donald Swanson, at Scotland Yard, was demanding results, which was easier said than done. Abberline was working day and night, sometimes even sleeping in his office overnight, which didn't bode too well with his wife, Emma. To add to his woes, he also had the press breathing down his neck, asking for interviews, and printing headlines that more or less labelled the police as incompetent fools.

The press were blaming everyone and anyone, with the Home Secretary, Henry Mathews, and Commissioner of Police, Sir Charles Warren, being described as 'Helpless, Heedless, and Useless'. As if to reiterate these comments against them, Sir Charles Warren came up with the ridiculous idea of using bloodhounds to track the killer down. How on earth they were going to be able to accomplish this, no one seemed to know. While on a trial run in Tooting Common, the two dogs, Barnaby and Burgho, ran away. Telegrams were sent to all London police stations to be on the look out for the pair of canine detectives. When the press picked up on this of course, the public were convulsed with laughter, and the police were ridiculed even more.

One needs to bear in mind that Inspector Abberline was at this time not just investigating a singular murder case he was still in charge (theoretically) of the Whitechapel murders as a whole, which now included, Emma Smith, Martha Tabram, Polly Nichols and now Annie Chapman, and still without one credible witness or suspect.

To make matters worse, if that were possible, a group of local businessmen had formed themselves into a group known as the Whitechapel Vigilance Committee, led by a local builder named George Lusk, who was elected chairman during the committee's first meeting on 10 September 1888. The purpose of the committee was to employ local volunteers to patrol the streets, mainly at night, in their search for the murderer. They said that the murders were affecting their businesses, and that the police were doing nothing whatsoever to help.

As chairman of the committee, George Lusk became something of a celebrity, with his name appearing in the national newspapers and on posters in Whitechapel, appealing for information concerning the identity of the murderer. Lusk also complained about the police's lack of foresight in not offering a reward for such information. In answer to this, Chief Inspector Donald Swanson immediately had an official police poster made up, stating: 'Ghastly Murder in the east end. – Dreadful mutilation of a woman. – Capture Leather Apron.' This absolutely infuriated Abberline, as John Pizer, the man the public knew as Leather Apron, had by this time already been cleared of any involvement in the murder, and to mention the name 'Leather Apron' again would, he felt, throw the public off the track completely. This was still, of course, before the name 'Jack the Ripper' was thrust into the public arena.

6

Searching for the Real Annie Chapman

*F*rederick George Abberline had not embarked on his career in the police force because he thought it was going to be an easy job, neither did he do it for the money, for a policeman's wages in those days were very poor by today's standards, and the only perk he was allowed was living accommodation at his local police station. Abberline had entered the police service because he was a decent and honest man. In today's parlance, he would probably be described as a man of the people.

Although born in the country, he never felt more at home than when he was in the East End of London; he became almost an honorary East Ender, and as such, had an empathy with his surroundings, and the people who lived and worked there. Unlike many other policemen of his day, Abberline was interested in the well-being of his fellow East Enders, and did not treat them simply as statistics; be they a local priest, a market labourer or a lowly prostitute, in his eyes they were all human beings, who deserved the same level of help, respect, and protection from the police as a Westminster politician would expect.

During his years in the police force, Abberline had seen many murders, but it was only when he was put in charge of what became known as the Ripper case that he saw anything so horrific; for these poor women had not just been murdered, they had been mutilated, and from the little evidence on hand, he could see no motive for the murders, other than that the women were all prostitutes.

Abberline decided to find out as much as possible about these women, from their early life onwards, and not just as lifeless corpses lying in some dirty alley in the East End. He felt that if he could learn more about them, it might just be possible to gain an insight into their lives, their friends, their fears and what motivated them. This, he hoped, might possibly lead to the murderer.

Starting with the most current, which was Annie Chapman, Abberline learned that she was born Eliza Ann Smith, on 22 February 1842, the daughter of George Smith, a soldier in the 2nd Regiment Life Guards, and his partner, Ruth Chapman. Annie was born out of wedlock; her parents didn't marry until nearly six months after she was born in Paddington. Although a soldier at the time of their marriage, Annie's father later became a domestic servant.

Annie Chapman was 27 years old when she married her cousin, John Chapman, a coachman, on 1 May 1869. They were married at All Saints church in the Knightsbridge district of London. They lived quite happily for a number of years at various addresses around West London, during which time they had three children, Emily Ruth Chapman, born 25 June 1870; Annie Georgina Chapman, born 5 June 1873; and John Alfred Chapman, born 21 November 1880.

The family moved in 1881 to Windsor, Berkshire, where John Chapman took a job as coachman to a farm bailiff. But instead of the idyllic lifestyle they had expected, this seemed to signal the start of their downfall. Their youngest child, John, had been born severely disabled, but instead of the country air and lifestyle helping him, it seemed to have the opposite effect, and he developed breathing problems. As if this wasn't enough to break Annie's heart, within months, their firstborn, Emily Ruth, developed meningitis, and died of it shortly after at the age of 12. There can be no denying that this tragedy, coupled with the ongoing effect of seeing their youngest child constantly gasping for breath, sent both Annie and her husband on the road to heavy drinking, and eventual separation in 1884.

John Chapman left the matrimonial home, leaving Annie to look after the two remaining children on 10s per week, which he supported her with. Ten shillings doesn't seem much by today's standards, but it was enough at that time, especially in the country, to provide her with a reasonable standard of living. The one big problem was, however, that Annie was still drinking heavily, and within a short time, had her youngest child, John, taken into the care of a local charitable school. At around this time, Annie's daughter, Annie Georgina, who by now was an adolescent, had also decided to leave the family home, and ran off to join a travelling circus in the French Third Republic.

Annie Chapman eventually moved to Whitechapel, where sometime around 1886, she moved in with a man named John Sivvey at a common lodging house at 30 Dorset Street, Spitalfields. It is unsure whether Sivvey was his real name or just a nickname, as he did work at making wire sieves. Whatever the outcome, Annie Chapman became known to many people at that time as Annie 'Sievey' or 'Siffey'.

This relationship didn't last long, however, as on Christmas Eve 1886, having not received her weekly 10s from her ex-husband, Chapman made a few enquiries, and found, much to her misfortune, that he had died that same week of alcohol-related causes. Not only had she lost her only source of income at that time, but within days, John Sivvey also walked out, in all probability due to the cessation of her weekly 10s income. One of her friends at the lodging house later testified that Chapman became very depressed after this and went rapidly downhill, drinking more than ever, when she could get the money that is. This in turn led to her friends calling her 'Dark Annie'.

Chapman earned a little money from crochet work, making antimacassars, but this just about managed to pay for her lodgings; if she needed money to buy drink, which she often did, then the only way she knew of obtaining this was to sell herself as a prostitute. By 1888 she was living at Crossingham's lodging house at number 35 Dorset Street, where she paid 8d a night for a double bed. She had two regular clients, one known as Harry the Hawker and the other, a man named Ted Stanley, a supposed retired soldier who was known to her fellow lodgers as 'the Pensioner'. As it later transpired, Stanley was neither a retired soldier nor a pensioner, but was in fact a bricklayer's labourer who lived at 1 Osborn Place, Whitechapel.

The majority of people who knew her at Crossingham's described her as very civil and industrious when sober, but added that she was often seen staggering and incoherent, especially after one of her drinking bouts. In the week before her death she complained of feeling ill after suffering several bruises to her face, including a black eye. This followed a fight with Eliza Cooper, a fellow resident in Crossingham's. The two women were allegedly rivals for the affections of Harry the Hawker, but Eliza Cooper denied this, and claimed the fight was over a borrowed bar of soap that Annie had not returned.

The more Abberline found out about Chapman, the more he empathised with her, especially when he discovered that at the time of her death, she was suffering from tuberculosis, for it was this very same illness which had tragically robbed him of his first wife, Martha. Abberline was not the sort of policeman to take his work home, so to speak, but he felt a compulsion to do so with this particular case, and even asked his wife Emma for her thoughts on why and how these women allowed themselves to live such degraded lives.

In a way, he was perhaps using his wife's thoughts and perceptions of these women, whom she saw on a day-to-day basis in the area in which they lived, in the same way as a modern-day psychological profiler, who records a person's behaviour and analyses their psychological characteristics in order to predict or assess their ability in a certain sphere or to identify a particular group of people. There is no record that Abberline ever used this direct line of thought in his investigative methods, but he certainly showed a very keen interest in the women, as human beings and not just victims. The closer he could get to them, the closer he might get to finding out the identity of their killer.

The night prior to Annie Chapman's death, more suggestive of October or November weather than September, it had been raining, with a cold wind blowing. This led to the streets of East London being almost empty, and consequently led to a distinct lack of trade for Chapman and the other women who worked there. After walking the deserted streets for nearly two hours, Chapman was cold and fed up, and decided to have a drink in her local pub to get dry, and with a bit of luck, she might even pick up a customer. The one drink, which she originally went into the pub to have, turned into three or four, and before she knew it, she was drunk and out of money.

Now penniless, and faced with the ever-worsening weather outside, she asked the landlord of the pub for one more drink, which she would pay him for the following day. The landlord, however, experienced these women all the time and point-blank refused her until she could pay for it. The time was about 1.45 a.m. when she finally left the pub and made her way back to her lodgings. Her misfortunes, however were not at an end yet, as when she finally did arrive at the lodging house, the lodging house deputy, Tim Donovan, refused her admission. 'Sorry Annie,' he told her. 'You know the rules, no money, no bed.'

The strict house rules didn't deter Chapman too much; she had been through this same scenario many time before, but always thought it was worth chancing her arm one more time. 'You never know,' she once told a friend. 'He might take a shine to me one day, and I'd be in there for free.' Poor Annie Chapman certainly wasn't a good judge of character, for the house deputy never took a 'shine' to any of the women who lodged there. The reason for this is unsure: some said that he was impotent, others, that he was homosexual.

At 2 a.m., Annie Chapman stepped out onto the streets of East London once again. At least it had stopped raining, which meant there might be a few lonely souls back out on the streets looking for company. From the limited information we have to hand, the lonely souls were indeed far and few between. It might have stopped raining, but it was still cold and windy, and the dark, narrow streets of Spitalfields were almost bereft of life. Chapman found herself shuffling along from one doorway to the next, pausing here and there for a while trying to keep warm, and hoping and praying that she might find a customer with a few pennies to spend.

It is unsure whether she did any business at all that night, as she certainly didn't return to the lodging house, but one of the witnesses, Mrs Elizabeth Long, who gave evidence at the inquest, later testified that she had seen Chapman talking to a man at five o'clock that morning, just past the backyard of 29 Hanbury Street, Spitalfields. Mrs Long said she was certain of the time, as she had heard the clock on the Black Eagle Brewery, Brick Lane, strike the half hour just as she had turned onto the street. As she passed them, she overheard the man ask, 'Will you?' To which Chapan replied, 'Yes.' Mrs Long described the man as in his forties, slightly taller than Chapman, of dark complexion, possibly foreign, 'shabby-genteel' in appearance, and wearing a deerstalker hat and dark overcoat.

Apart from the murderer, it seems very likely that Mrs Long was the last person to see Annie Chapman alive. Another witness at the inquest, Albert Cadosch, who lived nearby, had gone into the neighbouring yard at 27 Hanbury Street at about 5.30 a.m. to use the outside toilet. Whist there he heard voices in the yard next door, followed by the sound of something crashing against the adjoining fence. Cadosch didn't know it at the time, but in all probability this crashing sound was the noise of Annie Chapman's body as she was pushed up against the fence by the murderer.

It was still quite dark at six o'clock that morning, when John Davis, a market porter, left his home at 29 Hanbury Street, to go to work at nearby Spitalfields Market. As he came out of his back door into the yard, he saw something lying on the ground between the doorway and the garden fence, which he at first thought was a dog. As he got closer, he realised it was in fact the body of a woman, which was later identified as Annie Chapman.

Davis could see immediately that she was dead, by the position and the amount of blood on and around her body. He rushed back into the house and alerted several neighbours, before running off to Commercial Street police station to report what had happened. Abberline and several members of his team were on the scene within minutes. Nothing was to be touched, Abberline ordered, until he had spoken to as many witnesses as possible; but within minutes, Abberline's boss, Chief Inspector Donald Swanson, had also arrived on the scene. Completely ignoring Abberline, he publicly ordered an immediate search of all common lodging houses, to ascertain if anyone had entered that morning under any suspicious circumstances, or with blood on their hands or clothes. While Swanson strutted about giving out orders, and showing the press and the public exactly who was in charge of this case, Inspector Abberline quietly went about his duty speaking to local people and taking notes from anyone who could possibly throw some light on the case.

There were sixteen people living at 29 Hanbury Street, none of whom had seen or heard anything at the time of the murder. The passage led from the street door right through the house, and out to the backyard. It was never locked as it was frequented by the residents at all hours of the day and night, as the yard was the location of the only toilet in the house. The street door was wide open when Chapman's body was discovered, which was also quite normal. Another witness said he had often seen strangers, both men and women, in the passage of the house, using the yard's toilet as if it were a public one.

While the yard was still undergoing a thorough search, Abberline was busy noting all of Chapman's private belongings, which were pitifully lacking, to say the least. These items included a piece of muslin, a comb, and the coins and brass rings, which he had noted laid out around the feet of the corpse. Abberline discovered later that the bloodstained envelope also found in the yard, with the crest of the Sussex Regiment upon it, did in fact belong to Chapman. She had apparently picked it up from her lodgings and used it to carry two pills in, for her lung condition.

The coins and the brass rings, which Abberline had told his constable to make a note of, strangely went missing sometime between having been found and the time of the inquest. They were never mentioned again, not even in surviving police records. This could, of course, have been nothing more than an oversight or police incompetence, but during this period, medical students, who were not exactly paid large amounts of money, were known to polish farthings and try to pass them off as half sovereigns. As the rumours surrounding Jack the Ripper grew, so too did the assumption by many people that the Ripper was undeniably someone with a knowledge of surgery: a medical student perhaps?

After the preliminary police investigation at the scene of the crime, Dr George Bagster Phillips, the police surgeon, examined the body and noted that Chapman was probably killed sometime between 4 a.m. and 5 a.m. He also made several notes on her injuries and the position she was found.

The body was conveyed later that day to Whitechapel mortuary, in the same police ambulance that had been used for Polly Nichols. The inquest into Annie Chapman's death was opened on 10 September at the Working Lad's Institute, Whitechapel. The coroner was Wynne Edwin Baxter. Dr George Bagster Phillips described the body as he saw it at 6.30 a.m. in the backyard of the house at 29 Hanbury Street:

The left arm was placed across the left breast. The legs were drawn up, the feet resting on the ground, and the knees turned outwards. The face was swollen and turned on the right side. The tongue protruded between the front teeth, but not beyond the lips. The tongue was evidently much swollen. The front teeth were perfect as far as the first molar, top and bottom and very fine teeth they were. The body was terribly mutilated ... the stiffness of the limbs was not marked, but was evidently commencing.

The throat was disseevered deeply; the incision through the skin were jagged and reached right round the neck ... On the wooden paling between the yard in question and the next, smears of blood, corresponding to where the head of the deceased lay, were to be seen. These were about 14 inches from the ground, and immediately above the part where the blood from the neck lay.

Dr Phillips also commented on the instrument that was used to mutilate and murder Annie Chapman, stating that it must have been around 6–8 in in length, a very sharp and narrow blade, possibly the type used by a slaughterman which has normally been ground down in the sharpening process.

He ruled out the use of a bayonet or a sword type of weapon. He also discounted the possibility that it might have been an instrument used by a medical practitioner, as a knife of this particular shape would only be used for post-mortem purposes, and the ordinary surgical case would not contain such an instrument. However, he did go on to say that there were indications of anatomical knowledge.

Owing to the particularly cool weather for that time of year and the amount of blood Chapman had lost, it was very difficult to decipher the exact time of death as the body was cold when he first examined it. All he could say with any certainty was that there was no evidence of a struggle having taken place, and that he was positive the deceased had entered the yard alive.

Apart from the disappearing coins, another strange thing regarding Chapman's body was that, when she was found, there was a handkerchief tied around her throat: not a scarf, which might have possibly been worn to ward off the cold weather, but an ordinary small handkerchief. Dr Phillips testified that, in his opinion, the handkerchief was not tied on after the throat was cut. In other words, it was there when the killer struck, so firstly, why was the handkerchief there at all, and secondly, how could the killer have cut Chapman's throat while completely avoiding the handkerchief, and getting no blood on it whatsoever?

Her throat had been cut from left to right, and she had been disembowelled, with her intestines pulled out of her abdomen and placed over each of her shoulders. The morgue examination also revealed that part of her uterus was missing. Dr Phillips also concluded that Chapman's protruding tongue and swollen face led him to think that she may have been asphyxiated with the handkerchief around her neck before her throat was cut. He was certain that she was killed on the spot where she was found, as there was no blood trail leading from the street to the yard.

Dr Phillips formed the opinion that the murderer must have possessed some anatomical knowledge in order to have sliced out the reproductive organs in a single movement with such a relatively short blade. Dr Phillips' theory was, however, dismissed by other experts, who thought it more likely the organ had been removed by mortuary staff, who took advantage of bodies that had already been opened to extract and sell the organs as surgical specimens, in a lucrative market at the time.

It was also suggested in some circles that Chapman had been murdered deliberately to obtain the uterus. This theory was based on the premise that an American had made enquiries at a London medical school for the purchase of such organs. Both the *Lancet* and the *British Medical Journal* were dismissive of this idea; the *British Medical Journal* reported that the physician who requested the samples had left the country eighteen months before the murder and was a highly reputable doctor, although they didn't name him. The *Chicago Tribune* then picked up on this story and claimed the American doctor was from Philadelphia. This quickly led others to speculate that the man in question was the notorious Francis Tumblety, who had either lived in, or travelled to, almost every American state and later became a prime suspect in the Jack the Ripper case.

7

Arrests

t this point in the investigation, neither Inspector Abberline, nor any of his fellow officers, had any real suspects in mind. It was alleged that Abberline had been ordered direct from Scotland Yard: to start giving the public and the press what they were seemingly clambering for: arrests. There were far too many strange and suspicious-looking people on the streets, especially around the East End, and the public did not feel safe.

Abberline was far from comfortable with this method of working; he had been a policeman for far too long to issue casual arrest warrants based upon a person's looks or sometimes erratic behaviour. Using a special hand-picked team of men, he continued with his investigations in the manner he saw fit, while leaving what he termed these 'panic arrests' to lower ranked officers and other stations.

Not only was Abberline and his team working diligently to catch the killer, the ordinary citizens of the East End also did their best to assist the police as much as they could. They reported every suspicious person and every overheard piece of conversation which they deemed to be relevant to the case. These actions were commendable, but they also hindered the investigations to an extent, as every single witness statement that was reported to the police had to be recorded and looked into.

So great was the amount of extra work that this entailed that it actually took officers off the street. Abberline was under great strain and pressure to bring the murderer to justice, and with this now smaller team of detectives actually out on the streets, it meant that he would spend almost the whole day directing his staff, and then go out onto the streets himself, often in disguise.

He had been known to spend hours on the streets, often until the early hours of the morning. Then, feeling too weak to walk home, he would hail a hansom cab to finally arrive home, worn out and weary, at 5 a.m. Even then he was often deprived of sleep, as just as he was about to get into bed, he would often be sent a telegram, summoning him back to the East End to interrogate some lunatic or suspected person whom the inspector in charge would not take the responsibility of questioning.

While Abberline diligently carried on with his investigations, arrests by other officers were certainly being carried out. Men were pulled up on the street, questioned, and often arrested if they wore outlandish clothing, shouted or acted suspicious in any way. This would obviously include such unfortunates as the mentally handicapped.

One such incident involved a Swiss butcher, Jacob Isenschmidt, who matched the description of a bloodstained man seen acting strangely on the morning of the murder. The landlady of a public house, Mrs Fiddymont, had reported a 'strange looking man' with bloodstains on his clothing, acting very suspiciously close to the scene of the murder. When the police did pick him up, the only thing 'strange' about his appearance turned out to be nothing more than his large ginger moustache. There were indeed bloodstains on his clothing, but when it was checked out, these were found to be animal blood, obtained from his work as a butcher. He was found to have a history of mental illness, and after being examined by a police doctor, was detained in a mental asylum. When Abberline heard of this, and the fact that his alibi had been checked out and cleared him of any involvement in the murder, he felt that he couldn't stand back and watch such a travesty of justice take place and immediately ordered the man's release.

Other examples of this type of hysteria included a local street-market trader, Friedrich Schumacher, apothecary assistant Edward McKenna, medical student John Sanders, and Oswald Puckridge, who was undergoing treatment for mental health problems. All had undoubtedly acted in some seemingly strange way or another, but when investigated there was no evidence against any of them and all were released.

Not every suspect was, of course, suffering from some form of illness. Some were arrested purely for their 'strange' looks or so-called 'strange' behaviour. One such example was a ship's cook, William Henry Piggott, who was detained after causing a disturbance in the street which involved shouting at women and making misogynist remarks. When he was searched, the police found him to be in possession of a blood-stained shirt. He was arrested and taken to the police station, where he claimed that he had been bitten by a woman, which he said was the reason he was shouting in the street and that the blood on the shirt was his own. After spending a night in the cells he was thoroughly investigated and, like so many others, released without charge.

Another suspect, whose actions were more than a little strange, was a German hairdresser, named Charles Ludwig. He was arrested after an argument at a coffee stall, where he allegedly attempted to stab a man. The man had accused him of attacking a prostitute earlier, a charge which Ludwig firmly denied, along with the subsequent attempted stabbing charge. Ludwig was exonerated from all charges after another murder was committed while he was in custody. All these cases seemed to have one thing in common, which was that in every instance the suspect either looked strange or acted strange. None had any real connection to the actual case, and, much to Abberline's chagrin, wasted an awful lot of valuable police time.

While these so-called suspects were being arrested and questioned, the real work surrounding the crimes was, of course, still going on. At the inquest into Annie Chapman's death, John Pizer, the man the press had dubbed 'Leather Apron', and whom Inspector Abberline had long since ruled out as a suspect, was called as a witness. He was closely questioned and subsequently cleared of any involvement in Chapman's murder, and went on to successfully claim compensation from one of the newspapers that had named him as the murderer. Directly after his acquittal, the name 'Leather Apron' was to be supplanted by 'Jack the Ripper' as the media's favourite name for the murderer.

At this particular time, however, Jack the Ripper had not yet been invented. The three previous murders had certainly caused the people of East London to feel very worried when going about their business, particularly women, and especially if it involved being out after dark. The death of Annie Chapman, however, turned their fear into hysteria, with street mobs turning on anyone who looked or acted differently, and leading to a wave of anti-Semitism. Innocent Jews, or anyone with an unpronounceable name whom the angry crowd assumed to be Jewish, were attacked. The police were put on standby, expecting full blown anti-Jewish rioting at any time, after reports of harassment and attacks upon Jews and other foreigners were received. The general consensus upon the streets seemed to be that no Englishman could possibly be capable of such crimes.

Even though Pizer, who was a Jew, had been exonerated from the crime, anti-Semitic feelings were still riding high. As one newspaper reported: 'A touch would fire the whole district in the mood which it is now in', while the *Jewish Chronicle* warned: 'There may soon be murders from panic to add to murders from a lust for blood.'

As if to add to Abberline's woes, George Lusk and his Whitechapel Vigilance Committee suddenly appeared in the headlines again, as well as on posters around Whitechapel, appealing for information concerning the identity of the murderer. Not only did the posters appeal for information, they also allegedly scared the living daylights out of the local populace. According to the press, men spoke of the horrible murders with bated breath and pale-faced women shuddered as they read the ghastly details.

Hoardings became so graphic that they were denounced by *Punch* magazine thus: 'Imagine the effects of these gigantic pictures of violence and assassination, on the morbid imagination of imbalanced minds.' Paper boys on the streets called the headlines out to a public that seemed eager for yet more gory details and titillation. 'Another horrible murder and mutilation in Whitechapel,' they yelled, while dishing out more papers than they had ever sold in their lives.

The *Daily Telegraph* printed a letter from an irate reader, stating that he was fed up with 'hoarse voiced ruffians, yelling at the top of their hideous voices, "murder – mutilation – special murder edition".' The reader went on to say that in his opinion, 'It is monstrous that police are doing nothing to protect us from such flagrant and ghastly nuisances'.

Not only was Abberline and his team being berated for not catching the murderer, now they were being asked to deal with paper boys as well, for selling their newspapers too loudly.

Women were allegedly fainting, after reading the graphic accounts of the murders, and one publican in Whitechapel even blamed his bankruptcy on the incompetence of the police. 'If they were doing their job properly,' he said, 'the killer would have been caught by now, and people would be back on the streets of Whitechapel once again.'

Lusk also complained about the lack of a reward from the government for information. There is no doubt that Lusk's intentions were honourable, but he was also a shrewd businessman and, as such, knew how to manipulate the media. Not only was he doing his best to force the government into offering a reward, but he was also appealing to public sympathy, by saying that he had received threatening letters through the post, allegedly from the murderer.

Maybe he did receive such letters the public will never know for certain whether the letters he was said to have received were real or not. Some say they were created by a journalist in order to sell more newspapers; others have suggested that Lusk himself wrote them, but there is always the possibility that some of them were genuine.

During that autumn, hundreds of letters were sent to the police and local press purporting to be written by the Whitechapel killer. Most of these were discarded immediately as hoaxes, including one received at the Central News Agency on 27 September 1888. This was looked at, albeit briefly, and tossed aside with a number of other letters received that week from the alleged murderer.

Even though not much attention was paid to this letter at the time, it did include one thing that no other letter had contained before, which was the name 'Jack the Ripper'.

The transcript of that letter, which has since become known as the 'Dear Boss' letter, is as follows:

Dear Boss,

I keep on hearing the police have caught me but they wont fix me just yet. I have laughed when they look so clever and talk about being on the right track. That joke about Leather Apron gave me real fits. I am down on whores and I shant quit ripping them till I do get buckled. Grand work the last job was. I gave the lady no time to squeal. How can they catch me now. I love my work and want to start again. You will soon hear of me with my funny little games. I saved some of the proper red stuff in a ginger beer bottle over the last job to write with but it went thick like glue and I cant use it. Red ink is fit enough I hope ha. ha. The next job I do I shall clip the ladys ears off and send to the police officers just for jolly wouldn't you. Keep this letter back till I do a bit more work, then give it out straight. My knife's so nice and sharp I want to get to work right away if I get a chance. Good Luck.

Yours truly
Jack the Ripper

Dont mind me giving the trade name

PS Wasnt good enough to post this before I got all the red ink off my hands curse it No luck yet. They say I'm a doctor now. ha ha

Five days later, on 1 October 1888, the Central News Agency received yet another communication signed with the name 'Jack the Ripper'. This time it was a postcard, which became known as the 'Saucy Jacky' postcard. This in turn made direct reference to both the 'Dear Boss' letter and the murders, which were to become known as the 'Double Event'. The general consensus of opinion was that the postcard was genuine: it mentions the removal of Elizabeth Stride's ear and the Double Event before it had been published by the press.

The transcript of the 'Saucy Jacky' postcard is as follows:

I was not codding dear old Boss when I gave you the tip, you'll hear about Saucy Jacky's work tomorrow double event this time number one squealed a bit couldn't finish straight off. ha not the time to get ears for police. thanks for keeping last letter back till I got to work again.

Jack the Ripper

The letter and the postcard had both happened so quickly that the press hardly had time to act upon them, and were still hard at work besmirching Abberline and his team's efforts in failing to catch the killer, while at the same time increasingly taking up Lusk's cause.

8

When Evidence is not to be had – Theories Abound

*H*aving ascertained that the main investigating police officers in the Ripper case did not have a singular suspect in mind does not mean that there were no discernible suspects. As already pointed out, many arrests had been made over the course of the investigation. Following the murder of Annie Chapman on 8 September 1888, the *Daily Telegraph* reported: 'More than one person was detained on suspicion; one at Limehouse, another at Bethnal-green, and a third at Deptford, but in each case no tangible result followed.' The press reported many such stories throughout the years 1888–91, when various men were arrested on suspicion and later released. Very little, if anything, is known regarding the identity of these men, whom we can only assume to have been innocent with no connection to the murders.

Whenever and wherever murders are committed, the publicity surrounding them nearly always inspires a series of twisted individuals cum publicity seekers to emerge from the woodwork and claim responsibility for the crime or crimes. The Whitechapel murders were no exception to this rule, and inspired numerous individuals to hold their hands up to being Jack the Ripper.

ALFRED NAPIER BLANCHARD

On 5 October 1888, Alfred Napier Blanchard was drinking at the Fox and Goose tavern at Aston (Greater Birmingham). As with most drunks, the more he drank, the louder he became, as his main aim was to get people listening and taking notice of him. He finally got his wish by confessing that he was none other than Jack the Ripper. The landlord of the pub reported him to the police, and Blanchard was arrested and remanded in custody while the police checked up on his story. The confession was eventually found to be completely made up so he was charged in court with being drunk and wasting police time, and was fined and dismissed by the local magistrate, with the words: 'What a foolish man you have been.'

On the same day that Blanchard was trying to establish a name for himself in the annals of notoriety, a young medical student named William Bull walked into Bishopsgate police station and confessed to the murder of Catherine Eddowes. His so-called confession was looked into by the police, and it was decided that, as with Blanchard, he could not have possibly committed the crime. He was released without charge.

Other would-be Jack the Rippers included John Avery, William Wallace Brodie and George Payne who all confessed at various times, and as before, all were released without charges being brought against them, even though they had wasted valuable police time. Theophil Hanhart, however, was not so lucky. After confessing to the police that he was the Ripper, the police looked into his admission and decided, as with the others, that he could not possibly have been. They did, however, decide that Theophil Hanhart was of 'unsound mind', so instead of being charged with being the Ripper or wasting police time, he was incarcerated for an unspecified period in the nearest mental asylum.

THOMAS NEILL CREAM

In 1893 Thomas Neill Cream, a Scottish doctor, confessed to being the Ripper whilst standing on the platform of a scaffold, about to be hanged. He had been found guilty of murdering Matilda Clover on 15 November 1892. Just as the hangman released the lever to the trapdoor that Cream would plunge into, he was alleged to have uttered the words, 'I am Jack'; his last words were cut short by the hangman's noose. Whether he did utter these words or not, we will never know, but one fact that is known about Cream is that at the time of the Ripper murders, he was actually serving a prison sentence at the Illinois State Penitentiary in Joliet, Illinois, from 1881–91.

As well as the self-confessed killers popping up all over the place, there was also the popular press, who were more than eager to come forward with claims that they had unearthed the identity of Jack the Ripper. When Annie Chapman was murdered in September 1888 the press came out in force, in favour of John Pizer, a Jewish shoemaker with a criminal record and an apparent hatred of prostitutes, being the Ripper. Pizer was dubbed 'Leather Apron', a name that stuck in the public's imagination. At the exact time that Annie Chapman was being murdered, Pizer was deep in conversation with a police officer. After suffering months of accusations and humiliation at the hands of the press, Pizer went to court and won a libel action and damages against the newspapers that had named him.

THE FANATICAL ANARCHIST

By late November, early December 1888, the newspapers were getting desperate to keep the Ripper story going, and so the 'fanatical anarchist' story was born. Nikolay Vasiliev was said to have gone on a killing spree, murdering four prostitutes within the space of a fortnight in Paris 1872. He was quickly caught and placed in a mental asylum where he underwent treatment. After being declared cured on 1 January 1888, he was released and made his way to London; which of course placed him in the frame during the period of the Ripper murders. If the facts surrounding Vasiliev are true, then he indeed would be a fairly strong suspect in the Ripper murders, but there is no written evidence anywhere to suggest that Vasiliev ever existed. The whole story appears to have been invented by the press.

The Australian press published a story on 8 April 1892, with the *Melbourne Evening Standard* triumphantly stating in its headline: 'Jack The Ripper: Deeming At Aldgate On The Night Of The Whitechapel murders.'

Frederick Bailey Deeming had been arrested in Australia on 11 March 1892 on suspicion of murdering his wife, whose body had been discovered buried beneath the floor of the fireplace at their home in Melbourne. After the Australian police had interviewed him, they asked the English police to help by searching his former home at Rainhill in Liverpool. This search resulted in the discovery of the bodies of his previous wife and their four children buried under the floorboards. The decomposition of the bodies led the police to believe that they had been dead less than a year, which tied in perfectly with the time he left England and fled to Australia.

Deeming was certainly in Australia in December 1887, as he was facing bankruptcy charges at the time. In order to escape the charges, he fled to South Africa in January 1888 and remained there until at least March of that year. His exact whereabouts from that time until his reappearance at Hull in October 1889 are uncertain. Deeming was without a doubt insane, but not to the extent that he didn't make an attempt to hide his crimes by burying the bodies of his victims. This did not fit in at all with the known habits of Jack the Ripper, which once again begs the question: did the press exaggerate this story to fit in with a possible sales slump of their newspapers at the time?

Thomas Cutbush

Six years after the last official Ripper murder, in 1894, *The Sun* newspaper published a headline-blazing article stating that they had unearthed the identity of the Ripper. They named Thomas Cutbush, who had been arrested in April 1891 for maliciously wounding Florence Grace Johnson, and also attempting to wound Isabella Fraser Anderson at Kennington. Assistant Commissioner of Crime at Scotland Yard, Sir Melville Macnaghten, was dismissive of the notion that Cutbush could have been the killer. Macnaghten later noted: 'It was found impossible to ascertain Cutbush's movements on the nights of the Whitechapel murders.'

Cutbush was declared insane and confined at Lambeth Infirmary. Although no evidence was ever found to incriminate Cutbush in regard to the Ripper murders, his profile of an individual then safely incarcerated in a mental asylum, fitted the public's imagination perfectly at the time.

Unfortunately, or fortunately, depending on one's point of view, naming Ripper suspects did not end in the 1890s. It continued, and is still continuing to this day.

Doctor Stanley

In Leonard Matters'1928 book *The Mystery of Jack the Ripper*, Matters names a certain Doctor Stanley as being Jack the Ripper. According to this version, Doctor Stanley's only son had caught syphilis from Mary Kelly, which led Stanley to seek revenge by killing the woman who was to blame for his son's terrible disease. In doing so, Stanley killed four other prostitutes before he finally found his objective and duly slaughtered Mary Kelly.

After completing his gory tasks, Stanley left the country and ended up in Buenos Aires, where he died in 1927. Before he died, however, he allegedly confessed his crimes to the author Leonard Matters. The Doctor Stanley story was widely publicised by Matters in the American press in 1927 and later appeared in the first full-length book in English on the subject, *The Mystery of Jack the Ripper* published in 1928.

When Leonard Matters' book was first published, it was accepted as factual evidence, but the truth was that Doctor Stanley and his deathbed confession only ever existed in Matters' imagination. The basic concept, however, of a 'demented doctor' seeking revenge for some real or imaginary injury has become one of the most influential of the suggested solutions to the mystery of Jack the Ripper. Leonard Matters' concept of the Ripper being this mysterious mad doctor fits in perfectly with the many suggested theories that the murderer must have had some anatomical knowledge and skill with a knife to have carried out the type of mutilations and removal of organs from his victims as the Ripper did.

Sir William Gull

The medical connection theory has survived well over the years, from fictitious characters suggested by Leonard Matters, to prominent men such as Sir William Gull, the Queen's personal physician, who features heavily in what became known as the Royal Conspiracy Theory. One only has to delve into the factual evidence at the time to learn that Sir William Gull was in his seventies at the time of the murders, and most importantly, he was partially paralysed after suffering a stroke in 1887. He unfortunately suffered a number of other attacks following his stroke, and died on 29 January 1890 at the age of 73. Bearing in mind that the Ripper murders all happened in 1888, one year after his first attack and one year before his death, it hardly seems feasible that this man would have been chosen by his fellow conspirators to haunt the streets of the East End, looking for women to rip to pieces.

Joseph Barnett

The next name on our list did not have anything to do with the medical profession, and he was named as a suspect from day one. Joseph Barnett was the lover of Mary Kelly, the last of the Ripper victims, who was murdered on 9 November 1888. Barnett was arrested by the police immediately following the murder. He was questioned for four hours and then released, with the police being apparently satisfied that he had no connection with her murder or indeed any of the previous crimes.

Barnett may have been released without charge in 1888, but that hasn't stopped various writers during the twentieth century from suggesting that he was indeed the Ripper. The author Bruce Paley wrote an article in *True Crime* magazine in 1982, where he named Barnett as the Ripper. He elaborated on this theme in his later book *Jack the Ripper: The Simple Truth* in 1995.

Another author, Paul Harrison, also argued that Barnett carried out the murders. In his book, *Jack the Ripper: The Mystery Solved*, in 1991, Harrison's argument is based upon the theory that Barnett was so unhappy with the fact that Mary Kelly had turned to prostitution that he went on a murder spree, killing Nichols, Chapman, Stride and Eddowes in an attempt to frighten Kelly into abandoning her chosen profession. If there is any truth in this, it certainly did not work, as, in frustration and rage, Barnett turned up at Mary Kelly's flat in Miller's Court and slaughtered her. This, like so many other theories, could have been possible, but it could also have been entirely untrue, and just another theory in the long line that has surfaced since the anonymous killer struck, back in 1888.

JAMES MAYBRICK

As recently as 1993 we saw the publication of yet another exposé; this time it was the *Jack the Ripper Diary*, allegedly written by a Liverpool businessman named James Maybrick in which he confessed to being Jack the Ripper.

The diary is littered with errors and of dubious provenance, and is now regarded internationally as a forgery. It was supposed to be the handwritten account of James Maybrick, but when the handwriting in the original diary was checked by a handwriting expert, alongside the handwriting in Maybrick's last will and testament, it was proven without a doubt to have been written by a different hand.

When this was discovered, the so-called finder of the diary, Michael Barrett, admitted that it was a fake, and that he had forged it. Since then, however, he has retracted that confession and subsequently re-confessed at regular intervals.

The only fact linking Maybrick to the murders is that he was in London at that particular time, but so too were about 8 million other people; they couldn't all be Ripper suspects could they? James Maybrick died in suspicious circumstances in May 1889. His wife Florence was tried and convicted of murder by poisoning him with arsenic. The evidence against her was very flimsy and she appealed against her conviction. In 1904 she was released from prison.

CHARLES L. DODGSON

One of the most improbable suggestions for Jack the Ripper, if not the most, in my opinion, is that which Richard Wallace put forward in his 1996 book, *Jack the Ripper, Light-Hearted Friend*.

Wallace writes that Charles L. Dodgson and his friend Thomas Vere Bayne committed the Ripper murders. He bases this theory primarily on a number of anagrams derived from passages in two of Dodgson's works. Wallace claims that the books contained hidden but detailed descriptions of the murders.

Before we go any further, for those who do not know, Charles L. Dodgson wrote under the pen name of Lewis Carroll and the two books in question were *The Nursery Alice*, an adaptation of *Alice's Adventures in Wonderland* for younger readers, and from the first volume of *Sylvie and Bruno*.

Lewis Carroll first published both works in 1889, which was a year after the Ripper murders, and was probably still working on them during the period of the murders. Wallace's entire argument was based on his ability to take certain passages from Carroll's work and, by re-arranging the letters, construct statements that incriminated the author; these were, of course, coded confessions deliberately inserted into his work for the enlightenment of those not sufficiently knowledgeable to decipher them in the first place.

For a very short while, this theory gained enough attention to make Carroll a late but notable addition to the list of suspects, although not one that is taken very seriously, as this technique could be applied to almost any author's work and end with very similar results.

JAMES KELLY

In 1997 *The Secret Of Prisoner 1167 – Was This Man Jack The Ripper?* was published. It was written by James Tully, who claimed in the book that James Kelly, no relation of the victim Mary Jane Kelly, was in fact Jack the Ripper.

Kelly was perfect fodder for inclusion into the Ripper suspect files. He was married in his early twenties, and on 21 June 1883, aged just 23 years old, he stabbed his wife in the throat with a pocket-knife while in the midst of a violent argument. She died three days later, on 24 June, and Kelly was charged with her murder. He was subsequently convicted and sentenced to hang. His execution date was set for 20 August 1883, but doctors decided that he was insane, and was granted a reprieve and sent to Broadmoor Criminal Lunatic Asylum, as it was known at the time.

Whilst in Broadmoor, he found a piece of metal one day, while working in the asylum's kitchen garden, and fashioned a set of keys from it. On 23 January 1888 he put his keys to the test and subsequently escaped. A large search was organised for him throughout the country, but he was never found, until thirty-nine years later, on 11 February 1927, James Kelly, then aged 67, turned up at the gates of Broadmoor and gave himself up.

Whether his mental health had deteriorated even more during his years on the run or if he expected some sort of celebrity status when he returned to Broadmoor, he didn't seem to be too happy with his reception, whatever the circumstances were. Just two years later, in 1929, he made another escape attempt, but by this time security at Broadmoor had been much improved and his efforts were in vain. James Kelly died from double lobar pneumonia on 17 September 1929 at the age of 69.

There was no real case against Kelly, apart from the fact that he murdered his wife with a knife and was declared insane. There doesn't seem to be any records of witnesses picking him out as a Ripper suspect or even seeing him in the area at the time of the murders; in fact, his exact whereabouts for 1888 are unknown. James Tully's book and evidence against James Kelly seem to be based entirely on Kelly killing his wife and then being incarcerated in Broadmoor. Records from Victorian asylums would no doubt reveal hundreds, if not thousands, of similar cases to James Kelly, men who had murdered their wives and been certified as insane. This 'evidence' does not qualify them all as Ripper suspects.

WALTER SICKERT

For some reason, the artist Walter Sickert has surfaced on no less than three separate occasions with relevance to the Ripper murders. Firstly, as has already been pointed out, in connection to the Royal Conspiracy Theory. Secondly, with the painter's claim that he knew the identity of the Ripper because he occupied his former rooms.

Sickert was a member of a group of artists known as the Camden Town Group, and, as such, he took up lodgings in a house owned by an elderly couple in Mornington Crescent, Camden. This was several years after the Ripper killings, and the couple told him that the previous occupant of the rooms was Jack the Ripper. According to the couple, the mystery lodger was a veterinary student who would stay out all night and then rush out to buy the papers on the morning following the murders. He was also, they said, in the habit of burning his clothes. Eventually the lodger's health began to fail and he returned to his mother's house in Bournemouth where he died a short while after.

The couple told Sickert the lodger's name, which he allegedly wrote down in the margin of a copy of *Casanova's Memoirs* which he gave to fellow artist Harry Rutherford. Unfortunately, Rutherford could not decipher Sickert's handwriting and the book was eventually lost in the London Blitz during the 1940s.

Two connections to the Ripper murders are twice as many as most suspects ever got, but Walter Sickert now has a third, and that is as a candidate for the Ripper himself. In 2002, the author Patricia Cornwell published *Portrait of a Killer: Jack the Ripper – Case Closed*, which was also publicised in a television documentary to coincide with the book.

In her book, Cornwell decides there is a definite link between Sickert and the Ripper on the grounds that she had forensic tests carried out on two separate letters; the first was an example of Sickert's own correspondence, and the second was a letter allegedly sent by Jack the Ripper to Dr Thomas

Horrocks Openshaw at the London Hospital on 29 October 1888. Dr Openshaw had recently analysed an item of human flesh, which George Lusk of the Whitechapel Vigilance Committee had received in the post on Tuesday, 16 October 1888. When Lusk first opened the package, he was shocked to discover this small piece of rancid flesh, which was later identified as part of a human kidney. Also enclosed was a note, which later became known as the 'From Hell' letter.

The tests showed a match of DNA profiles in the two pieces of evidence. Cornwell says that she is 100 per cent certain that Walter Sickert was Jack the Ripper, and even goes so far as to stake her reputation upon this claim.

The Openshaw letter, however, is universally regarded as a hoax and had therefore no connection with the real killer. The DNA profiling might indeed show at best that Sickert was the author of one of the many hoax Ripper letters. The worst scenario, however, is that at some point in time, both sets of evidence were handled by two people who were in some way distantly related. Cornwell never managed to obtain a reference sample of Sickert's own DNA, which means there is absolutely no proof whatsoever that any of the DNA samples were connected to the artist in the first place.

Last but not least, in this particular assertion, is that all the available evidence points to the fact that Walter Sickert was actually in France between August and October 1888, when the murders took place.

BLACK MAGIC

When the press couldn't find a new suspect to hang the Ripper name on, which wasn't very often, they delved into the realms of fantasy and black magic, which were always a good ploy to sell a story. The Ripper murders were perfect for such scaremongering; even the very nature of the killings fitted in perfectly with the belief that there was something ritualistic about them, and that they were linked to black magic.

Believers in the occult have long held the belief that the 'Hand of Glory' or 'Thief's Candle' was something that could empower the holder with special magical powers. The Hand of Glory is the dried and pickled hand of a man who has been hanged, often specified as being the left (Latin: sinister) hand, or else, if the man was hanged for murder, the hand that 'did the deed'.

According to old European beliefs, a candle made of the fat from a malefactor who died on the gallows, virgin wax and Lapland sesame oil – lighted and placed (as if in a candlestick) in the Hand of Glory, which comes from the same man as the fat in the candle – would have rendered motionless all persons to whom it was presented. The candle could only be put out with milk. In another version the hair of the dead man is used as a wick; also the candle is said to give light only to the holder. The Hand of Glory also purportedly had the power to unlock any door it came across. A Thief's Candle is very similar, except that it does not necessarily have to come from a man.

In October 1888 the *East London Advertiser* suggested that the Ripper murders were carried out in order to obtain the necessary body parts to manufacture what they described as *Diebslichter,* which is German for a Thief's Candle.

The following month the *Pall Mall Gazette* ran an article suggesting that the murders were being conducted in accordance with a medieval spell that would permit the murderer to attain 'the supreme black magical power'.

In 2001 Ivor Edwards published his book *Jack the Ripper's Black Magic Rituals,* in which he argues that each of the five murders were carried out at a specific location, in order to map out the shape of a sacred symbol known as the *Vesica Piscis,* as part of a black magic ritual. Edwards went on further to name the magician-killer in question as Robert Donston Stephenson (alias Roslyn D'Onston Stephenson), who was a journalist and writer interested in the occult and black magic. He admitted himself as a patient at the London Hospital in Whitechapel shortly before the Ripper murders started, and left shortly after they ceased. He authored a newspaper article which claimed that black magic was the motive for the killings.

This was not the first time that Robert Donston Stephenson had been named as the murderer. Aleister Crowley (known as the world's wickedest man) had claimed that Stephenson was the killer based on information supposedly provided by his friend Baroness Vittoria Cremers. Crowley is hardly the most credible of witnesses to anything, and Stephenson's interest in the occult was centred on his attempts to revive the worship of female deities, a point of view that seems rather at variance with the activities of Jack the Ripper.

Although Ivor Edwards provides us with a great deal of information concerning the magic symbols and their use throughout history, there is nothing that actually connects such symbols to the Ripper murders.

WAS JACK THE RIPPER A WOMAN?

Not such a preposterous notion as it might seem upon first being presented with the idea. Most people automatically assume when hearing of a murder that the culprit is a man, and indeed most murders are carried out by men, but there is also a proportion that are carried out by women.

When Inspector Abberline was investigating the murder of Mary Kelly, he interviewed a number of witnesses, including Mrs Caroline Maxwell, who lived in the area. Mrs Maxwell testified that she had seen Mary Kelly twice on the morning of Friday 9 November 1888. The first occasion was between 8 a.m. and 8.30 a.m., at which time Mrs Maxwell claimed that Kelly looked quite ill as she stood near the entrance to Miller's Court. Mrs Maxwell stated that she was sure of the time because her husband returned from work at around eight each morning. The second time Mrs Maxwell saw Kelly was an hour later, when Mrs Maxwell claims she saw her speaking with a man outside the Britannia public house.

These sightings do not appear to be strange or unusual in any way, until we take into account the medical evidence supplied by both the police doctor and the coroner, who both state that the time of death for Mary Kelly was estimated to be between 3.30 a.m. and 4 a.m. on Friday 9 November 1888. This time was estimated based on the medical evidence such as temperature of the body and stiffness of the joints.

If the medical evidence is accurate, and we have no reason to suppose otherwise, then it would have been impossible for Mrs Maxwell to have seen Kelly at these two later times, as by then she would have been dead for at least four hours!

Mrs Maxwell also vividly described the clothes she saw on the woman she believed to be Kelly that morning: 'A dark shirt, velvet bodice and a maroon-coloured shawl.' When asked if she had ever seen Kelly in this outfit before, she replied that she definitely remembered her wearing the shawl.

Abberline had no reason to distrust Mrs Maxwell as a witness, but maybe she had made a mistake with the times and clothing? Mrs Maxwell, however, was adamant that both the times and the clothing were as she had said. The problem definitely perplexed Abberline; so much so, in fact, that he allegedly approached a colleague about it, and asked if he thought that they should be looking elsewhere, as maybe it was a case not of Jack the Ripper at all, but of Jill the Ripper.

Abberline's assertions were based upon the fact that it was possible that the killer dressed up in Kelly's clothes in order to disguise herself, therefore accounting for Mrs Maxwell's later sightings of Kelly that morning.

According to Donald McCormick, author of *The Identity of Jack the Ripper*, published in 1959, the colleague of Abberline whom he spoke to regarding this theory was a man he called Abberline's mentor, Dr Thomas Dutton. McCormick goes on to say that Dutton answered that he believed it was doubtful, but that if it were a woman committing the crimes, the only kind of woman capable of doing so would be a midwife.

The main problem with Donald McCormick's version of these events is that there doesn't seem to be any record of Abberline knowing anyone named Dr Thomas Dutton, or being mentored by such a person.

This does not necessarily mean, however, that the theory of Jill the Ripper, as opposed to Jack the Ripper, is out of the question; in fact, there are several points which add credibility to the theory. Firstly is the fact that whilst all of London was searching for Jack the Ripper, his female counterpart would be free to walk the streets of Whitechapel with considerably less fear of capture or discovery than a man would. Secondly, if she was a midwife, as has been suggested, it would be a perfectly common sight to see her no matter what time of the day or night. Thirdly, based on the theory that the murderer must have a good knowledge of anatomy, a midwife would fit into this category perfectly.

Another writer, William Stewart, was one of the first to write about the possibility of Jill the Ripper in his book *Jack the Ripper: A New Theory*, published in 1939. Stewart's theory, in following with the conversation between Abberline and Dutton over fifty years earlier, was that the killer had been a midwife, possibly an abortionist. He claims that it is perfectly feasible that 'She might have been betrayed by a married woman whom she had tried to help, and sent to prison, and as a result, this was her way of revenging herself upon her own sex'.

Stewart also suggests that a midwife would have had the knowledge to have been able to produce a state of almost instant unconsciousness in a patient, and particularly in a person who had been drinking. This method was frequently used on patients in those days by midwives, and involved pushing on the pressure points until the patient, or possibly the victim, passed out.

Mary Kelly was three months pregnant at the time of her death, and according to Stewart, she could barely afford her lodgings, let alone a baby, so she decided to terminate her pregnancy by calling in an abortionist. The abortionist/midwife was admitted into the room by Kelly, which is why Kelly was found stripped naked, as she had taken her clothes off in readiness for the abortion.

The abortionist killed Kelly almost immediately, cutting and hacking at her body until hardly anything recognisable was left of her. When she had finished her grizzly work, she took off her bloodstained clothes and burnt them in the open fireplace. She then dressed herself in Kelly's clothes, which had been neatly folded and left on a chair, and escaped the scene.

This could possibly explain the sighting by the witness, Mrs Maxwell, who said she saw Kelly at eight the next morning, and again about an hour later. We know she couldn't have seen Kelly at these times, but she could have seen someone else, possibly the midwife/abortionist, dressed in Kelly's shawl, which she said she was sure she had seen Kelly wearing on other occasions.

But why would the midwife/abortionist want to remove organs from her victims?

Stewart claims that the particular mutilations practised by the killer held a psychological fascination and horror for all women, and the midwife would be no exception to this rule.

Stewart was not content with just naming the type of person he thought the Ripper was, but continued his assertions by suggesting that the modus operandi between his mad midwife theory and a woman named Mary Pearcey were too similar not to be taken seriously. In October 1890 Pearcey had stabbed her lover's wife and child to death and cut their throats. She then placed their bodies onto a handcart and wheeled them into a secluded street.

The two striking similarities here, according to Stewart, were, firstly, the savage throat cutting, and secondly, the modus operandi of killing in private and then dumping the bodies in a public place. This, he says, also explains why there were no witnesses who heard any of the Ripper victims scream.

Sir Arthur Conan Doyle, creator of Sherlock Holmes, had his personal theory on the possibility of the Ripper being a woman. He said he was sure the Ripper was a man, but that he disguised himself as a woman in order to avoid capture and become more readily accessible to other women. Contrary to this suggestion, a potential female Ripper would not be more accessible to other women; in fact, she would be at something of a disadvantage to her male counterpart. As far as the Whitechapel murders were concerned, the victims were all prostitutes, and as such they would be plying their trade to men, not women. Prostitutes are willing to go with men who are complete strangers to them, but are usually wary of women, unless they personally know them. Bearing this in mind, there seems to be no good reason for believing that Jack the Ripper was a woman.

INSPECTOR ABBERLINE AND THE POLICE FORCE

As far as I know, no one thus far has suggested that Inspector Abberline was Jack the Ripper, or that the murders were the result of a police conspiracy to embarrass the then unpopular Commissioner of the Metropolitan Police, Sir Charles Warren, and force him into resigning. If no one has brought up these theories, then you might well ask why I have brought it up.

The simple reason I have used these two examples as possible future theories, is that no one has any real proof as to the identity of Jack the Ripper, and in all probability, no one ever will.

On 26 June 1976 an article was first published in the *Evening News* and later re-published in the book. *The Ripper and the Royals* by Nigel Morland, where the author recalled visiting Abberline when the inspector was living in retirement in Dorset. Morland claimed that Abberline told him that the case was shut. 'I've given my word to keep my mouth permanently closed about it,' said Abberline. 'I know and my superiors know certain facts. The Ripper wasn't a butcher, Yid or foreign skipper, you would have to look for him not at the bottom of London society at the time, but a long way up.' Given Abberline's other statements about the identity of the Ripper not being known, this alleged statement should be treated with considerable scepticism and caution.

On 10 November 1888, which was the day subsequent to the final Ripper murder of Mary Jane Kelly, *The Times* newspaper: proclaimed in its editorial: 'When evidence is not to be had, theories abound.' Even with all the modern – day technology we now have, no further evidence has surfaced regarding the true identity of the Ripper, and just as *The Times* stated all those years ago, theories are still continuing to abound.

9

The Double Event

hree days after the arrival of the 'Dear Boss' letter, yet another event took place which shook not just the public's imagination but also that of Inspector Abberline and indeed the whole police force. What happened on this date was to later become known as the Double Event. It started at approximately 1 a.m. on Sunday 30 September 1888.

26-year-old Louis Diemschutz, a Russian Jew who lived with his wife in rooms above the International Working Men's Educational Club, had been hard at work all day as a stallholder, selling cheap imitation jewellery. He travelled by pony and cart to various markets around London and this particular Sunday had been set up in a street market at Westow Hill, Crystal Palace. Street markets around this time would often last late into the night, and the Westow Hill Market had not finished until almost midnight, which then left Diemschutz quite a long drive home.

By the time Diemschutz drove his pony and cart into Berner Street it was almost 1 a.m. As he turned the cart into Dutfield's Yard, all he could think of was unloading his unsold stock and hopefully having something to eat, before taking his pony and cart back to the stables at George Yard, Cable Street. He looked up at the International Working Men's Educational Club, which was on the corner of Dutfield's Yard and Berner Street, and smiled to himself as he heard the singing and laughing coming from an open window there. He would have liked to have joined in, but by the time he had taken his pony and cart back to the stables and walked home, it would probably be closed; even though he acted as a sort of steward there, he couldn't control the opening hours, much to his chagrin.

There was no street lamp near to the entrance of the yard, so Diemschutz didn't notice that the gates were wide open until he had jumped down from his cart with his key, ready to open them. No one else normally used the yard that late at night, but who was he to complain, he thought, as he jumped back up onto the cart again and ordered the horse on.

Just a few steps into the yard, his pony suddenly shied to the left and started whinnying, refusing to go any further. Diemschutz started to get angry, as he had had a terrible day's trading and now just wanted to get his work done and eventually have something to eat with his wife, before retiring for the night. He shouted at the horse a couple of times, trying his best to coax it further into the yard, but it was useless, it just wouldn't move. 'Stupid animal,' he grumbled, 'probably nothing more than a damned rat or something.'

By this time, however, his eyes were starting to grow accustomed to the darkness and he could just make out something lying in the yard. He was not able to distinguish exactly what it was, but it certainly wasn't a rat; it was something much bigger and it wasn't moving. He prodded the object with his whip, noting that it was heavy but soft to the touch. He then got down from his cart, struck a match, and cupped it with his hands to prevent the wind blowing it out. In the flickering light, he could just about make out the horribly mutilated body of a woman lying on the ground.

Diemschutz gazed in disbelief for a moment or two, holding his hand over his mouth in order to stop himself throwing up. As soon as he had composed himself, he rushed straight into the club, shouting at the top of his voice to make himself heard. His wife was the first to see him and rushed over to see what was wrong. He told her, and two other men who were standing nearby, about the woman lying in the yard next door. At this point, he still wasn't certain if she was dead, even though he had seen some of her injuries. He quickly obtained a candle from behind the bar, and led the other two men out into the yard, where, by the flickering illumination, they could all see a stream of blood running from the woman's body, which had by then formed a large pool on the ground.

The three men decided to all go off in different directions to alert the police. Within a few minutes Police Constable Henry Lamb and another constable were on the scene. PC Lamb felt the woman's face, which he later described as still warm, but couldn't detect any sign of a pulse. He sent the other constable off to find a doctor while he continued to examine the corpse, noting that he did not see any signs of a struggle, and neither were the woman's clothes unduly disturbed, which was unlike the earlier victims, whose skirts had been raised up above their knees.

By 1.16 a.m., Doctor Frederick Blackwell, whom the police had used on several occasions before, had arrived on the scene and started making a detailed examination of the body, the details of which were read out at the later inquest, as follows:

The deceased was lying on her left side obliquely across the passage, her face looking towards the right wall. Her legs were drawn up; her feet close against the wall of the right side of the passage. Her head was resting beyond the carriage-wheel rug, the neck lying over the rut. The neck and chest were quite warm, as were also the legs, and the face was slightly warm. The hands were cold. The right hand was open and on the chest, and was smeared with blood. The left hand, lying on the ground, was partially closed, and contained a small packet of cachous [popular Victorian breath sweeteners] wrapped in tissue paper.

The appearance of the face was quite placid. The mouth was slightly opened. In the neck there was a long incision which commenced on the left side, 2 inches below the angle of the jaw, and almost in a direct line with it, nearly severing the vessels on that side, cutting the windpipe completely in two, and terminating on the opposite side.

While Dr Blackwell was examining the body, he was joined by the official police surgeon, Dr Phillips. Between them, they estimated the time of death to be between 12.36 a.m. and 12.56 a.m.

A number of police officers were called in to continue with routine investigations and searches, but no senior detectives at this point were drafted in. Abberline was furious when he found out the following day; he had not even been woken from his bed, even though he could have been on the scene within minutes, which, as he later pointed out, could have helped immensely with the investigation. A search of the yard and immediate area was undertaken by the officers at hand, but nothing in the way of clues or weapon were found. It was noted, however, that the chairman of the International Working Men's Educational Club had walked through the yard around 12.40 a.m., which was roughly twenty minutes before the body was discovered, and he had seen nothing suspicious or anyone loitering nearby. The story was the same with Diemschutz, who had discovered the body when he had pulled into the yard at 1 a.m. The yard, he said, was completely deserted, apart from the body, which was later identified as the body of Elizabeth Stride.

While all this was going on in Whitechapel, just a quarter of a mile away in Mitre Square, which comes under the jurisdiction of the City of London, another gruesome find was about to be uncovered. Catherine 'Kate' Eddowes, who also worked as a prostitute, had just been released from Bishopsgate police station.

She had been arrested on Aldgate High Street at around 8.30 p.m. the previous night for being drunk and disorderly. The arresting constable said that she was trying to entertain passers-by with a drunken rendition of a very popular song at the time called, *Any Old Iron*; it has been alleged that she was doing an imitation of a fire engine, but that is very doubtful as fire engines at that time were horse drawn and had a single bell, not a siren as they have today, and how anybody would attempt to imitate such a vehicle is a mystery. As she finished her inebriated performance, Eddowes tried to take a bow, but was so drunk that she couldn't stand up again and just toppled over onto the pavement, where she tried to go to sleep. The constable lifted her to her feet and propped her against a wall, but every time he tried this she just slid back down to the floor again. At this point, the constable saw another police officer and got him to help take Eddowes to Bishopsgate police station.

Eddowes was so drunk that when they got her to the police station and asked for her name, she either couldn't remember it or couldn't be bothered to tell them, her answer to that question being, 'No one'. She was obviously not in a position to be able to look after herself, so it was decided to place her in a cell until she sobered up. An officer checked on her several times over the next few hours but each time found her to be sleeping soundly.

At 12.30 a.m. the duty officer in charge on the main desk heard her shouting, asking when they were going to let her out of there. The officer smiled to himself, remembering the state she was in when she was brought in; he called back to her, saying, 'When you can look after yourself.' To which she replied back, 'I can do that right now.'

The duty officer finished off some paperwork he was working on, and then went along to Eddowes' cell, which he opened up. By this time it was 12.55 a.m. She certainly looked like she had sobered up; at least she was standing, and not staggering. 'One last thing before I let you go,' he said, 'your name and address, what is it?' Eddowes paused for a few moments, before replying 'Mary Ann Kelly'; she then gave her address as 6 Fashion Street.

Prostitutes often gave false names and addresses when picked up by the police, but Eddowes did often use the name Kelly, as it was the name of a man, John Kelly, whom she'd had a relationship with a couple of years earlier. But why did she choose 'Mary Ann' and why the fictitious address of 6 Fashion Street? She was living at a common lodging house on 55 Flower and Dean Street at this time.

The duty officer led her along a passageway, to a door that led out to the street. As he pushed the door open for her, she asked him the time, to which he replied, 'Too late for you to get any more drink.' She said it wasn't more drink she was after; she was worried she would get a beating from her man when she got home so late. She was probably making all this up in order to make him believe her fictitious name and address, and that she was an ordinary married woman. The duty officer was not exactly sympathetic, whatever her circumstances, and replied to her, 'Serves you right – you have no right to get drunk.' He then turned to walk back inside, telling her to make sure she shut the door. Even after being treated so appallingly by the duty officer, Eddowes still managed a smile as she waved cheerily to him and said, 'Good night old cock', before stepping out onto the street and turning left in the direction of Houndsditch and Mitre Square.

Mitre Square is situated just inside the City of London boundary. At this time, it was an enclosed square which housed three imposing warehouse buildings, three uninhabited houses and a shop, which backed onto its south-west corner. There were also two more smaller houses, which nestled between the warehouses, one of which was occupied by a City of London police constable, Richard Pearse. During the day the square was a little hive of industry, but when night fell and the workers left their premises, the square became a dark and usually deserted area.

Mitre Square had three entrances, the first being a fairly wide street which led from Mitre Street, the second being St James Place (known locally as the Orange Market), which was much narrower and not much more than an alley really, and the third, in the south-east corner of the square, being the long and narrow Church Passage, which stretched into the square from Duke's Place.

Police Constable Edward Watkins, of the City of London Police, paced his beat through Mitre Square, as he did almost every other night. The only sounds to be heard were the echos of his own boots on the pavement, as well as that of a local cat meowing as it always did when he passed. It took Watkins approximately fifteen minutes to patrol the square. It was then 1.30 a.m. and, as usual, all was quiet. So quiet, in fact, that he used to say to his colleagues that you could hear a pin drop.

About five minutes after Watkins had left the square, three Jewish gentlemen, Harry Harris, Joseph Hyam Levy and Joseph Lawende, left the nearby Imperial Club on Duke Street. As they passed Church Passage they noticed a woman talking quietly with a man. The woman had her back to them, but they noticed that the couple were very close to each other, and the woman's hand was resting on the man's chest.

Being the gentlemen that they were, the three men did not like to see this type of thing happening, quite brazenly, on a street corner. Levy was more worried for his own safety than that of the others, so told his friends that with characters like that about they should stay together as a group, rather than go their separate ways home. He hurried past the couple as quickly as he could, trying to pay them as little attention as he could. When asked later if he could give the police a description of either of them, all he could say with any accuracy was that he thought the man was possibly about 3 in taller than the woman.

Joseph Lawende, however, was a little less disgusted than his friend, and a little more observant. Although he hadn't seen the woman's face, he was almost certain of what she was wearing. When later shown the clothing Catherine

Eddowes had been wearing, he was absolutely certain that it was the same as worn by the woman he had seen that night.

The street lighting wasn't particularly good in the square, but he had caught a brief glimpse of the man's face and was able to provide police with a description. He described the man as aged about 30, 5 ft 9 in tall and of medium build. He went on to say that the man had a fair complexion, a small fair moustache and was dressed in a dark jacket, red neckerchief and a grey, peaked, cloth cap.

One would think that to describe someone so accurately, Lawende must have got a very good view of him indeed, but he later said that he only caught a brief glimpse of the man as he passed by, and since the couple were doing nothing particularly suspicious, he didn't exactly pay either of them too much attention. When asked if he thought he would be able to recognise or identify the man if he were to see him again, he replied that he doubted it.

By 1.44 a.m. PC Watkins had returned to his starting position in the square. The only thing on his mind, at this time, was getting back to the police station and clocking off for the night. It was at this point, as he started to walk away, that he noticed a dark bundle on the ground, close to a corner of the square. It certainly couldn't be the cat, as it was quite large; he lifted his lantern and shone it in the direction of the bundle. He reeled back in horror at the sight that confronted him, for it was the body of a woman, who was later identified as Catherine Eddowes. This was the second murder in one night, and just forty-five minutes apart, not that Watkins would have known that at this moment in time; all he was aware of was the ghastly sight that now confronted him.

Catherine Eddowes was lying on her back in a pool of blood; her throat had been cut open, almost from ear to ear, and her clothes were up above her waist, exposing all of the lower half of her body. Her stomach had been slashed and ripped open, leaving her intestines and bowels protruding.

PC Watkins had been in the police force for a number of years, during which time he had witnessed all types of crimes, including murder and rape, but he had never seen anything as horrific as this before. So bad were her injuries that he had to steady himself against the wall for a moment, and take in a breath of fresh air, before running across the square for help. He banged on the doors of Kearley and Tongs tea warehouse, which dominated the northern side of the square, where he knew a retired Metropolitan Police officer named George Morris was working as a nightwatchman.

George Morris barely had time to open the door before PC Watkins grabbed him. 'Quick,' he shouted, 'grab your lamp and come with me, there's a woman been cut to pieces over there.' The two men ran across the square to where Eddowes' body was lying. George Morris could hardly believe his eyes, and had to be shook back to reality by Watkins, who told him to run as fast as he could and fetch help. This was not an easy task for Morris, who was not exactly young at the time, but he nevertheless did as he was told and made his way to Aldgate, where he enlisted the help of two more constables, PC James Harvey and PC Holland.

PC Watkins, who had assumed charge of the operation until a senior officer arrived on the scene, immediately sent PC Holland to fetch a local doctor, Dr George Sequira, from his house on nearby Jewry Street. It was 1.55 a.m. when Sequira reached Mitre Square and examined Eddowes' body. He later gave evidence at the inquest regarding his opinion on how she had been killed, and the time of death.

A short while later they were joined by more police officers from the City of London Police. Inspector Edward Collard arrived from Bishopsgate police station and ordered an immediate search of the neighbourhood, instructing that door-to-door inquiries were to be made of the area around Mitre Square. He was quickly followed by a number of detectives from the City of London Police, headed by Superintendent James McWilliam, head of the City of London Police Detective Department.

Officers from both police stations began to fan out through the streets of Whitechapel and the surrounding area. Anyone who looked even remotely suspicious was stopped and questioned, but no arrests were made. The killer, it seemed, was beginning to take on the mantle that the popular press had given him, which was that of a phantom, a ghostly figure who seemed to be able to appear and disappear into the night, without anyone ever seeing him. Directly opposite where the body of Eddowes was found lived City Police Constable Richard Pearce; his bedroom window looked directly down onto the murder scene, yet he neither heard nor saw a thing that night.

By 2.18 a.m. a police doctor, Frederick Gordon Brown, had also arrived on the scene and made a quick examination of the body. He certified that the victim's throat had been cut, her torso had been ripped open and her intestines had been pulled out and laid over her shoulder. The killer had cut deep V shapes into her cheeks and eyes. The tip of her nose had been sliced off and her ear lobes had been nicked through with the blade. In addition, the killer had carefully removed her left kidney and her uterus, and taken them with him when he fled the scene. One rather strange item that was also missing was a portion of her apron, which had been ripped or torn from the article as a whole and also removed from the scene. Dr Brown later testified at the inquest that the body was still relatively warm when he examined her, and that there were no signs of rigor mortis having taken place at that point. He further testified that, in his opinion, Catherine Eddowes must have been killed within half an hour prior to him being called to the scene.

The police search turned up nothing: no witnesses or clues, and most certainly no suspects. No money was found on the corpse and there was no evidence that she had struggled with her killer, which left the police with absolutely nothing to go on. When one considers the enormously high number of police officers in the direct vicinity of the square that night, and at that exact time, it is amazing that no one saw or heard a thing.

It wasn't exactly turning out to be a good night for the police: two prostitutes had been murdered within half an hour of each other, one of which was murdered in the City of London of all places, which was certainly not known for this type of thing. Add to this the abnormally large police presence, a witness who forgot what a possible suspect looked like almost immediately after accurately describing him to the police and a police officer who lived directly opposite the scene of the crime and did not hear or see a thing. This was turning into a newspaper reporter's dream!

Under the eyes and ears of the police, the murderer had somehow tracked his victim into the square, killed her, mutilated her body and escaped completely, in total silence, and all in the space of fifteen minutes. But the night was far from over.

At 2.55 a.m., PC Long was patrolling his beat in Goulston Street, Spitalfields, which is just over a third of a mile away from Mitre Square. As he passed the entrance to 108–119 Wentworth Model Dwellings, he noticed a piece of material with bloodstains on it, lying on the floor near to the staircase. Although he did not know it at the time, the piece of material was the portion of the apron that had been ripped from the clothing Catherine Eddowes had been wearing when she was found dead in Mitre Square.

The piece of material looked very suspicious to PC Long as it had a considerable amount of blood and faeces on it, and was wet along one side. PC Long's first thoughts were that the blade of a knife had apparently been wiped on it, which he thought could be consistent with maybe a fight or an attack of some sort. He had passed this spot just thirty-five minutes earlier and had not noticed anything there then, which led him to surmise that it must have been left there very recently. As PC Long bent down to pick the piece of material up, he noticed a message, written in chalk, on the wall just above it, which he also did not remember seeing before. He copied the wording down into his notebook, as follows:

The Juwes are the men that will not be blamed for nothing

PC Long then searched all six staircases in the buildings, in the hope that he might possibly find a weapon, a body, bloody footprints or even a trail of blood, but unfortunately he didn't find anything. As he started to make his way back to the police station, he bumped into another police officer, who was from a different station to him. The police officer told him that a murder had been committed in Mitre Square, which in turn made PC Long even more suspicious of what he had found. Long told the other constable of what he had discovered, and left him in charge of the building, telling him to keep a close observation on the dwelling, to see whether anyone left or entered, while he was away. PC Long then took the piece of the apron along to Commercial Street police station, where he reported it to the inspector on duty, along with his report, which included a copy of the writing he found on the wall.

Could the piece of bloodstained apron have held a clue which has long been overlooked? It has never been established why the piece of apron was cut from Eddowes' clothing in the first place or why it was dumped in the doorway of the flats in Goulston Street. It has been alleged that the Ripper may have used it to wipe Eddowes' blood from his hands and face as he fled the scene, but when Abberline looked into this theory, he thought it highly unlikely, as the distance between Mitre Square and Goulston Street is approximately one-third of a mile, and would probably take about eight to ten minutes to walk. He argued that the murderer would never have seriously contemplated walking that distance through the London streets, whilst wiping away the blood from himself, knowing full well that the streets were full of policemen looking for anyone and anything suspicious at the time.

The second theory as to why he took the piece of apron was to hide his knife. This again, Abberline argued, just doesn't hold water; why would he suddenly need something to conceal his knife in? What did he use to hide his knife before he murdered Eddowes? This then leaves the third theory, which was that he used the piece of apron to take away some of Eddowes' internal organs. This, said Abberline, was the most likely of the three theories, but it is let down somewhat by the fact that it was dumped in Goulston Street, meaning that the Ripper either lived there in Model Dwellings, and dumped the piece of apron on his own doorstep so to speak, which would be highly unlikely, or he found a more suitable method of transporting the organs at that point, and transferred the grizzly contents of the apron to his newly found carrier. Once again, said Inspector Abberline, it just didn't add up.

It is more likely that the Ripper, who you must remember was working very quickly in Mitre Square, cut himself badly whilst ripping open Eddowes' body, and then used the piece of her apron to bandage his hand or arm, which he could then stuff into a pocket of his coat, thus making sure that he would not leave a bloody trail. By the time he had reached Goulston Street, he was in all probability, not too far from where he lived and felt safe enough to dump the bloodstained piece of apron.

Not only is this theory much more plausible then the other three, but it could also explain the reason why there was a pause of nearly six weeks between the murders of Eddowes and Kelly, which I will delve into later. In my opinion, the Ripper injured his hand or arm so badly that he couldn't go about his work for this period.

Another police officer, who also confirmed that he had not seen the piece of apron or the writing on the wall of the Wentworth Model Dwellings, was DC Halse, who had been at Mitre Square just after the discovery of Eddowes' body. He had also been part of the team sent off to comb the complex of streets around Whitechapel, in search of the fugitive. He later stated that at 2.20 a.m. he had passed along Goulston Street and was pretty sure neither the apron nor the writing were there then. He said he was sure he would have noticed these as he had specifically stopped and searched the entrance to Wentworth Model Dwellings and found nothing of interest.

After PC Long had submitted his report, he returned to Goulston Street to find a number of senior officers now on the scene. The time was now about 5 a.m. and he noticed a number of officers gathered around the doorway gazing at the graffiti and apparently discussing it amongst themselves.

When news of the two murders was broke to Inspector Abberline the following morning, he was firstly very angry that he had not been informed of such an important new development immediately, and he was also very worried regarding the location of where the piece of apron was found. Wentworth Model Dwellings not only stood in a largely Jewish locality but was also inhabited almost exclusively by Jews, and within a few short hours would see the opening of the vast Wentworth Street and Petticoat Lane markets, which were run almost entirely by Jews.

Abberline was very aware of the strong feelings of anti-Semitism that had surfaced in this area in the wake of the Leather Apron scare, and as much as he realised the importance of this piece of evidence, he also knew that if the graffiti was left for all to see, it would undoubtedly lead to a resurgence of racial unrest in the area, and the consequences could be severe indeed. This was, after all, an area that Inspector Abberline had more expertise on, than any other police officer on the case, and this is why he came up with his suggestion, that the only option was that the graffiti must be erased from the wall immediately.

Detectives from the City of London Police, however, begged to differ; the murder, they said, had been carried out in their jurisdiction, and as such both the portion of the apron and the graffiti pertained to their investigation, and should remain untouched until they decided otherwise. The City of London Police wanted the graffiti to be photographed, but Inspector Abberline pointed out to them that this would mean waiting until it was light, by which time the crowds would be arriving in their thousands to purchase from the Jewish stallholders at Petticoat Lane, Wentworth Street and Goulston Street Sunday markets.

Above: Inspector Frederick George Abberline, taken from a group photograph of H Division at Leman Street police station in London *c.* 1886. (Wikimedia Commons)

Above right: Caricature of Lord Arthur Somerset, taken from *Vanity Fair*, 19 November 1887. (Wikimedia Commons)

Right: Prince Albert Victor. (Wikimedia Commons)

Left: A sketch of Charles Hammond.
(Author's collection)

Below: A sketch of the boy witnesses appearing in court to testify against Hammond.
(Author's collection)

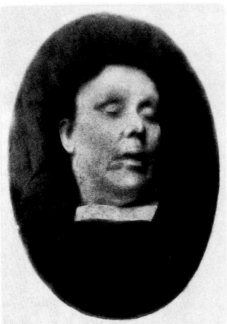

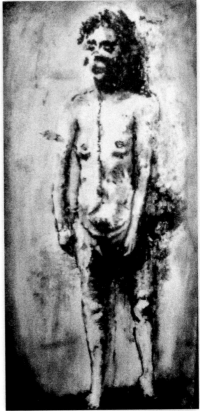

Left: Miller's Court, the location of the murder of Mary Kelly. (Wikimedia Commons)

Right: A cartoon criticising the police for their inability to find the Whitechapel murderer appeared in *Punch* on 22 September 1888. (Wikimedia Commons)

The infamous 'Dear Boss' letter. (Wikimedia Commons)

FINDING THE MUTILATED BODY IN MITRE SQARE

Right: The front page of *The Illustrated Police News* on 22 September 1888. (Author's collection)

Below: A map of the seven murder sites. (Wikimedia Commons)

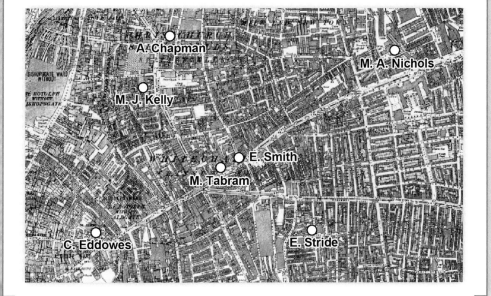

GHASTLY MURDER IN THE EAST-END.
DREADFUL MUTILATION OF A WOMAN.

Capture : Leather Apron

Another murder of a character even more diabolical than that perpetrated in Back's Row, on Friday week, was discovered in the same neighbourhood, on Saturday morning. At about six o'clock a woman was found lying in a back yard at the foot of a passage leading to a lodging-house in a Old Brown's Lane, Spitalfields. The house is occupied by a Mrs. Richardson, who lets it out to lodgers, and the door which admits to this passage, at the foot of which lies the yard where the body was found, is always open for the convenience of lodgers. A lodger named Davis was going down to work at the time mentioned and found the woman lying on her back close to the flight of steps leading into the yard. Her throat was cut in a fearful manner. The woman's body had been completely ripped open and the heart and other organs laying about the place, and portions of the entrails round the victim's neck. An excited crowd gathered in front of Mrs. Richardson's house and also round the mortuary in old Montague Street, whither the body was quickly conveyed. As the body lies in the rough coffin in which it has been placed in the mortuary   the same coffin in which the unfortunate Mrs. Nicholls was first placed   it presents a fearful sight. The body is that of a woman about 45 years of age. The height is exactly five feet. The complexion is fair, with wavy brown hair; the eyes are blue, and two lower teeth have been knocked out. The nose is rather large and prominent.

Left: A newspaper broadsheet of 1888, published immediately after the murder of Annie Chapman, referring to the Whitechapel murderer as 'Leather Apron'. (Wikimedia Commons)

Right: A police copy of the writing found in Goulston Street. (Wikimedia Commons)

While the two forces clashed, it was gradually getting lighter. Inspector Daniel Halse of the City of London Police suggested a compromise whereby only the top line, The Juwes are, would be erased. Abberline was against this idea, as was Superintendent Arnold of the Metropolitan Police, who later pointed out in a report: 'Had only a portion of the writing been removed the context would have remained.'

Tempers flared, voices were raised and accusations started to fly between the two opposing teams. At one point, it is alleged that Inspector Abberline lost his temper completely, which he had never been seen to do before, and shouted at Inspector Halse, telling him that if the graffiti was not removed within the next five minutes, it would almost certainly lead to a full-scale riot against the Jews, and that he would hold Halse personally responsible.

At 5.30 a.m. Sir Charles Warren arrived at the scene. The doorway, he declared, stood on Metropolitan Police territory, which made his word final. He had a brief talk with Inspector Abberline and then ordered the message to be erased without delay. He completely ignored calls from the City of London Police to at least wait until their photographer got there. 'It will be light by then and will have been seen by numerous people,' bellowed Warren. 'Remove the writing now.'

This would prove to be the most controversial order Warren gave during the entire investigation. Major Smith, the acting City Police Commissioner at the time, considered it 'a blunder of massive proportions' and could barely disguise his contempt for Warren's actions in the days and weeks that followed.

Such was the furore that followed Sir Charles Warren's controversial decision, that on 6 November, in a report to the Home Office, he defended his action with the following:

Warren's Report to the Home Secretary
6 November 1888

4 Whitehall Place, S.W.
6th November 1888

Confidential
The Under Secretary of State
The Home Office

Sir,

In reply to your letter of the 5th instant, I enclose a report of the circumstances of the Mitre Square Murder so far as they have come under the notice of the Metropolitan Police, and I now give an account regarding the erasing of the writing on the wall in Goulston Street which I have already partially explained to Mr. Matthews verbally.

On the 30th September on hearing of the Berner Street murder, after visiting Commercial Street Station I arrived at Leman Street Station shortly before 5 A.M. and ascertained from the Superintendent Arnold all that was known there relative to the two murders.

The most pressing question at that moment was some writing on the wall in Goulston Street evidently written with the intention of inflaming the public mind against the Jews, and which Mr. Arnold with a view to prevent serious disorder proposed to obliterate, and had sent down an Inspector with a sponge for that purpose, telling him to await his arrival.

I considered it desirable that I should decide the matter myself, as it was one involving so great a responsibility whether any action was taken or not.

I accordingly went down to Goulston Street at once before going to the scene of the murder: it was just getting light, the public would be in the streets in a few minutes, in a neighbourhood very much crowded on Sunday mornings by Jewish vendors and Christian purchasers from all parts of London.

There were several Police around the spot when I arrived, both Metropolitan and City.

The writing was on the jamb of the open archway or doorway visible in the street and could not be covered up without danger of the covering being torn off at once.

A discussion took place whether the writing could be left covered up or otherwise or whether any portion of it could be left for an hour until it could be photographed; but after taking into consideration the excited state of the population in London generally at the time, the strong feeling which had been excited against the Jews, and the fact that in a short time there would be a large concourse of the people in the streets, and having before me the Report that if it was left there the house was likely to be wrecked (in which from my own observation I entirely concurred) I considered it desirable to obliterate the writing at once, having taken a copy of which I enclose a duplicate.

After having been to the scene of the murder, I went on to the City Police Office and informed the Chief Superintendent of the reason why the writing had been obliterated.

I may mention that so great was the feeling with regard to the Jews that on the 13th ulto. the Acting Chief Rabbi wrote to me on the subject of the spelling of the word 'Jewes' on account of a newspaper asserting that this was Jewish spelling in the Yiddish dialect. He added 'in the present state of excitement it is dangerous to the safety of the poor Jews in the East [End] to allow such an assertion to remain uncontradicted. My community keenly appreciates your humane and vigilant action during this critical time.'

It may be realised therefore if the safety of the Jews in Whitechapel could be considered to be jeopardised 13 days after the murder by the question of the spelling of the word Jews, what might have happened to the Jews in that quarter had that writing been left intact.

I do not hesitate myself to say that if that writing had been left there would have have been an onslaught upon the Jews, property would have been wrecked, and lives would probably have been lost; and I was much gratified with the promptitude with which Superintendent Arnold was prepared to act in the matter if I had not been there.

I have no doubt myself whatever that one of the principal objects of the Reward offered by Mr. Montagu was to show to the world that the Jews were desirous of having the Hanbury Street Murder cleared up, and thus to divert from them the very strong feeling which was then growing up.

I am, Sir,

Your most obedient Servant,
(signed) C. Warren

It is easy to sympathise with Sir Charles Warren on this matter — Inspector Abberline certainly seemed to — as local feelings were still running high regarding the Jews, who most certainly dominated this particular area at the time. The press had not helped the situation, of course, with their anti-Semitic characterisations of people they alleged were suspects, such as the now infamous Leather Apron, and now this graffiti actually naming the Jews as 'The men that will not be blamed for nothing'. This could provide the spark which was all that was needed to set the whole of East London ablaze.

Could there have been another reason why Warren wanted the graffiti removed so promptly? There are some who say yes to this, giving their explanation as a Freemason's conspiracy, which involved a member of the royal family. Astonishing as this might seem, it does have a ring of authenticity about it, and involves the actual wording of the graffiti, but more about this later. At this point there was still one more Jack the Ripper victim to fall foul of his knife, but with one inconsistency, this being that up to this point there were gaps of approximately one week in between each murder. The final Jack the Ripper murder was that of Mary Jane Kelly, which took place on Friday 9 November, almost six weeks after Catherine Eddowes' murder.

During the period between these dates, George Lusk and his Whitechapel Vigilance Committee had also been somewhat busy. On 30 September 1888, the same day as the Double Event took place, Lusk wrote on behalf of his committee to the Prime Minister, Lord Salisbury, pleading with him to offer a reward for information leading to the apprehension of the killer. He eventually received a reply from the Home Secretary, Henry Matthews, who turned down his request, saying that such matters were not a part of government responsibility. Lusk was so angry at this rebuke that he organised a public fund from within his committee and proceeded to offer their own reward. The committee also employed two private detectives, Mr Le Grand and Mr J.H. Batchelor, to investigate the murders without the involvement of the local police.

Needless to say, there was great deal of resentment between the police and members of the Whitechapel Vigilance Committee, for Lusk was now starting to publicly say that the police were just not doing their job. So unhappy was Lusk and the general public, according to him, with the level of protection that the community was receiving from the police, that the committee introduced its own system of local patrols using hand-picked unemployed men to walk the streets of the East End every evening from midnight to between 4. a.m. and 5 a.m.. The men, who were paid a small wage, patrolled a particular beat just like a police officer would do, and were armed with a police whistle, a pair of galoshes and a heavy stick. Committee members met each evening at 9 p.m. in the Crown public house, where they would discuss any possible leads that might have been made, before allocating the patrols for the evening. These patrols were shortly to be joined by those of the Working Men's Vigilance Committee.

On 16 October, George Lusk received a 3in square cardboard box in his mail, which contained half a human kidney preserved in spirit, alongside a short letter to him. Convinced the contents of the box, and the letter, were a practical joke, Lusk placed the box and the kidney in his desk drawer, and didn't think much more about it until he held a meeting of the Vigilance Committee at his home, a day or two later. He suddenly remembered it, and showed it to other members of the committee, saying that he had kept it to show them and thought he should now throw both the box and its contents away. One of the committee members, however, took the whole thing much more seriously and persuaded him to take it to Dr Frederick Wiles, who had a surgery nearby on the Mile End Road.

Unfortunately Dr Wiles was out, so his assistant suggested taking the box and its contents to Dr Thomas Horrocks Openshaw, a pathologist at the nearby London Hospital. Openshaw conducted tests on the kidney and stated that, in his opinion, it had almost certainly come from the body of Catherine Eddowes. Openshaw's findings stated that the kidney was human and had been removed from the left side of the body of a woman within the last two weeks. The woman, he stated, would be approximately 45 years of age (Eddowes was 43). The kidney was 'gin sodden' (Eddowes' favourite drink was gin). The kidney also showed an advanced state of Bright's disease. Eddowes was suffering from Bright's disease. Probably the most significant factor in proving the kidney had come from the body of Catherine Eddowes was the fact that the renal artery attached to the kidney is 3in in length altogether 1in was found still attached to the kidney, while 2in were found still intact within Eddowes' body.

Lusk was visibly shaken by these findings, and took both the box and its contents, along with the letter, to the City of London Police, in whose jurisdiction Catherine Eddowes had been murdered.

The transcript of the note, which was also inside the cardboard box and later became known as the 'From Hell' letter, read as follows:

From Hell.

Mr Lusk,

Sor

I send you half the Kidne I took from one woman and prasarved it for you tother piece I fried and ate it was very nise. I may send you the bloody knif that took it out if you only wate a whil longer

signed

Catch me when you can Mishter Lusk

To say George Lusk was shaken by this event could be classed as something of an understatement, for while he relished in his new-found celebrity status, his name had also started to attract a different kind of 'fan', who today would possibly be termed as a stalker!

Just over a week before receiving the 'From Hell' letter and kidney, a man, described as aged between 35 and 40, medium height, with a florid complexion, bushy brown beard, sideburns and moustache, called at Mr Lusk's house in Alderney Street, Mile End. Lusk wasn't at home at the time, but his housekeeper told him that he was at a nearby tavern, owned by his son. The man went to the pub, where he found Lusk and started asking him all sorts of questions; he then tried to induce Lusk to enter a private room with him, but Lusk was repulsed by the man's strange and somewhat foreboding appearance and felt that it would be better to talk where they could be observed by other people.

The man, who did not give his name, said he was interested in the work of Lusk's Vigilance Committee, but all the time Lusk was talking to him, Lusk said he noticed the man's eyes never stayed still for a moment, darting to and fro, as if his mind was elsewhere. The man then suddenly drew a pencil from his top pocket, as if he was about to take notes. He then dropped it onto the floor, which Lusk later said he thought was done on purpose, and quickly asked Lusk to pick the pencil up for him. Lusk thought this strange, as the man wasn't particularly old or impaired in any way that he could see, so why had he asked him, instead of picking it up himself? Lusk, nevertheless, bent down to pick the pencil up, and as he did so he noticed the man make a sudden movement with his right hand towards his side coat pocket. Lusk became scared as he saw the man start to draw out an object from his pocket; it could have been a knife or a gun. Lusk didn't wait to find out, and quickly got to his feet. The man by this time could see that whatever it was he had been intending to do, he had now been detected, and other people were also looking in his direction. The man swiftly took his now empty hand out of his pocket and gave Lusk a strange smile; he then got to his feet and mumbled something, which Lusk later said he thought sounded like, 'Another time maybe'. The man then nonchalantly asked Lusk where the nearest coffee and dining rooms were. Lusk gave him directions to dining rooms in the Mile End Road and the man left. Lusk was so suspicious of the man by this time that he enlisted the help of one of his committee members, and together they followed the man. They unfortunately lost sight of him, but nevertheless went directly to the dining rooms that Lusk had described to the man, only to find that he was not there and never had been.

A few days after this incident, Lusk was seemingly targeted again. This time it involved yet another sinister-looking character who was seen acting suspiciously outside his house. Fearing for not just his own safety, but that of his family as well, Lusk reported the character to the police and a full description of him was circulated.

On 12 October Lusk received a letter in handwriting that some experts thought could be the same as the 'Dear Boss' letter.

The transcript of this letter is as follows:

I write you a letter in black ink, as I have no more of the right stuff. I think you are all asleep in Scotland Yard with your bloodhounds, as I will show you to-morrow night (Saturday). I am going to do a double event, but not in Whitechapel. Got rather too warm there. Had to shift. No more till you hear me again.

JACK THE RIPPER.

The Vigilance Committee had posters offering a reward for information about the murders almost everywhere in East London, and the little shop selling leatherwear in Jubilee Street, just a short distance from the London Hospital, was no exception. The young lady, Miss Marsh, who worked in the shop for her father, smiled and asked if she could help the man that came in that day, on

15 October, for she didn't feel that she had anything to be afraid of, as he was wearing a clerical collar of the type the clergy might wear.

The man said he was interested in the Vigilance Committee's reward poster in the shop window and asked if she knew the address of Mr George Lusk. Miss Marsh didn't know this, but suggested he should enquire at the nearby Crown public house. The man was polite and even apologetic as he insisted he didn't want to go into a pub. Miss Marsh understood, and obligingly got out a newspaper that gave Lusk's address, although not the actual house number, but the man nevertheless made a note of what was there. Miss Marsh later described the man as being in his mid-forties, with an Irish accent, 6ft tall, of slim build, with a dark beard and moustache.

No one answering the man's description ever called upon Lusk, but on the following evening, Tuesday 16 October, a small package, wrapped in brown paper and bearing an indistinct London postmark, was delivered to Lusk's house. The package was addressed to Lusk by name, along with his address. There was one thing missing: the house number. This package turned out to be the now famous 'From Hell' letter, and the box contained the kidney. Could the man in the clerical collar, who called into the leatherwear shop, have possibly been the same man who sent the package? Could he have been Jack the Ripper himself?

Lusk and his Vigilance Committee seemed at this point to be doing more than the police were; that is if one took notice of the newspapers. Lusk himself had received visits from shady-looking characters, offered rewards and had allegedly received letters and threats through the post, not to mention what could possibly be vital pieces of evidence.

Abberline felt thwarted; his bosses at Scotland Yard were telling him one thing, whilst the general public, egged on by the newspapers and Lusk's Vigilance Committee, were telling him another. Not only was this affecting his work, it was also affecting his home life. He was having trouble sleeping, when he did manage to get home, and was arguing more with his wife as she was worried that it was affecting his health.

Ever the pragmatist, Emma listened to Abberline and told him he must do what he does best, and that was detective work; to pay no attention to rumours and scaremongers, and to get on with his work, for when it was finished, and the Jack the Ripper crimes, as they were now known, had been solved, then, and only then, could they return to normality in their daily lives once again.

10

The Final Ripper Victim

The Ripper's final victim was Mary Jane Kelly, who was approximately 25 years old at the time of her death although there doesn't seem to be any record of her actual birth date, she would have been born sometime around 1863. She was said to be attractive to men, with blonde hair, blue eyes and a fair complexion. She was 5ft 7in tall, and described as buxom.

She was born in Limerick, Ireland, but moved to Wales with her family as a young child. By the time she was just 16 years old, she married an equally young coal miner named Davies. They were apparently happy, but just two years later Davies was killed in a pit explosion.

Kelly was distraught with grief and moved away to Cardiff, where she moved in with a cousin, who worked as a prostitute. This was probably where Kelly started out on her ill-fated career, although the Cardiff police have no record of her ever being arrested. By 1884, however, she had seemingly heard of the riches she could earn in London, and so moved there, allegedly working in a high-class brothel in the West End. There are, of course, no records to prove exactly what Kelly did, or where she actually stayed during her time in London, and it has been said that she was somewhat prone to exaggeration. Others who knew her later testified that at this time she was staying with nuns at the Providence Row Night Refuge on Crispin Street. One of the provisions for being allowed to stay at the Providence Row Night Refuge was that she would have had to scrub floors and carry out general menial tasks. Whatever the truth, Kelly was eventually placed, probably by the refuge, into domestic service in a shop in Cleveland Street, in the West End.

The other side to the story, which she often told friends, regarding her arrival in London, was that she had befriended a French woman who lived in Knightsbridge, and that it was this woman who encouraged her to pursue the lifestyle which would ultimately lead to her death. Kelly claimed that while she was with the company of this woman she would often be driven about London in a carriage. She also claimed to have made several journeys to Paris with a man she described only as a 'gentleman'. In other words, if her story is to be believed, Kelly was at that time living the life 'of a lady'.

For some reason, which she never explained to anyone, she met a woman named Mrs Buki, who in all probability was either a prostitute herself, a madam, or maybe even both. Mrs Buki lived in a house on St George's Street, just off Ratcliffe Highway in the East End. Kelly moved into the house, which was a very big step downwards after living in Knightsbridge. It is thought that Kelly and Mrs Buki started working together as prostitutes. Just a week or two after moving into the St George's Street house, Mrs Buki and Kelly went to the French lady's house in Knightsbridge, where Kelly demanded a large clothing box containing a number of very expensive dresses, which Kelly claimed belonged to her. Kelly and Mrs Buki left in something of a hurry, minus the dresses, when the French lady threatened to call the police.

The relationship between Kelly and Mrs Buki isn't quite clear; did Kelly befriend Mrs Buki purely because she had nowhere else to stay at that time or did Mrs Buki use her, possibly thinking that she had access to money? Probably the latter, as within weeks of visiting the French lady's house in Knightsbridge, and being threatened with the police, Kelly found herself looking for somewhere else to stay once again.

Like so many women who take up prostitution, Mary Kelly always seemed to be searching for the one true love that she hoped would one day come her way. This is hard to imagine ever happening in the course of her chosen profession and an environment such as the East End of London at that time. From Mrs Buki's, she drifted to another lodging house in Breezer's Hill, and from there to a house close to Stepney Gasworks which she shared with a man named Morganstone.

Love, however, was still nothing more than just a remote memory to her, for the only real love she had ever known was that of her young husband. From Morganstone, she moved on to a man named Joseph Fleming, a stonemason from Bethnal Green, but again, this didn't last, even though Fleming was very fond of her and still visited her from time to time, right up to just before her death.

By 1886 she had started drinking heavily and found that she needed to move to cheaper lodgings. Spitalfields at this time was full of doss houses and cheap lodgings, which were usually not much more than filthy hovels. Cooley's lodging house in Thrawl Street was one such place, and it was here that Kelly then rented a solitary room.

Now needing money more than ever, in order to feed her drink habit as well as pay the rent, Kelly was walking the streets on Good Friday, 8 April 1887, when she bumped into a man and started chatting to him. The man was Joseph Barnett, an Irish fish porter, who took her for a drink and then arranged to meet her the following day. Kelly could hardly believe her luck: Barnett was such a nice man, kind and considerate, and seemed to want her for who she was, rather than just for sex. Within hours of their second meeting, Barnett had asked her to live with him, and she had agreed.

Within days they had moved into lodgings in George Street, off Commercial Street, and from there to a larger flat in Little Paternoster Row off Dorset Street; but six weeks later, they were evicted for not paying the rent and for being drunk and making too much noise. Drink was their downfall as a couple; friends, who remembered them from this time, said they were a friendly and pleasant couple who gave little trouble, unless they were drunk. In fact, records for Thames Magistrate Court show that on 19 September 1888, a Mary Jane Kelly was fined 2s 6d for being drunk and disorderly.

Since she had moved in with Barnett, Kelly had given up prostitution and they had relied solely on his wages. Unfortunately the money he earned as a fish porter only just about fed and clothed them, and paid the rent, which left hardly anything for their ever-increasing drink habit. Their only option at this time was to move into cheaper accommodation, which they did; firstly in one room in Brick Lane, which was infested with rats, and from there, in March 1888, to Miller's Court off Dorset Street. Again this was only a single room but at least it was reasonably clean and without rats. This new address was listed as 13 Miller's Court.

In September 1888, Barnett was fired from his job for consistent lateness and time off, which was, once again, probably due to his drinking habits. Now faced with no money coming into the household at all, Kelly decided to do the only thing she knew, which was to return to the streets again; and if this wasn't enough, she also decided to rent out a spare bed to other prostitutes. Barnett couldn't stand this, as he now looked upon Kelly as his wife and absolutely hated the thought of any other man touching her. They had a blazing row, in which he told her that either she gave up the street life altogether or he would leave her. In defiance, Kelly grabbed a quarter-full bottle of gin from the sideboard and swigged it back in one go, before walking out smiling and waving goodbye to Barnett as she went. When she did return, some four hours later, Barnett was gone and Kelly broke down in tears, thinking she would never see him again. This wasn't true, as Barnett still apparently loved her, and although he couldn't bear to see her selling herself to other men, he continued to visit her and give her money whenever he could.

Throughout October, and into early November, at least two other prostitutes shared Kelly's room with her, one being a woman known only as Julia and the other a woman named Maria Harvey.

At the later inquest into Kelly's death, her ex-partner Joseph Barnett testified that it was because Kelly had allowed these other prostitutes to stay in their room that they had broken up. He stood up for her right to the end, saying that she would never have gone wrong again if it hadn't been for the prostitutes staying at the house. She only let them stay there, he said, because she was so good hearted and did not like to refuse them shelter on cold bitter nights. He added that they had lived comfortably until Kelly had allowed a prostitute named Julia and then Maria Harvey to sleep in the same room.

The last known dates that Kelly was seen were on Monday 5 November, when Maria Harvey left her room and found lodgings elsewhere, and then again on Wednesday 7 November, when Kelly went to McCarthy's, a local shop, to buy a candle for her room. Later that same evening she was seen in Miller's Court by Thomas Bowyer, a pensioned soldier who also happened to work in McCarthy's shop.

Bowyer later stated at the inquest that on Wednesday night he saw a man speaking to Kelly in Miller's Court. Bowyer's description of the man, matched almost exactly, to a witness' description of the man who was seen talking to Elizabeth Stride on the night of her death. He described the man's appearance as very smart, and drew special attention to his very white cuffs and large white shirt collar, which came down over the front of his long black coat. The man was not carrying a bag or a package of any description.

A number of witnesses saw Kelly on Friday 9 November, including her ex-partner, Joseph Barnett, who called in to see her at about 7.45 p.m., but he couldn't speak to her at any length as she was talking to another woman. Maria Harvey later said that she was the woman Kelly was speaking to, and that she had left her about ten minutes later. There is some discrepancy about this, however, as firstly, Barnett knew Harvey and would have instantly recognised her, and secondly, another woman, Lizzie Albrook, who lived at 2 Miller's Court, said it was her who Kelly was talking to when Barnett had arrived. She said that Kelly had said to her, 'What ever you do Lizzie, don't you go doing wrong and turn out as I did'. Albrook said that Kelly was a very caring person and had often spoken to her in this way. She went on to say that Kelly had warned her against going onto the streets, as she had done. She had apparently said that she was heartily sick of the life she was leading and wished she had enough money to go back to Ireland where her family lived.

November that year was a very cold and damp month, and housing conditions in London's East End were far from adequate, especially amongst the poor. One needs to remember that what we today class as our normal everyday rights were practically non-existent during this time. There was no television or radio or central heating; in fact, people were lucky to be able to afford coal or wood to burn on their open fires, if they indeed even had a fireplace. Entertainment was restricted to a visit to the local pub, when one could afford it; other than that there was nothing, which meant that many people tucked themselves up into their beds, sometimes as early as 8 p.m. during the cold weather, in order to escape their humdrum existence, and to try to keep warm.

The streets of Whitechapel that Friday night, 9 November, were particularly quiet, with just the odd straggler here and there. The scene inside the Ten Bells public house, which was on the corner of Commercial Street and Fournier Street, and just a stone's throw from Kelly's lodgings, was a completely different story. Bearing in mind that, being a Friday night, when most workers got paid, the pub was absolutely thriving and heaving with customers.

The Ten Bells was a very popular pub, which the women who worked the streets used quite often. Being directly opposite Spitalfields Market, it naturally attracted a great deal of market workers, who not only supplied the ladies with a few free drinks, but also some extra custom to their trade. Kelly was seen in this pub drinking with a well-known prostitute from the area, Elizabeth Foster; the exact time isn't known, but there didn't seem to be any men with them. It was just the two women, chatting and having a drink.

By 11 p.m., Kelly had moved on to another nearby pub, the Britannia, where she was seen drinking with a youngish man, with a dark moustache, and described as quite well dressed. The witness said that by this time Kelly appeared to be very drunk.

Another prostitute, 31-year-old Mary Ann Cox, who lived close to Kelly at 5 Miller's Court, was just returning home at about 11.45 p.m. after a very unsuccessful night. It had now started to rain and all Cox could think about was getting indoors and hopefully warming herself up a little. As she turned into Dorset Street from Commercial Street, she noticed Kelly and a man walking ahead of her. The man was carrying a pail of beer, and Kelly was carrying a package, which looked like it could be fish and chips. Cox described the man as rather stout, with a blotchy face, small sideburns and a ginger coloured moustache.

Mary Ann Cox wasn't exactly enamoured by the man's looks, but then who was she to pick and choose on such an awful night, and at least Kelly looked happy with her fish and chips and pail of beer. Cox smiled and called goodnight to Kelly as she passed her. Kelly smiled back and started to sing as she opened her door for the man and herself to go in.

About half an hour later, and probably still thinking about the beer and fish and chips, Cox decided to go out and try her luck on the streets again. As she went, she could still hear Kelly singing from inside her room. She was singing an old-time music-hall song called *A Violet from Mother's Grave*. The song had very poignant lyrics, which brought tears to Cox's eyes as she heard it, and probably also had a special meaning to Kelly as well. The first verse went as follows:

> *Scenes of my childhood arise before my gaze,*
> *Bringing recollections of bygone happy days.*
> *When down in the meadow in childhood I would roam,*
> *No one's left to cheer me now within that good old home,*
> *Father and Mother, they have pass'd away;*
> *Sister and brother, now lay beneath the clay,*
> *But while life does remain to cheer me, I'll retain*
> *This small violet I pluck'd from mother's grave.*

When Cox returned yet again, around 1 a.m., still without money, drink or food, she could still hear Kelly singing, and there was a light showing from beneath her door, so presumably all was still well within Kelly's lodgings at this time.

About an hour after this, at approximately 2 a.m., George Hutchinson had just returned from Romford, where he had been working as a labourer. As he got to Commercial Street, where his lodgings were, he noticed a man standing on the corner of Thrawl Street, which he thought was strange, as it was still very cold and raining quite heavily by this time, and the man wasn't even trying to shelter from it. Hutchinson shook his head, thinking to himself how silly some people are, standing in the pouring rain like that.

As Hutchinson reached Flower and Dean Street, he suddenly bumped into Kelly, who he vaguely knew. She looked very drunk and clung onto his clothes, saying she was so pleased to see him, and could he possible lend her sixpence. Hutchinson was only a labourer, and made it a rule never to lend anyone money; he made an excuse to Kelly, who thanked him and went on her way, in the direction of Thrawl Street.

Hutchinson felt sorry for Kelly and somewhat guilty that he hadn't helped her by lending her the sixpence she required. He watched her go towards Thrawl Street, where she started talking to the man Hutchinson has passed a little earlier. He saw them talking and laughing together, with the man putting his hand on Kelly's shoulder and whispering something in her ear. Kelly apparently laughed at whatever it was the man had said to her, nodded her head and told him it was all right. Kelly and the man then walked off towards

Dorset Street, the man with his right hand on Kelly's shoulder. In his left hand, he carried a small parcel.

By this time, Hutchinson had got a good look at the man, and described him later as such:

> He had a pale complexion, a slight moustache turned up at the corners, dark hair, dark eyes, and bushy eyebrows. He was of 'Jewish appearance.' The man was wearing a soft felt hat pulled down over his eyes, a long dark coat trimmed in astrakhan, a white collar with a black necktie fixed with a horseshoe pin. He wore dark spats over light button over boots. A massive gold chain was in his waistcoat with a large seal with a red stone hanging from it. He carried kid gloves in his right hand and a small package in his left. He was 5 feet 6 inches, or 5 feet 7 inches tall and about 35 or 36 years old.

Hutchinson continued to watch and follow them, as Kelly and the man crossed Commercial Street and turned into Dorset Street, where they stopped outside Miller's Court and spoke for a few minutes. Kelly was heard to say, 'All right, my dear', to the man, 'come on then, you'll be comfortable with me'. They then kissed and went into Miller's Court together. At this point, which was then 3 a.m., there was nothing left for Hutchinson to see, and so he left.

Elizabeth Prater, who also lived in Miller's Court, hadn't had a particularly good night's sleep that night, owing to the heavy rain which had been dripping through her ceiling all night. At around 4 a.m., she had just managed to get to sleep when she was suddenly awoken by her kitten, which had climbed onto her bed, and at the same time she heard a distant cry of 'Murder, oh murder' from outside somewhere. Another young woman, Sarah Lewis, who was staying with friends in Miller's Court, also heard the cry, but unfortunately, neither woman took any notice of it, as it was a common cry in the district.

The rest of the night was reasonably quiet, apart from the consistent rain battering against the windows, and in some cases pouring through the holes in them. It wasn't until 10.35 a.m. that John McCarthy, the owner of McCarthy's Rents, as Miller's Court was known, decided to send his rent collector, Thomas Bowyer, to Kelly's room, to collect the arrears in her rent.

Bowyer knocked on the door quite loudly, trying his best to imitate a police-knock, as that usually scared the tenants enough into opening the door for him. After receiving no reply, he rapped on the door again, and then tried the handle, but the door seemed to be locked. He was starting to get angry at this point, believing Kelly to be in and just trying to avoid him. The window next to the door had a large broken hole in it, which he then went to peer through, but the curtain inside was blocking his view. He pushed the curtain aside and called Kelly's name, but as he looked through into the gloomy interior of the room, the sight that greeted him caused him to retch; it was most certainly a human body, but not like anything he had ever seen or heard of before in his life.

Bowyer ran as fast as he could to McCarthy, and informed him of what he had seen. After quickly seeing the body for himself, McCarthy then ran to Commercial Street police station, where he spoke with Inspector Walter Beck, who returned immediately with him to the court.

Within minutes Inspector Abberline was on the scene, along with his team and many ordinary police officers, who absolutely swamped the area. When asked by one of his team what he should do next, Abberline lost his temper and shouted at the man, telling him to question his fellow police officers if he thought it would do any good. Abberline felt so frustrated; he had been given strict instructions by Scotland Yard not to allow anyone to enter the scene of the crime until the police bloodhounds, Barnaby and Burgho, had arrived.

Abberline classed these dogs as a silly intrusion, which only served to hamper his inquiries, rather than help them. After waiting over an hour, he decided enough was enough and instructed one of his men to smash in the door with an axe handle.

The ghastly scene that befronted the police officers who entered Kelly's room that morning is something that can only be appreciated by reading the actual post-mortem report by Doctor Thomas Bond, a distinguished police surgeon from A Division. His report read as follows:

> The body was lying naked in the middle of the bed, the shoulders flat but the axis of the body inclined to the left side of the bed. The head was turned on the left cheek. The left arm was close to the body with the forearm flexed at a right angle and lying across the abdomen.
>
> The right arm was slightly abducted from the body and rested on the mattress. The elbow was bent, the forearm supine with the fingers clenched. The legs were wide apart, the left thigh at right angles to the trunk and the right forming an obtuse angle with the pubes.
>
> The whole of the surface of the abdomen and thighs was removed and the abdominal cavity emptied of its viscera. The breasts were cut off, the arms mutilated by several jagged wounds and the face hacked beyond recognition of the features. The tissues of the neck were severed all round down to the bone.
>
> The viscera were found in various parts viz: the uterus and kidneys with one breast under the head, the other breast by the right foot, the liver between the feet, the intestines by the right side and the spleen by the left side of the body. The flaps removed from the abdomen and thighs were on a table.
>
> The bed clothing at the right corner was saturated with blood, and on the floor beneath was a pool of blood covering about two feet square. The wall

by the right side of the bed and in a line with the neck was marked by blood, which had struck it in a number of separate splashes.

The face was gashed in all directions, the nose, cheeks, eyebrows, and ears being partly removed. The lips were blanched and cut by several incisions running obliquely down to the chin. There were also numerous cuts extending irregularly across all the features.

The neck was cut through the skin and other tissues right down to the vertebrae, the fifth and sixth being deeply notched. The skin cuts in the front of the neck showed distinct ecchymosis [large bruise]. The air passage was cut at the lower part of the larynx through the cricoid cartilage [attachments for the various muscles in the neck].

Both breasts were more or less removed by circular incisions, the muscle down to the ribs being attached to the breasts. The intercostals between the fourth, fifth, and sixth ribs were cut through and the contents of the thorax visible through the openings.

The skin and tissues of the abdomen from the costal arch to the pubes were removed in three large flaps. The right thigh was denuded in front to the bone, the flap of skin, including the external organs of generation, and part of the right buttock. The left thigh was stripped of skin fascia, and muscles as far as the knee.

The left calf showed a long gash through skin and tissues to the deep muscles and reaching from the knee to five inches above the ankle. Both arms and forearms had extensive jagged wounds.

The right thumb showed a small superficial incision about one inch long, with extravasation of blood in the skin, and there were several abrasions on the back of the hand moreover showing the same condition.

On opening the thorax it was found that the right lung was minimally adherent by old firm adhesions. The lower part of the lung was broken and torn away. The left lung was intact. It was adherent at the apex and there were a few adhesions over the side. In the substances of the lung there were several nodules of consolidation.

The pericardium was open below and the heart absent. In the abdominal cavity there was some partly digested food of fish and potatoes, and similar food was found in the remains of the stomach attached to the intestines.

Dr George Bagster Phillips was also present at the scene, and gave the following testimony at the inquest:

The mutilated remains of a female were lying two-thirds over towards the edge of the bedstead nearest the door. She had only her chemise on, or some underlinen garment. I am sure that the body had been removed subsequent to the injury which caused her death from that side of the bedstead that was nearest the wooden partition, because of the large quantity of blood under the bedstead and the saturated condition of the sheet and the palliasse at the corner nearest the partition.

The blood was produced by the severance of the carotid artery, which was the cause of death. The injury was inflicted while the deceased was lying at the right side of the bedstead.

11

Hell

The police were not completely surprised when they burst into the room, as some of them had managed to get a brief glimpse of what was in store for them through the broken window. When true horror hits one in the face, however, it can have such an impact that it often renders grown men speechless, as was the case of one of the first officers on the scene, who collapsed and had to be taken to hospital, where he didn't say a word for ten days.

Abberline later admitted that he had never seen anything so terrible in his life before. 'It was like hell in there,' he said.

The investigation nevertheless had to continue, with notes, drawings and diagrams being taken. The official police photographer also had, almost certainly, the worst job of his career. One of the first things that struck Abberline, apart of course from the mutilation, was Kelly's clothes, which were neatly folded and placed on a chair in one corner of the room. Her boots were placed in front of the fireplace, probably in order to dry them out after the rain of the previous day.

Abberline reasoned that when Kelly had placed these items so neatly and carefully in her room, assuming that it was her who had done this, she must have felt completely at ease with whoever it was she was sharing her bed with that night.

Another very important thing that Abberline noted was that the door lock had not been forced in any way. In fact, when the police had smashed through one of the door panels with their axe, they still had to reach in and turn the door handle in order to open the door. Considering that Kelly had been murdered indoors, the only Ripper victim not to be killed on the street, this meant that the killer had either been invited in, in all probability by Ms Kelly as a paying customer, or that she had forgotten to lock her door and her killer had just walked in. This last scenario is highly unlikely, as it would then point to a random killing. The slaughter of Mary Kelly was certainly the most horrific of all the Jack the Ripper murders, but there can be no doubt in anyone's mind that it was most definitely the work of the same killer, and it is a well-established fact that the Ripper did not work on a random basis.

The problem Abberline had with the theory of the killer being invited in is that there was only one witness who said he saw Kelly with a man on the night of her death, and that was George Hutchinson. When Abberline went back over Hutchinson's original statement, however, he noticed one vital flaw, which was that Hutchinson had said he got a good look at the man. This is a very detailed description indeed, especially considering the fact that it was raining heavily at the time and also very dark, as London, during this period in time, was lit only by the occasional gas lamp. To be able to pass a man in the early hours of the morning and be able to pick out the direction his moustache turned, the colour of his eyes, his bushy eyebrows, even his ethnicity, and add to this what pin he was wearing in his necktie and upon his watch chain, is almost an impossibility. To make Hutchinson's description even more implausible is the fact that he said the man 'Was wearing a soft felt hat pulled down over his eyes'. Surely, Abberline argued, such a hat, pulled down over the man's eyes, would have obscured most of his facial features completely, let alone the colour of his eyes and the bushiness of his eyebrows.

There is also the fact that when Hutchinson first saw the man standing on the corner of Thrawl Street and Commercial Street, he said he was making his way home after just returning from Romford, where he had been working as a labourer, and that it was then 2 a.m. When he last saw the man, who was by this time with Mary Kelly just outside Miller's Court, it was then 3 a.m. The distance between Thrawl Street and Miller's Court is less than a mile, probably no more than ten to fifteen minutes' walking distance at the very most, so how come it took Hutchinson an hour to complete this journey? He said he was an ordinary working man, who had finished a hard day's work and was on his way home at the time. I personally find it implausible for a labourer to be returning home at 2 a.m., and even more implausible that he would hang around in the cold, dark and pouring rain at such a time whilst following a prostitute and her client, and that it should take him a whole hour to do so.

This was the only alleged sighting of a man with one of the victims just before their death; a man who could well be Jack the Ripper. However, with just this one, rather unreliable witness statement to go on, Abberline found himself frantically going back over all the old evidence, witness statements and possible suspects.

The main suspects were Aaron Kosminski, Michael Ostrog, Dr Francis Tumblety and Montague John Druitt. Abberline's own prime suspect, however, was Severin Klosowski, alias George Chapman.

12

The Suspects

AARON KOSMINSKI

The first suspect was Aaron Kosminski, who was born in the Polish town of Klodawa, which was then in the Russian Empire. His parents were Abram Jozef Kozminski, a tailor, and his wife Golda *née* Lubnowska. Kosminski left home in 1882, when he was just 17 years old, and immigrated to England, where he embarked on a career as a barber in the Whitechapel area of East London. This was an area that many Jewish refugees chose, many of whom were fleeing pogroms and economic hardship in Eastern Europe and Tsarist Russia at the time. It was an impoverished slum area but at least it was cheap and they could afford a room there. A short while after he settled in, his sisters, brother and widowed mother also left Russia and joined him in Whitechapel.

In July 1890 and again in February 1891, Kosminski was placed in Mile End Old Town Workhouse because of what was termed as 'his insane behaviour', although this 'behaviour' was never explained at the time. When he was discharged from the Mile End Old Town Workhouse on the second occasion, he was dispatched immediately to Colney Hatch Lunatic Asylum, where he remained for the next three years until he was admitted on 19 April 1894 to the Imbeciles Asylum at Leavesden.

Case notes indicate that Kosminski had been mentally ill since at least 1885. His insanity took the form of auditory hallucinations, a paranoid fear of being fed by other people that drove him to pick up and eat food dropped as litter in the street, or on the floor, as well as a refusal to wash or bathe. The cause of his insanity was recorded as 'self-abuse', which is thought to be a euphemism for masturbation. Because of his poor diet, he was always in a state of emaciation.

For some strange reason, the police didn't seem to have a stable address for Kosminski, which might have been due to the fact that he moved in and out of various lodging houses. The police had been watching Kosminski for some time while he was living at his brother's home in Whitechapel. They eventually took him, with his hands tied behind his back, to the workhouse and then to Colney Hatch Linatic Asylum, where he eventually died shortly after. When asylum records were checked later, however, they only showed Aaron Kosminski as living in Whitechapel, but they also noted the name and address of one, Isaac Kozminski, who may have been Aaron's brother, residing at 76 Goulston Street. All the Ripper's victims were murdered within walking distance of Goulston Street, and the bloodstained piece of apron that came from one of the Ripper victims, Catherine Eddowes, was also found there.

Aaron Kosminski's case notes indicate that he was a paranoid schizophrenic, a fact that today is recognised in most serial killers.

Apart from his obvious mental illness, there was no real reason to connect Kosminski with the Ripper murders, other than his supposed 'great hatred of women and his strong homicidal tendencies'.

MICHAEL OSTROG

Number two on the list of suspects was Michael Ostrog, a Russian Jew, who was born in 1833, probably in Russia, but we are not sure. Ostrog was also known as Bertrand Ashley, Claude Clayton, Dr Grant Max Grief Gosslar, Ashley Nabokoff, Orloff, Count Sobieski and Max Sobiekski.

Ostrog was what we would probably call today a career criminal. This is not to say that he actually made a living from his crimes, because most of them were very petty to say the least:

1863 While using the alias Max Grief (Kaife) Gosslar, Ostrog committed theft at Oxford College, and was soon after sentenced to ten months in prison.

1864 Convicted at Cambridge and sentenced to three months in prison. In July, he appeared in Tunbridge Wells under the name Count Sobieski. Imprisoned in December and sentenced to eight months.

1866 Acquitted on charges of fraud in January. On 19 March he stole a gold watch and other articles from a woman in Maidstone. He committed similar thefts in April and was duly arrested in August, and sentenced to seven years in prison.

1873   Released from prison in May, he committed numerous other thefts, and subsequently was arrested by Superintendent Oswell in Burton-on-Trent. He produced a revolver at the police station and nearly shot his captors.

1874   Convicted in January and sentenced to ten years in prison.

1883   Released from prison in August.

1887   Arrested for theft of a metal tankard in July and sentenced to six months' hard labour in September. He was listed as suffering from 'mania' on 30 September.

1888   Released on 10 March as 'cured'. He was mentioned in *Police Gazette*, in October, as a 'Dangerous man, who failed to report. He was sentenced to two years' imprisonment in Paris for theft on 18 November.

For the next sixteen years, Ostrog continued to court the attention of the authorities for one reason or another:

1891   Committed to the Surrey County Lunatic Asylum.

1894   Charged for theft at Eton.

1898   Charged in Woolwich for the theft of books.

1900   Imprisoned for theft of a microscope at London Hospital, Whitechapel. He was known to be partially paralysed by this time.

1904   Released from prison and entered St Giles Christian Mission, Holborn. Nothing further is known of Ostrog after this time.

Not a very impressive record at all, but like Kosminski, not one to particularly connect him as a suspect to the Ripper murders. Police records (not Abberline) had Michael Ostrog down as 'A mad Russian doctor and a convict and unquestionably homicidal maniac'. Ostrog was said to be 'Habitually cruel to women, and for a long time was known to have carried about with him surgical knives and other instruments; his antecedents were of the very worst and his whereabouts at the time of the Whitechapel murders could never be satisfactorily accounted for'. This account does not seem to tie in at all with the rather pathetic criminality we see in his criminal record.

Ostrog was certified insane while in Wandsworth prison, and was sent to the Surrey pauper mental asylum on 30 September 1887, where he was described as '50 years of age, Jewish, a surgeon, married and suffering from mania'. He was released on 10 March 1888 and continued his criminal career.

If the records of his birth were true, it would have made him at least 55 years of age at the time of the Whitechapel murders. This would make him much older than any of the eyewitness sightings of a Ripper suspect, who was usually described as 28 to 35 years old. Ostrog also did not match the suspect's build or general description, which described the Ripper as a short, stout man, just a little taller than his victims, with fair to medium brown hair; whereas Ostrog was dark skinned with dark brown eyes, grey hair and was 5ft 11in tall.

The notes that Ostrog was a doctor, had some sort of medical training or carried surgical knives, and was habitually cruel to women, are also completely unfounded. There is absolutely no evidence throughout his long criminal career that Ostrog used violence on anyone, particularly women.

The whole case against Ostrog, as with Kosminski, seems to be based on his mental instability and ethnicity.

FRANCIS TUMBLETY

Number three on the list of suspects was neither Jewish nor mentally disturbed; Francis Tumblety was born in Ireland in 1833, and along with his family, including ten brothers and sisters, immigrated to Rochester, New York, just a few years after his birth. Nothing much is known of his early years in the USA, but by the time he was in his early thirties, he was making a very good living by posing as an 'Indian Herb' doctor throughout the United States and Canada, and was commonly perceived as a misogynistic quack.

During the mid-1860s one of his patients died in mysterious circumstances. The police instigated an investigation into Tumblety and his methods, but not enough evidence could be found to link him to the woman's death, and the case was eventually dropped. In 1865, he was arrested in St Louis and held in prison for three weeks, accused of being a conspirator in the assassination of Abraham Lincoln. He was eventually released without charge, as he was found to be using an alias similar to the name of a wanted man at the time.

By 1888, the year of the Ripper murders, Tumblety had left the USA and had set up home in England. On 7 November of that year he was arrested and charged with engaging in a homosexual act, which was illegal at the time. He was granted bail while awaiting trial, which was scheduled to take place on the next magistrates' court sitting on the 16th of the same month. Tumblety was re-arrested on the 14th and re-bailed on the 16th.

These dates are important, as they show that Tumblety was actually on the streets of London on 9 November, the date Mary Kelly was murdered.

Tumblety didn't wait around for his trial to begin, and sometime between 14 and 16 November, he fled to France under an assumed name, and from there to the USA.

Tumblety's notoriety preceded him, and the US newspapers soon discovered his whereabouts and printed reports of how his arrest in England was connected to the Ripper murders. The American press also claimed that Scotland Yard were trying to extradite him back to England, but these allegations were not confirmed by the British press or the London police, who stated: 'There is no proof of his complicity in the Whitechapel murders, and the crime for which he is under bond in London is not extraditable.'

As with all of the suspects, there was no concrete evidence linking Tumblety to the Ripper murders but there was an abundance of circumstantial evidence; so much so, in fact, that the senior police officer in charge of Tumblety's case was given the assistance of six English detectives and two clerks. This led to Tumblety becoming one of the major suspects in the Ripper case. After all, Scotland Yard would hardly assign a team of six detectives to a case where the suspect was only accused of an indecency charge. This action by the police threw suspicion on Tumblety of something far worse.

A former Union colonel from the Civil War period gave an interview with a newspaper, where he recalled attending a dinner party that Tumblety had thrown, in which he had showed guests to a small attic room where he kept what he referred to as his anatomical museum. The room was filled with glass jars and cases. Tumblety lined up a number of the jars on a table, and told his guests that they contained the wombs of women of every social class. He then proceeded to break into a long and vehement speech, in which he revealed that he had once been married to an older woman who had let him down badly when he found out that she was in fact a prostitute. He denounced all women, especially those he described as 'fallen women', like his ex-wife.

Tumblety was, if nothing else, a fantasist. He used to boast of having met Charles Dickens during his frequent trips to London, though there was no proof of this whatsoever.

When Tumblety arrived in London in 1888, he took lodgings in Batty Street, which is just a couple of minutes walk away from Whitechapel, which, in turn, is right in the heart of what was to become known as Ripper territory.

The landlady of the lodging house in Batty Street later reported that one of the lodgers had vanished after asking her to wash a shirt, which was steeped in blood. She never identified Tumblety as this lodger, but it is a very strong coincidence that he happened to be a lodger at that same address.

Tumblety was also alleged to be an Irish-American Fenian and possibly part of a plan to assassinate Arthur James Balfour, who at the time of the alleged plot was Chief Secretary of Ireland. Balfour later served as Prime Minister of the United Kingdom from July 1902 to December 1905.

It is also believed that he had a role in what became known as the Phoenix Park murders, which was the name given to the assassination on 6 May 1882 of Lord Frederick Cavendish, British Secretary for Ireland, and Thomas Henry Burke, his undersecretary, in Phoenix Park, Dublin. They were stabbed to death by members of the 'Invincibles', a terrorist splinter group of the Fenian movement.

A number of different men were arrested and tried for these murders, two of whom turned state's evidence, five were hanged and three were sentenced to penal servitude. One man, who was apparently never caught, was someone whose description matched very closely to that of Francis Tumblety.

Being a misogynist or a fantasist, or even a member of an extremist political group, might well be damning features, if indeed proven to be true, but these features do not prove or disprove Tumblety's involvement in the Ripper case. There was no doubt that there were some very strong indications that Tumblety was in some way involved in this case, which made Abberline, and the police in general, very suspicious of him; but it was not until after his death in 1903 that several other vital and very damning pieces of evidence came to light.

When an inventory of his personal belongings was taken after his death, it was noted that he had several pieces of extremely expensive jewellery, $1,000 in bonds and over $430 in cash. He also had two very cheap fake gold rings, which didn't fit in at all with his general style and demeanour; their value was approximately $2, and they matched exactly the description of the rings that were taken from the body of Annie Chapman.

To sum up the evidence pointing to Tumblety's involvement in the case, we have the following:

1. Tumblety was known for his hatred of women.
2. His wife had worked as a prostitute whilst married to him.
3. He had a wide knowledge of anatomy and collected body parts in jars, which he readily showed to guests.
4. The murders ceased when he fled the country.
5. He was noted on police files at the time as a person of bad character.
6. It was a fact that Scotland Yard contacted the New York Police Department for a copy of his handwriting. This was just after Catherine Eddowes' death, which indicates that he was high on their suspect list.
7. The rings thought to have belonged to Annie Chapman were found in Tumblety's inventory after his death.
8. He lived in the Whitechapel area at the time of Mary Kelly's death.

These are all very strong points that add to the case against Francis Tumblety. There were other lesser points which nevertheless still scored against him, such as his use of aliases and the fact that Scotland Yard pursued him to New York after he jumped bail on what was a relatively small misdemeanour. If we add to these the other allegations, such as his involvement in the Fenian movement and the death of one of his patients in mysterious circumstances when he was posing as an 'Indian Herb' doctor during the mid-1860s, then I would say the case against him is very strong indeed.

Tumblety eventually returned to the USA and settled down with a female relative, whose house also served as his office. He died in 1903 of heart disease at the age of 73.

MONTAGUE JOHN DRUITT

Next on our list is Montague John Druitt, who came from a distinguished medical family, from Wimborne, Dorset. His father, William, was the town's leading surgeon and his uncle Robert and cousin Lionel were also doctors.

In 1870 Druitt won a scholarship to Winchester College and later graduated to the University of Oxford. On 17 May 1882, two years after graduation, Druitt was admitted to the Inner Temple, one of the qualifying bodies for English barristers. He paid his membership fees with a loan from his father, which was secured against an inheritance legacy of £500 he had promised him (equivalent to about £45,000 today).

Druitt was called to the Bar on 29 April 1885, and set up a practice as a barrister. Five months later, in September 1885, Druitt's father died suddenly from a heart attack. He left an estate valued at £16,579, which would be equivalent to approximately £1.5 million today.

Unfortunately for Montague Druitt, most of his father's estate went to his wife Ann, three unmarried daughters, Georgiana, Edith and Ethel, and his eldest son William. Druitt senior had even instructed the executors of his will to deduct the £500 he had advanced to his son from his legacy, leaving very little money, if any at all, for Montague Druitt, although he did receive some of his father's personal possessions.

Druitt rented legal chambers at 9 King's Bench Walk in the Inner Temple. During this period, it was mostly just the very wealthy who could afford to take out legal action, and only one in eight qualified barristers was able to make a living from the law.

To supplement his income Druitt found work as an assistant schoolmaster at George Valentine's Boarding School, 9 Eliot Place, Blackheath, London.

The school had quite a long and prestigious history, with such distinguished students as Benjamin Disraeli. Druitt's post came with accommodation in Eliot Place, and the long school holidays gave him time to follow up his law studies and pursue his interest in cricket.

Druitt continued his work at the school for the next three years, while simultaneously continuing with his legal career. People who knew him, including staff at the school, said that he seemed very happy during this period. He had a busy social life centred around sport, and was the secretary and treasurer of the local Blackheath Cricket Club as well as regularly turning out for other various teams.

In 1888, his mother's health started to deteriorate, but unfortunately it was not just her bodily health, but her mental health as well. In July of that year, she attempted to commit suicide, which led to her being permanently hospitalised in a number of private asylums and clinics until her death. In trying to sum up Druitt, we need to remember that this was the same year that the Ripper murders began. It has been known in other such cases that losing a parent in such a way can have a significant bearing on an offspring's life, and could even act as a catalyst for their descent into mayhem and murder. Mental illness certainly ran in Druitt's family: his maternal grandmother and aunt had committed suicide and his sister was also to do so, although many years later.

By early December of that same year, Druitt's brother William began to get worried about him, as he hadn't heard from him for nearly two weeks, and normally they spoke on a regular basis. He contacted Druitt's chambers, where he was told that he had not been seen for over a week. He then travelled immediately to the school in Blackheath, where he learned that his brother had got into serious trouble at the school and been dismissed nearly two weeks earlier. A note written by Druitt and addressed to William was found in Druitt's room in Blackheath. It read: 'Since Friday I felt that I was going to be like mother, and the best thing for me was to die.'

On Monday 31 December, Henry Winslade, a Thames waterman, discovered the decomposed body of Montague Druitt at approximately 1 p.m., floating in the water just off Thorneycroft's Wharf, near Chiswick. He took the body ashore and notified the authorities. Police Constable George Moulston made a complete listing of possessions found on the then unidentified corpse:

1. Four large stones in each pocket.
2. £2 17s 2d.
3. A cheque for £50 and another for £16.
4. Silver watch on a gold chain with a spade guinea as a seal.
5. Pair of kid gloves.

6. White handkerchief.
7. First-class half-season rail ticket from Blackheath to London.
8. Second-half return ticket from Hammersmith to Charing Cross dated 1 December 1888.

At the inquest into his death, a verdict was returned of suicide while of unsound mind.

William Druitt's first thoughts on the subject were that his brother had been unable to cope with the loss of both his parents within the short space of three years. But then he started to hear rumours about why Druitt was dismissed from his post at Blackheath school. The authorities at the school would not divulge the reason, but after speaking to friends and colleagues of Druitt, William started to form his own ideas that his brother was dismissed for homosexual tendencies and for molesting students. This was, of course, nothing more than pure conjecture on William's part, but as far as he was concerned, it could quite well have been the reason behind his brother's suicide; the straw that broke the camel's back, so to speak.

If we accept this as fact, we have Montague John Druitt, a reasonably successful barrister, suddenly overcome with grief about being dismissed from his job at the school; what would happen if his vice was discovered by his friends and family? How would it be taken by his colleagues in chambers? Would he still be able to practise law at his firm? And probably more important to him, would he be able to bear the embarrassment of it all?

We now know that he was awarded some sort of job settlement payment from his school, so if these conjectures are correct, he would have left the school with his two settlement cheques in his pocket, as indeed was found on his body when it was fished from the Thames. He would have skulked home with thoughts of suicide entering into his mind. The next morning, after writing the suicide note to his brother, he then would have headed towards the Thames, pausing only to gather some stones, four of which he placed in each pocket. A slight pause maybe, and then he would have thrown himself into the icy waters of the Thames, his body not to be discovered until 31 December, almost three weeks later.

These assertions all sound very laudable, but they have never been proven; they are nothing more than assertions. Also, they most definitely do not link Druitt to the Ripper murders in any way, yet the chief constable of Scotland Yard, Melville Macnaghten, considered Druitt to be his prime suspect; a theory which no other police officer, including Abberline, supported.

Macnaghten's suspicions of Druitt seemed to be based entirely on the fact that Druitt killed himself very shortly after the last Ripper murder, of Mary Kelly, and that the murders stopped immediately after that. Add to this the fact that, at the inquest into Druitt's death, a verdict was returned of suicide while of unsound mind. As we know, almost anyone of an unsound mind at that time was classed as a possible suspect, so in that respect Druitt was the perfect suspect in Macnaghten's mind. In Macnaghten's memoranda that was published later he describes Druitt as being 'sexually insane'.

It was possible that Druitt's mind was slowly deteriorating. The death of both his parents within a relatively short period, and the committal of his mother, might well have played a heavy part in the matter. Mental illness certainly seemed to have played a large role in the Druitt family. Ann Druitt, his mother, was later to die at the Manor House Asylum in Chiswick in 1890, after suffering from depression and paranoid delusions. Her mother before her had committed suicide, and her sister had also tried to kill herself. Even Druitt's oldest sister ended up killing herself in old age by jumping from an attic window.

When all the facts are weighed up, there is no real evidence to support Macnaghten's theory of Druitt being the Ripper, other than that he vaguely fitted some witness descriptions of average height, between the ages of 30 to 35, and had a moustache. This is a description that probably would have fitted half the population of London at the time.

If we add to this the fact that Druitt was living at his school accommodation in Blackheath at the time of all the murders, this alone would have made it almost impossible for him to commit the crimes, and then commute back to Blackheath in the early hours of the morning, sometimes possibly covered in blood, without anyone even noticing him. We also need to bear in mind that there was no all-night train service between London and Blackheath during this period. In 1888 the last train left Blackheath for London at 12.25 a.m. and the first train leaving London for Blackheath was at 5.10 a.m.

As all the Ripper murders were committed in the early hours of the morning, this would have meant the killer, if it were Druitt, either had to remain relatively close to the area until daybreak, when the first train was ready to leave, or had to walk home, which would have taken him several hours. If he was also covered in blood, it would have been almost impossible for him not to have been discovered.

With so many factors pointing against his theory, why then did Macnaghten stick so adamantly to his claim that Druitt was the Ripper? There have been allegations that Macnaghten was not kept up to date on all the information regarding the Ripper case, as he didn't join the force until a year after the first Ripper murder, in the summer of 1889; as such he had to rely completely on reading police reports, rather than actual groundwork, which other detectives such as Inspector Abberline could.

If the allegations against Macnaghten were true, then he certainly would not have wanted to be thought of as some newcomer to the case, and so decided to stamp his authoritative view on it. In his memoranda, Macnaghten says:

'From private information I have little doubt but that his [Druitt's] own family believed him to have been the murderer.'

There was absolutely no evidence on record of any member of Druitt's family, or anyone else of any significance, ever making such a statement. As everyone knows that all witness statements made to the police have to be entered in police records, and as none exist to support this claim of Macnaghten, we can only assume that it was fabricated by someone at some point.

Whatever Macnaghten's reasons for laying the blame of the Ripper murders on Montague John Druitt, whether it was to show his apparent inside knowledge of the case or to finally wind it up as far as Scotland Yard were concerned, Abberline was most definitely not in agreement with him.

In an interview with the *Pall Mall Gazette* in 1903, when Abberline was asked if he agreed with Macnaghten that the Ripper was known to have been dead soon after the autumn of 1888, Abberline replied as follows:

> You can state most emphatically that Scotland Yard is really no wiser on the subject than it was fifteen years ago. It is simply nonsense to talk of the police having proof that the man is dead. I am, and always have been, in the closest touch with Scotland Yard, and it would have been next to impossible for me not to have known all about it. Besides, the authorities would have been only too glad to make an end of such a mystery, if only for their own credit.

Macnaghten's document on the subject, then, contains nothing more than his personal opinions, and is not the official view or definitive solution.

13

Abberline's Number One Suspect

SEVERIN KLOSOWSKI

Throughout his period of working on the Ripper case Inspector Abberline had a chance of going through the details of every one of the dozens of suspects. Most were no more than just a name, bandied about by locals: someone of strange appearance or, as previously pointed out, maybe mentally unbalanced; but there were also those, such as the names we have just been through, who, rightly or wrongly, at least attracted a modicum of serious suspicion. There was one man, however, whom Abberline classed as his number one suspect, and that man was Severin Klosowski.

If a modern profiler were to try to paint us a picture of the man known as Jack the Ripper, Klosowski would fit that picture almost perfectly. Severin Klosowski, also commonly known as George Chapman, was a man who had all the makings of a serial killer. He poisoned three of his wives, demonstrating beyond doubt that he was capable of senseless, cold-blooded murder while remaining completely emotionless. Even the investigators present at his trial would later describe him as a real villain who was capable of almost anything.

Severin Klosowski was born on 14 December 1865 in a small village in Russian-occupied Poland. In 1880, after leaving school, he trained in what was known as a feldscher, which was an occupation combining the roles of barber and minor surgeon, which consequently qualified him to perform small operations by himself and to assist in major operations carried out by fully qualified surgeons.

By the time Klosowski was 19, he left his small town and travelled to Warsaw, where he enrolled in a course on practical surgery at the Hospital of the Infant Jesus. To help pay for his studies, he took a job as an assistant to a barber-surgeon, but it was around this time that he met and married his first wife, who almost immediately became pregnant. He promptly finished his studies and started to look for a full-time job in order to provide for his new family. It is unclear where he lived or if he did manage to find a job in Warsaw, but the next we hear of him is when he turned up alone in London, sometime in the spring of 1888, having left Poland.

Shortly after arriving in London, Klosowski introduced himself to a Polish barber, as a hairdresser and qualified doctor, using the alias Ludwig Zagowski. The Pole gave him a job as his assistant, and even let him stay above the premises for a while, as his son was ill and Klosowski pretended to care for him. This arrangement didn't last long, however, when the Pole found out that his son was actually getting worse under Klosowski's supposed care.

Klosowski was undaunted by this rejection, and soon found himself another job with a barber whose shop was in the basement underneath a public house on Whitechapel High Street.

During the early hours of the morning on 7 August 1888, Albert George Crow, a resident of George Yard Buildings, Whitechapel, was returning home after a night's work as a cab driver, when he noticed the body of a woman, later identified as 35-year-old prostitute Martha Tabram, lying on a landing above the first flight of stairs in his building; she had been stabbed thirty-nine times. Martha Tabram was a victim of the Whitechapel murders, and sometimes referred to as the first victim of Jack the Ripper.

The murder occurred within yards of Klosowski's place of work, and when he was questioned by the police, they found out that at the time of this murder Klosowski had rented rooms in George Yard Buildings; the very building in which Tabram was found murdered.

The police questioned a number of local people regarding the Tabram murder, including Klosowski on a number of occasions. Despite regular questioning, nothing ever came of the investigation surrounding the murder. Klosowski was allowed to walk free, and the identity of the murderer remained unknown.

Klosowski not only walked away from this without a stain on his character, but he also reverted to his real name, and in June 1889 he opened his own barber's shop. It was during this period that he met Lucy Baderski, and married her just five weeks later. What he had unfortunately forgotten to tell his new wife was that he was still legally married to his first wife, who was still living in Poland.

Somehow or other, Klosowski's first wife heard the news of his new marriage, and rushed to London as quickly as she could in an attempt to reclaim her marriage and get rid of this other woman. As usual, Klosowski took the whole thing in his stride, and somehow managed to bring the two women together, telling them they should be friends. His plan worked, and for a while both women cohabited with Klosowski. This happy threesome ended, however, when Baderski bore Klosowski a son in September 1890. This was too much for his first wife to bear, and after a blazing argument, she walked out and returned to Poland.

A few months later Klosowski's son fell ill and sadly died of pneumonia. Needless to say this put a terrible strain on their relationship, with Baderski threatening to walk out on Klosowski. In order to save their marriage, the couple decided to immigrate to New Jersey just one month later in order to try to establish a new life.

Within a couple of months of arriving in the United States, Klosowski had set up his own barber shop, but his relationship with his wife was far from on course, and fights between them began to lead to serious violence on his behalf. During the later trial against Klosowski, Baderski claimed that he threatened her on numerous occasions, at one point with a knife and saying that, if he had any more trouble, he would make her disappear and simply tell everyone that she had returned to London.

During this period, four murders occurred in the area he was living in. These were not just ordinary murders, but resembled very closely the Jack the Ripper murders of a few years earlier in London. One murder in particular was that of an elderly prostitute named Carrie Brown, or 'Old Shakespeare' as she was known, for her fondness of quoting the Great Bard himself when she was drunk. She was murdered in a common lodging house in Jersey City, on 24 April 1891. At the inquest into her death, it was established that she had been strangled first and then, 'savagely mutilated' in exactly the same manner as the Ripper victims. A suspect was arrested for the murder at the time, but he was later acquitted and the true culprit was apparently never found.

The American police didn't have any reason at the time to look into Klosowski as a potential suspect. It wasn't until some years later, when he was being investigated regarding the murders of his wives/partners, that the police realised he was a possible suspect.

It must be noted that Inspector Abberline did not have all these facts to hand when he first suspected Klosowski, as much of his suspicious activity happened some years after the initial Ripper investigations. What Abberline did know of Klosowski was that he had surgical expertise, a blatant disrespect for women in general, and had demonstrated violence with a knife, especially towards his wife. After extensive checking, Abberline also found out that Klosowski's movements coincided perfectly with the times of the Ripper murders.

Klosowski eventually returned to London, where he once again found himself a position as an assistant in a barber's shop. He also found the company of a young lady named Annie Chapman, which was also, strangely enough, the name of one of the Ripper victims. Klosowski asked Chapman if she would consider working for him as his housekeeper, for which he would pay her and provide her with a room at his house. Chapman agreed and moved in with him in November 1893. Their relationship soon blossomed into more than employer/employee, and within a very short time they began calling themselves husband and wife, even though they had never legally married.

Klosowski, however, was still the womaniser he had always been, and when he brought home another woman, telling Chapman that she was to share their bed, Chapman grew impatient and angry, and consequently left him. She returned a few weeks later, however, when she discovered that she was pregnant with his child. She gave Klosowski two options: either he married her and throw the other woman out or he should support her and the baby when it was born.

Klosowski simply refused either, denying that the baby was his and telling her that he was moving out of London soon anyway. There was nothing Chapman could do as they were not legally married, so she left him for good in February 1894. From this point on, he used the name George Chapman, which seemed a very strange thing to do, especially as he had professed to having no feelings for Annie Chapman whatsoever; or could it have been some strange fascination with the name of an earlier Ripper victim?

Following his split with Annie Chapman, Klosowski also walked out on the other woman and began posing as a well-off American. He posed quite an elegant figure in his smart suits, and found no difficulty in attracting yet more women. His next conquest came in the form of a young divorcee named Mary Spink, whose husband had left her and taken their son, allegedly because of her heavy drinking. Klosowski and Mary Spink joined hands in a fake marriage and he managed to talk her into signing over a £6,000 legacy to him, which she had inherited from her grandfather. He used part of the money to lease a barber's shop in a poor area of Hastings, but soon moved to a more salubrious area, where he also purchased a piano, which Mary would play while he serviced the customers. This provided a very good income for a while, and Klosowski found himself living the type of life he had long been searching for. He even bought himself a sailing boat, which he christened the *Mosquito*.

The business was successful but their life together started going down the same path as most of his other relationships. Neighbours reported hearing them arguing and hearing Mary crying and screaming with pain in the middle of the night. They also said they saw abrasions and bruises on her face, and on one occasion noticed marks around her throat.

At Klosowski's later trial, Mr William Davidson, a chemist, gave evidence that on 3 April 1897 Klosowski had purchased a 1oz dose of tartar emetic from his shop. Tartar emetic is a poison in the form of a white powder, easily soluble in water, containing antimony, which is colourless, odourless and almost tasteless. Its effects were little known in the late nineteenth century. Given in large doses, antimony is likely to be regurgitated and expelled almost immediately from the body, but in smaller, regularly timed doses, it would cause a slow and very painful death. Another aspect of the drug, which was also unknown at the time, is that it preserves the body of the deceased for many years after their death.

Mary was still alive when Klosowski decided to give up the barber's shop and move back to London, where he took on the lease of the Prince of Wales pub off City Road in Bartholomew Square. It was here that Mary started complaining of severe stomach pains and nausea. A doctor was called in, but failed to diagnose her condition. Mary died on Christmas Day of that year. Her cause of death was registered as consumption.

A witness who was there at the time of Mary's death said Klosowski seemed very sad and called to the dead body of his wife, asking her to speak to him. He then wept for a few minutes before drying his eyes and going downstairs to open the pub as usual. Klosowski didn't seem to care one iota what anyone else thought about his apparent lack of emotion following his wife's death. He was so wrapped up in his own thoughts and intentions that on 20 May 1899, he calmly decided to send Mary's orphaned son, Willie, to the Shoreditch Workhouse, and would never see him again.

It is difficult to work out if it was sex or making money – or maybe an amalgamation of both which came first in Klosowski's life. Within weeks of his wife's death, he had hired Bessie Taylor, whom he had met in a restaurant where she had worked. Bessie was given a room above the pub, but their work relationship soon blossomed into yet another romance, which in turn led to another bogus marriage.

Within a very short time, the old pattern of Klosowski's relationships began to emerge again, and he began abusing and beating her, just as he had done his previous partners. On one occasion he was seen by a witness to have threatened Bessie with a revolver. Notwithstanding this, Bessie began suffering the same symptoms that had killed her predecessor; tongues began to wag and Klosowski decided to move out of the area, possibly to avoid any sort of police investigation. The couple moved to Bishop's Stortford for a while, where he claimed the country air would help his wife's condition, and after a few months there they returned to London, where Klosowski leased the Monument Tavern in the borough.

The country air certainly had not helped Bessie's condition, and during the short time she spent at their new pub she grew steadily worse. When a close friend of hers, Mrs Painter, went to visit, she found Klosowski far from sympathetic when she asked about her friend's health; in fact, Klosowski would joke about it and tell her that Bessie was dead, which at that time she was not. On 15 February, however, when this same friend came to call again, Klosowski told her that his wife was much the same as usual. Mrs Painter later found out that Bessie had died the previous day Valentine's Day, 1901. The cause of death this time was given as 'exhaustion from vomiting and diarrhoea'.

Six months later Klosowski was up to his old tricks yet again. The pub was not earning him enough money to keep him in the lifestyle he had become accustomed to, and the lease was also soon to expire. Sex, however, seemed to play a dominant role in his life. When he saw an advert in a local newspaper, written by 18-year-old Maud Marsh, who was seeking a job as a barmaid, Klosowski responded to it immediately.

When Maud Marsh turned up at the pub for an interview, however, Klosowski found himself not only confronted with Maud, but her mother as well, due, she explained, to her daughter's young age. Klosowski explained to Maud that she would be required to live on the premises, above the pub, so she would be available for work at all times. Mrs Marsh was somewhat sceptical of this arrangement, but was reassured by Klosowski, who told her that Maud would be living with a family that rented rooms in the lodgings above the pub. Mrs Marsh was happy and her daughter accepted the job. All Klosowski had to do next was speak to the family above the pub, and get them to prepare Maud's room for her. He did speak to the family, but not to tell them to get a room ready, but to evict them. When Maud did arrive to take up her position in the pub, she found herself and Klosowski to be the only two residents in the building.

Klosowski wasted no time in showering non-stop attention on Maud, and within a few months she had agreed to marry him, but only on the condition that they would not share a bed until after the wedding. On 13 October 1901, the couple donned their best clothes and set off to be married at a Roman Catholic church, or so Klosowski alleged; for when Maud's mother later asked to see the marriage certificate, Maud told her that she could not find it at that moment, as Klosowski had put it away somewhere with his other paperwork. This explanation seemed to satisfy Mrs Marsh, for she never asked for sight of it again.

His sex life might have been back on form, but Klosowski was still desperately short of money, and the pub was still not producing a decent income for him. Klosowski's next plan was to set fire to his pub in the hope of collecting the insurance money, but when the insurance investigators called and started looking into what had happened, they discovered that all of the furniture and valuables had been removed from the premises before the fire occurred. The insurance company couldn't prove that Klosowski had deliberately tried to defraud them, but they nevertheless refused to pay him.

In desperation, Klosowski and Maud moved out of the pub without telling a soul, and he obtained the lease on another pub, as far away as possible. Shortly after moving, Klosowski began beating Maud, just like he had done with the others, but in April, Maud became pregnant. Klosowski was not very happy when he heard this, as he would not only lose a barmaid, but it could also dampen his womanising and sexual exploits. A few weeks into the pregnancy, Klosowski persuaded Maud to allow him to carry out an abortion on her, by syringing her womb with a dilute solution of Phenol. (Phenol is also known as carbolic acid, its vapours are corrosive to the eyes, the skin, and the respiratory tract. In other words, it can be a very dangerous chemical to use.)

Strangely enough, Maud did recover from the abortion, and within days, Klosowski had her working behind the bar in the pub again. In fact, one evening, while making his wife work behind the bar, he took another barmaid, Florence Rayner, upstairs to his flat where they made love, and he revealed his plans to leave London and go to America. He asked Florence to go with him, to which she refused, telling him that he already had a wife downstairs and that she had heard her screams when he beat her. According to Florence, Klosowski laughed when she said this and clicked his fingers, saying that is all it would take for his wife to be no more.

Florence was lucky; she walked out of Klosowski's bedroom that night and never returned to her job at the pub again. Maud however, was not so fortunate; following Florence's departure, Maud's condition deteriorated rapidly. The symptoms she started suffering mirrored those of her predecessors, and worried her mother so much that she started paying daily visits to oversee her daughter's welfare.

It was while Mrs Marsh was at her daughter's bedside that she noticed how Klosowski insisted on administering Maud's medicine himself. Mrs Marsh insisted on her daughter staying in a hospital despite Klosowski's protestations. When she was discharged from the hospital a few weeks later, she showed a great improvement, and for a while everything seemed to be back on track as far as her mother was concerned.

Klosowski, however, wasn't finished yet, and quickly set Maud back to work in the pub again, preparing meals for her to eat while she was working at the bar. Needless to say, these meals were not prepared for Maud out of the goodness of his heart, and within no time at all she fell extremely ill yet again. Klosowski maintained his façade by going to see a local doctor and asking for some medicine. He made the great mistake of confiding in the doctor that he and Maud were not legally married, which would later come back to haunt him.

Klosowski insisted that everything that Maud ate and drank must only be administered by him, obviously so that he could slip large amounts of poison into her food and drink. Maud's parents found this behaviour extremely worrying and suspicious to say the least, and called in their own doctor as a result. The doctor that Mr and Mrs Marsh called in happened to be the very same doctor that Klosowski had confided in. This must have rung alarm bells for the doctor, for he immediately informed the Marsh family that their daughter was not married, and in his opinion, unfortunately approaching her death.

Mr Marsh never told Klosowski what the doctor had confided in him, and said that he believed his daughter would get well again. Klosowski shrugged his shoulders in a very callous way when he heard this, and responded by saying, 'She will never get up no more'.

Klosowski, however, was more worried than he liked to show, and as soon as Mr and Mrs Marsh had left his home, he administered his wife with an enormous dose of the poison which killed her within hours. By the following morning, 22 October 1902, she was announced by the doctor as dead; but the doctor refused to issue a death certificate until a post-mortem had taken place. At the post-mortem traces of arsenic and 7.24 grains of antimony were found in Maud's stomach, bowels, liver, kidneys and brain. It was found to be the antimony which had actually killed her; the arsenic was only there as an impurity in the antimony.

Once again, Klosowski opened the pub only thirty minutes after Maud's death, and carried on as if the death had not occurred at all, thus showing his cold-blooded enjoyment of watching someone die a slow and horrible death.

Klosowski had got away with two murders prior to Maud's death, but this time it wasn't just the victim he had to deal with, it was her family. Mr and Mrs Marsh's suspicions resulted in a full investigation of Klosowski's past life, and on 25 October 1902, Klosowski was arrested by Inspector George Godley of Southwark Police, who charged him under the name of George Chapman. It was only discovered later, when the investigation got under way, that Severin Klosowski and George Chapman were one and the same person.

When the bodies of Klosowski's two previous wives were exhumed in November and December 1902, they were both remarkably well preserved. Bessie's body had a mouldy growth upon it but was otherwise fresh, while Mary (having been buried five years) was very well preserved. It was, of course, the large amounts of metallic antimony found in the bodies of both women that caused this preservation and also helped to convict Klosowski.

Klosowski was charged with the murders of Maud Marsh, Mary Spink and Bessie Taylor, but he was convicted only of Maud's death. On 20 March 1903, the jury deliberated for just eleven minutes before coming to a verdict of guilty. Up to this point, Klosowski had assumed an almost careless attitude to the trial, but as sentence was being passed upon him he suddenly broke down completely and wept. Klosowski lodged an appeal, and while waiting for it to be heard, his lawyer visited him in the condemned cell. He said Klosowski was busy writing out a lengthy statement of some kind that he said would explain all, but because it wasn't finished he would not let his lawyer see it.

The document never re-surfaced again; it was not among his personal effects, which came to light after his execution, and even his lawyer was at a loss as to what had happened to it. There has been speculation that Klosowski had decided to reveal himself in this document as one of the most infamous serial killers of all time. That he was indeed Jack the Ripper.

Whether the missing document would have proven once and for all the identity of the Ripper is pure conjecture, as it has never been found. Klosowski's appeal was eventually turned down by the Home Secretary, and he was hanged at Wandsworth prison on 7 April 1903.

Inspector George Godley had worked under Inspector Abberline on the Ripper murders, and the two men had remained good friends ever since. When Abberline heard the news that Godley had arrested Klosowski and charged him with murder, he immediately went to see him and congratulated him with the words: 'You've got Jack the Ripper at last.'

Klosowski had always been Abberline's number one suspect as Jack the Ripper, and Abberline felt thwarted that he had never been able to bring him to justice.

Abberline was interviewed by the *Pall Mall Gazette*, which published the following interview on 24 March 1903:

Should Klosowski, the wretched man now lying under sentence of death for wife-poisoning, go to the scaffold without a 'last dying speech and confession,' a great mystery may for ever remain unsolved, but the conviction that 'Chapman' and 'Jack the Ripper' were one and the same person will not in the least be weakened in the mind of the man who is, perhaps, better qualified than anyone else in this country to express an opinion in this matter. We allude to Mr. F. G. Abberline, formerly Chief Detective Inspector of Scotland Yard, the official who had full charge of the criminal investigations at the time of the terrible murders in Whitechapel.

When a representative of the Pall Mall Gazette called on Mr. Abberline yesterday and asked for his views on the startling theory set up by one of the morning papers, the retired detective said: 'What an extra-ordinary thing it is that you should just have called upon me now. I had just commenced, not knowing anything about the report in the newspaper, to write to the Assistant Commissioner of Police, Mr. Macnaghten, to say how strongly I was impressed with the opinion that "Chapman" was also the author of the Whitechapel murders. Your appearance saves me the trouble. I intended to write on Friday, but a fall in the garden, injuring my hand and shoulder, prevented my doing so until today.'

Mr. Abberline had already covered a page and a half of foolscap, and was surrounded with a sheaf of documents and newspaper cuttings dealing with the ghastly outrages of 1888.

'I have been so struck with the remarkable coincidences in the two series of murders,' he continued, 'that I have not been able to think of anything else for several days past–not, in fact, since the Attorney-General made his opening statement at the recent trial, and traced the antecedents of Chapman before he came to this country in 1888. Since then the idea has taken full possession of me, and everything fits in and dovetails so well that I cannot help feeling that this is the man we struggled so hard to capture fifteen years ago.'

'My interest in the Ripper cases was especially deep. I had for fourteen years previously been an inspector of police in Whitechapel, but when the murders began I was at the Central Office at Scotland Yard. On the application of Superintendent Arnold I went back to the East End just before Annie Chapman was found mutilated, and as chief of the detective corps I gave myself up to the study of the cases. Many a time, even after we had carried our inquiries as far as we could–and we made out no fewer than 1,600 sets of papers respecting our investigations–instead of going home when I was off duty, I used to patrol the district until four or five o'clock in the morning, and, while keeping my eyes wide open for clues of any kind, have many and many a time given those wretched, homeless women, who were Jack the Ripper's special prey, fourpence or sixpence for a shelter to get them away from the streets and out of harm's way.'

'As I say,' went on the criminal expert, 'there are a score of things which make one believe that Chapman is the man; and you must understand that we have never believed all those stories about Jack the Ripper being dead, or that he was a lunatic, or anything of that kind. For instance, the date of the arrival in England coincides with the beginning of the series of murders in Whitechapel; there is a coincidence also in the fact that the murders ceased in London when "Chapman" went to America, while similar murders began to be perpetrated in America after he landed there. The fact that he studied medicine and surgery in Russia before he came here is well established, and it is curious to note that the first series of murders was the work of an expert surgeon, while the recent poisoning cases were proved to be done by a man with more than an elementary knowledge of medicine. The story told by "Chapman's" wife of the attempt to murder her with a long knife while in America is not to be ignored, but something else with regard to America is still more remarkable.'

'While the coroner was investigating one of the Whitechapel murders he told the jury a very queer story. You will remember that Dr. Phillips, the divisional surgeon, who made the post-mortem examination, not only spoke of the skilfulness with which the knife had been used, but stated that there was overwhelming evidence to show that the criminal had so mutilated the body that he could possess himself of one of the organs. The coroner, in commenting on this, said that he had been told by the sub-curator of the pathological museum connected with one of the great medical schools that some few months before an American had called upon him and asked him to procure a number of specimens. He stated his willingness to give £20 for each. Although the strange visitor was told that his wish was impossible of fulfilment, he still urged his request. It was known that the request was repeated at another institution of a similar character in London. The coroner at the time said: "Is it not possible that a knowledge of this demand may have inspired some abandoned wretch to possess himself of the specimens? It seems beyond belief that such inhuman wickedness could enter into the mind of any man; but, unfortunately, our criminal annals prove that every crime is possible"!'

'It is a remarkable thing,' Mr. Abberline pointed out, 'that after the Whitechapel horrors America should have been the place where a similar kind of murder began, as though the miscreant had not fully supplied the demand of the American agent.'

'There are many other things extremely remarkable. The fact that Klosowski when he came to reside in this country occupied a lodging in George Yard, Whitechapel Road, where the first murder was committed, is very curious, and the height of the man and the peaked cap he is said to have worn quite tallies with the descriptions I got of him. All agree, too, that he was a foreign-looking man, but that, of course, helped us little in a district so full of foreigners as Whitechapel. One discrepancy only have I noted, and this is that the people who alleged that they saw Jack the Ripper at one time or another, state that he was a man about thirty-five or forty years of age. They, however, state that they only saw his back, and it is easy to misjudge age from a back view.'

Altogether Mr. Abberline considers that the matter is quite beyond abstract speculation and coincidence, and believes the present situation affords an opportunity of unravelling a web of crime such as no man living can appreciate in its extent and hideousness.

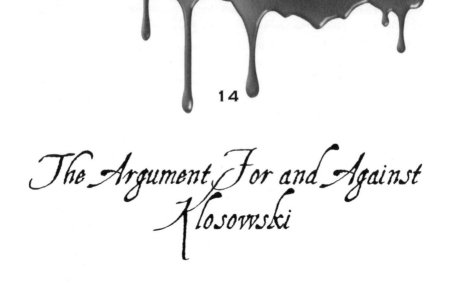

14

The Argument For and Against Klosowski

bberline was ecstatic when he first heard of Klosowski's arrest and even more so when he listened to the Attorney General, as he made his opening statement at Klosowski's trial, where he traced the events leading up to Klosowski coming to England in 1888. The pieces were all beginning to fall into place, and Abberline was as certain as he was ever going to be that Klosowski was the man he and his team had struggled so hard to capture fifteen years earlier.

Probably the main source of any argument against the probability of Klosowski being the Ripper is that most criminologists and behavioural therapists today maintain that the vast majority of serial killers continue their modus operandi, and that this is what links so-called signature crimes. As a general rule, poisoners are usually cold blooded and calculating, whereas those who go about their ghastly deeds using the method of brutish mutilation are more likely to show tendencies of being mentally unbalanced. Some say that this conclusion is incorrect, that subjects can and will change their modus operandi as they gain experience – a condition known as learned behaviour.

The next step in the argument against Klosowski being the Ripper is that according to a number of witness statements from people who claimed to have heard the Ripper actually conversing with his victims just before the crimes, they all understood very clearly what he was saying, and some even mentioned that he spoke in what they described as an 'educated manner'. We must bear in mind that this was in the autumn of 1888, and that Klosowski had only just immigrated to London one year previously. It could, of course, be possible for an educated Polish immigrant to have learned perfect English in such a short period of time, but there are no records of Klosowski having such an education, or even having private lessons in English. This then, according to the disbelievers in the Klosowski theory, rules him out completely as a Ripper suspect.

Another piece of information in the case against the Klosowski theory also comes from witnesses. In 1888, Klosowski would have been just 23 years old. Not one single witness described the man they alleged to be Jack the Ripper as that young. The majority of witnesses described the person they saw as between 35 and 40 years of age, while the youngest estimates were by PC Smith, who described him as 28, and Schwartz and Lawende, who thought he looked about 30. Klosowski's first wife, Lucy Baderski's brother and sister all claimed that Klosowski's appearance changed very little over the entire period they knew him. If what they say is true, and there does not seem to be any reason not to believe them, then perhaps it would be possible for Klosowski to have looked somewhat older than his age.

Even Inspector Abberline admitted that this did pose something of a stumbling block regarding his theory of Klosowski being the Ripper, but, as he later pointed out, almost every witness stated that they only saw the suspect's back, and it is easy to misjudge age from a back view.

Finally, we come to the subject of the 'similar murders committed in America' often referred to as evidence that Klosowski was indeed the Ripper. In actual fact, there was only one murder during the period that Klosowski was alleged to have been there, and that was of an elderly prostitute named Carrie Brown, or 'Old Shakespeare' as she was known. The assistant housekeeper at the lodging house where Carrie Brown was murdered, described the man she had seen Brown with as about 32 years of age, 5ft 8in tall, of slim build, with a long, sharp nose and heavy moustache of a light colour. He was dressed in a dark brown coat and black trousers, and wore an old and much-dented black derby hat. She said he had a foreign accent, and was possibly German.

The description could possibly fit Klosowski but it was so loose that it could have fitted almost any other foreign immigrant. The important question here, however, is Klosowski was even in Jersey City at this particular time.

On 5 April 1891, when the English census was taken, Klosowski was listed as still living in Tewkesbury Buildings, Whitechapel. The next listing for Klosowski being in England is shown as a whole year later, when he returned from America. When American records were searched, they did not show Klosowski being in Jersey City before 24 April, which seems to rule out completely his involvement in the Carrie Brown murder. But if we cast our minds back, it was the death of their son in March that prompted Klosowski and Baderski to move to America. Therefore it would be logical to assume that they moved to

America as soon as possible between the date of his death on 3 March and after the census register of 5 April. That leaves just nineteen days for Klosowski and Baderski to pack their possessions and move to Jersey City. Nineteen days to settle in and for him to murder Carrie Brown. For most people such a tight fit would be almost impossible, but we must remember this was Klosowski, and a short study of his modus operandi shows that, with him, nothing is impossible!

More on the positive side, as far as Abberline was concerned, were a number of facts. The first was that the date of Klosowski's arrival in England coincided exactly with the start of the series of murders in Whitechapel; the murders also promptly ceased in London when Klosowski went to America, where a series of similar murders began to happen. There was also the fact that he studied medicine and surgery in Russia before immigrating to England, where a number of experts agreed that the Whitechapel murders were the work of someone with a detailed knowledge of surgery. It was also stated that the recent poisoning cases were proven to have been carried out by someone with more than an elementary knowledge of medicine.

Another striking similarity that arises between the two sets of murders is that most experts agreed that the Ripper must have had a regular job, since all the murders occurred on weekends. The Ripper was, in all probability a single man, with no family ties, hence his propensity for staying out at all hours of the night. At Klosowski's trial, his first wife, Lucy Baderski, brought up the fact that her husband had been in the habit of staying out into the early hours of the morning. She even described how he once attempted to murder her with a long knife while they lived in America.

It was also a well-known fact that Klosowski had an enormous sexual appetite, and although the Ripper never actually committed any normal sexual acts with any of his victims, he was still classed as a sexual serial killer, for the simple reason that he always mutilated his victims' sexual organs. Klosowski was a known mass murderer, which should be taken into account. There were many men who fitted the description of the Ripper in 1888, but few who were known to be able to commit murder, and fewer still who were known to be capable of committing mass murder.

Klosowski was a man who seemingly took pleasure in watching his wives being slowly tortured to death by poison. Apart from the poisoning, he was capable of almost anything; even the attempted stabbing of his first wife, in such a cold-blooded manner, while they were living in New Jersey makes Abberline's theory of him being guilty of both sets of crimes seem all the more plausible.

Some experts expound the theory that someone who takes lives on a wholesale scale finds it impossible to stop until they are either arrested or die. The argument against this is the dissimilarity of character in the crimes, but the ghastliness is never eradicated. The victims in both cases continue to be women, but they are of different classes, and therefore call for different methods of dispatch.

Some years later, another police officer, ex-Superintendent Arthur Neil, also endorsed his belief that Abberline's theory regarding Klosowski was right. He urged that Klosowski took to poisoning his women victims as part of his diabolical cunning or insane urge to satisfy his inordinate vanity.

To sum up the verdict for or against Klosowski: he was a misogynist with medical skill and American experience; he was of foreign extraction, very similar in looks and general description, apart from age, to witness descriptions at the time; he lived and worked in the immediate area of the murders throughout the autumn of 1888 when the Ripper murders took place; the Ripper murders ceased the moment he moved to America; another Ripper-style murder took place in America almost as soon as Klosowski moved there. Everything falls into place, with the exception of his modus operandi. One question remains unanswered, probably forever, and that is whether a frenzied and savage mutilator of women can, in any way, turn his modus operandi around and become a calculating poisoner just seven years later.

15

Highly Implausible?

We have been through a list of the main suspects in the Ripper case, and we have explored the pros and cons of Inspector Abberline's number one suspect, Severin Klosowski. The most talked about, written about and romanticised name in any book, film or discussion about Jack the Ripper, however, is invariably Prince Albert Victor, known as 'Eddy' to his friends, and how the Freemasons allegedly came to his aid.

By their very nature, Freemasons have always been a target for gossip and insinuation. Even the Goulston Street graffiti was said by some to be linked to them, mainly because of the spelling of the word 'Juwes', which, it has been alleged, referred not to 'Jews', but to Jubela, Jubelo and Jubelum, the three killers of Hiram Abiff, a semi-legendary figure in Freemasonry. This then, said the conspirators, must be part of a Masonic plot.

Actual evidence implicating the Freemasons in the Ripper case was far and few between. The legend grew that a group of highly placed members of the brotherhood were actually involved in a murderous conspiracy to suppress knowledge of a secret and illegal marriage between Prince Albert Victor (Eddy), heir presumptive to the throne, and a shop assistant named Annie Crook, who duly delivered the prince a child.

Their conspiracy involved finding the only other person who knew of this tryst, which was Mary Kelly, an old friend of Annie Crook, who had been employed by the couple as their nanny. When the group of Freemasons found out that both Crook and Kelly had worked as prostitutes in the East End, their target was enlarged, and they set out to silence Kelly and anyone who might have known her or that she might have related the story to.

As unbelievable as it seems, this was accepted as fact by quite a number of people. In fact, it was this version of events that were used in numerous films and television series. The Freemasons' version ends with them, having completed their ghastly deeds, withdrawing back into the shadows; and although the case was never really closed, no one was ever caught for the crimes and so the legend of Jack the Ripper lives on to this day.

To accept that a group of highly placed, intelligent men sought to suppress knowledge of a secret royal marriage by means of a series of sensational and highly publicised murders is to accept the unbelievable.

Although the East End of London was a large sprawling place, it was also reminiscent of a village, in the fact that most of the inhabitants were in the same boat, so to speak: nearly all were poor, many were out of work, and all of the victims were heavy drinkers or alcoholics who spent most of their free time in public houses. In such an environment, it would have been impossible for tongues not to wag. Also, bearing in mind that the victims and their friends were all prostitutes and shared a common bond, gossip such as Prince Eddy's supposed secret marriage to a low-class girl from the East End would have raced through the pubs of Whitechapel like wildfire, and no power on earth, least of all the Masons, could have prevented it.

Upon initiation, a Freemason takes an oath, stating that the secrets of another Master Mason 'Shall remain as secure and inviolable in my breast as in his own, when communicated to me, murder and treason excepted; and they left to my own election'.

When the well-known actor and manager of London's Lyceum Theatre, Henry Irving, was elected as a Master Mason, he took the oath, which would last for the rest of his life, to keep any secrets he may have learned, 'Secure within his breast'.

During the early autumn of 1888, the Lyceum Theatre was running a very successful version of the German drama *Faust*, which strangely enough, when used as the adjective, is often described as an arrangement in which an ambitious person surrenders moral integrity in order to achieve power and success: the proverbial 'deal with the devil'.

The Lyceum, under Henry Irving's management, was doing good in the box office, and *Faust* was playing to packed houses. Irving, however, suddenly announced that he intended to discontinue its run and replace it with the Scottish play *Macbeth*, which was to open on 29 December with Ellen Terry as Lady Macbeth and Irving repeating the lead role in which he had hitherto been only partially successful.

So why had Irving suddenly taken *Faust* off, when it was so obviously a commercial success? He was a friend of the great and the good, many of whom waited eagerly for an invitation to supper in his private room at the Lyceum, known as the Beefsteak Room. A year earlier, Irving had helped found another Mason's lodge called the Savage Club Lodge, which was composed almost exclusively of literary and theatrical artistes. Members of this new lodge were also honoured on some occasions to meet the Prince of Wales, who had been Chief Mason, the Most Worshipful Grand Master of England, for the past fifteen years, in addition to being a patron of the Lyceum Theatre.

Taking into account the turmoil over the alleged association of the Freemasons and the Whitechapel murders, it is easy to see Irving's reasoning behind his decision to drop the still-popular *Faust* from the Lyceum programme, and replace it with *Macbeth*.

The public waited with baited breath for *Macbeth* to start. On the opening night, the leading Shakespearean actress Ellen Terry, commented on Irving's gaunt look, with his straggling moustache, saying he was, 'Like a great famished wolf' as he padded across the shadowy hall in Dunsinane, thrust aloft the glittering bloodstained daggers and hissed triumphantly to his fellow conspirator, and to the enthralled audience, 'I have done the deed!'

Sir Charles Warren, who was head of the London Metropolitan Police at the time of the Ripper murders, was also the first Worshipful Master of Quatuor Coronati Lodge, the premier research lodge in the world. On 9 November 1888, the Quatuor Coronati Lodge held its quarterly meeting, while on this same night Mary Jane Kelly, the final victim of Jack the Ripper, was found murdered. Sir Charles Warren resigned as London Metropolitan Police chief immediately following this event.

In summing up these events, we have a period of political unrest in the country as a whole: the previous autumn 100,000 unemployed had clashed with the army and police in Trafalgar Square. Rumours were starting to circulate of the imminent collapse of the established order, and London's Masonic lodges were far from immune to such talk. So worried had they become that they had sent to their own Worshipful Grand Master a series of letters, imploring him to behave, as he might become a future monarch worthy of the title.

Whether there is any real truth in the conspiracy theories surrounding the Masons' involvement in the Ripper killings is still very much debatable, but we still need to look further into Prince Eddy and his alleged involvement.

Eddy was born in 1864 to Prince Albert Edward, who was the son of Queen Victoria. Albert Edward, who was known as Bertie, would later become King Edward VII. He was not particularly well liked by the general public as he had a reputation of a ladies' man, and was alleged to have been involved in a number of scandals. His wife, Princess Alexandra, on the other hand, was a sort of equivalent to the late Princess Diana. The public loved her and had great sympathy for her, for having to put up with the antics of her husband.

It seemed that while Bertie was gallivanting and womanising, his son Eddy was sadly missing out on the parental love and control which most children take for granted. He had no formal education, and consequently became known as a 'slow' child. Being 'slow' did not mean he was deficient in any way, for he was, in every other aspect, a dear and loving child, but he lacked drive and tenacity. When he went to Cambridge, he had to have a private tutor, but this might have been due to his partial deafness.

In 1891, Eddy was given the title of Duke of Clarence and Avondale, and was in line to follow his father to the throne. In that same year he became engaged to Princess May of Teck, but in 1892, just six weeks after the announcement of the engagement, a large-scale influenza epidemic broke out, which Eddy fell victim to and subsequently died. The following year, Princess May became engaged to Albert Victor's next surviving brother, George, who subsequently became King George V.

The Ripper murders happened in 1888, four years prior to these events, when many names were being bandied about as possible suspects; but Prince Albert was never named as a suspect by anyone.

It wasn't until the 1960s, long after the principal characters in the theories were dead, that Eddy's name as an alleged suspect came to the fore. The first allegation came in a book entitled *Edouard VII* by Phillippe Jullien, in which the author states that Prince Albert and the Duke of Bedford were rumoured to be responsible for the Ripper murders, although there does not seem to be any evidence, prior or current, to support this theory.

A few years later, in 1970, British surgeon Dr Thomas E.A. Stowell published an article in the November issue of *The Criminologist*, entitled 'Jack the Ripper, A Solution?' Stowell's article states that the Ripper was an aristocrat who had contracted syphilis during a visit to the West Indies, and that it had driven him insane. His brain became addled by the disease and in this state of mind had perpetrated the five Jack the Ripper murders. Throughout his article, the killer is referred to as 'S', but there is enough internal evidence to identify Eddy as his chief suspect. Stowell even described in detail the suspect's family and his physical appearance, leaving little doubt, if any, that the person he was referring to was none other than Queen Victoria's grandson, Prince Albert Victor.

Stowell's article stated that following the Double Event murders on 30 September 1888, the suspect's family had him committed to a private mental hospital in the south of England. Assuming that Eddy was the suspect Stowell was referring to in his article, he then, according to Stowell, escaped from the institution and on 9 November, committed yet another murder, before ultimately dying of syphilis.

Stowell claimed that the information to back his theory had come from the private notes of Sir William Gull, a reputable physician who had treated members of the royal family. Stowell also claimed that his suspect drew his knowledge of anatomy and surgery, which most people accepted the Ripper must have had, from the disembowelment of deer that he had shot on the royal estates.

Stowell's claims seem ludicrous to say the least. It is a fact that Sir William Gull had died before Eddy had, and so could not have possibly known about Eddy's death. It is also a fact that three doctors attended Eddy at his death in 1892, and they all agreed that he had died of pneumonia. If Eddy had died of syphilis, he would have had to have contracted the disease at least fifteen years earlier for it to have progressed to his brain, as syphilitic insanity. This would have meant that Eddy was infected at the age of 9, in about 1873, six years before he visited the West Indies.

Phillippe Jullien and Thomas Stowell's theories regarding Eddy being the Ripper are blown completely out of the water when one looks at the dates the murders were committed. They both seem to have overlooked the obvious and most important thing surrounding their theory, which was that on every single date on which a murder was committed, Eddy was not in London, and therefore could not have possibly committed them.

Examination of court and royal records reveal exactly where Eddy was on the important murder dates:

29 August to 7 September 1888: The Prince was staying with Viscount Downe at Danby Lodge, Grosmont, Yorkshire. (Polly Nichols was murdered on 31 August.)

7 to 10 September 1888: The Prince was at the Cavalry Barracks in York. (Annie Chapman was murdered on 8 September.)

27 to 30 September: The Prince was at Abergeldie, Scotland, where Queen Victoria recorded in her journal that he lunched with her on 30 September. (Elizabeth Stride and Catherine Eddowes were murdered between 1 a.m. and 2 a.m. on 30 September.)

1 November: Arrived in London from York.

2 to 12 November: The Prince was at Sandringham. (Mary Kelly was murdered on 9 November.)

The above dates show without a doubt that Eddy could not have possibly been the Whitechapel murderer, but the theorists still seemed to like the idea of a royal connection, which would obviously sell books, and later, films and television programmes.

In 1973 the theory of Prince Albert Victor's involvement in the Ripper case was taken even further, when the BBC programme *Jack the Ripper* was aired. It was in this adaptation that the Royal Conspiracy Theory first appeared. In the programme, two fictional modern-day detectives finally solve the Ripper mystery through a series of conspiracies and cover-ups. It was alleged that whilst researching the story for the programme, the producers were contacted by a man named Joseph Sickert who said he knew about a secret marriage between Eddy and a poor Catholic girl named Annie Crook. Sickert's story involved Eddy, Lord Salisbury, Sir Robert Anderson, Sir William Gull and even Queen Victoria!

Joseph Sickert was the son of the famous artist Walter Sickert, from whom he allegedly got the story. Walter Sickert had lived in the East End during the time of the Ripper murders and was supposedly a close friend of Princess Alexandra, who was a fellow compatriot from Denmark. The Princess asked Sickert to take Eddy under his wing and teach him about art and introduce him to the artistic set; in other words, she wanted Eddy to come out more as a man about town.

Sickert introduced Eddy to a lot of things, but the one thing that allegedly got him involved in the Ripper case was his introduction to a poor girl named Annie Crook, who worked in a shop in Cleveland Street, London. Eddy and Annie Crook began an affair, and she became pregnant with his baby. Eddy set up a flat for her and her baby, Alice, and paid all the bills. News of this tryst soon got back to the Queen, however, and she demanded that her grandson's indiscretions should be terminated immediately. Annie was both a commoner, and a Catholic, which the Queen believed could spark a revolution if the people ever got to hear of it.

With this in mind, the Queen turned the matter over to her Prime Minister, Lord Salisbury. Salisbury then enlisted the aid of Sir William Gull, who was the Queen's personal physician. Then, according to Walter Sickert, Salisbury and Gull hatched a plot in which they organised a raid on Eddy and Annie's love nest. Eddy was taken away to a secret destination, to be kept there until things had calmed down, while Gull had Annie taken away and locked up in a mental institution, where he then performed experiments on her which made her lose her memory, become epileptic and slowly go insane.

Eddy and Annie's child, however, escaped the raid unharmed with her nanny, Mary Kelly, who had been found by Walter Sickert in one of the poor houses in the East End. Sickert had taken pity on Kelly and took her to the tobacconist's shop in Cleveland Street, to help Annie. Kelly loved children and soon became Alice's nanny. Kelly was there with the child when the raid took place and, as all of the attention was focused on Eddy and Annie, she managed to slip out of the house with the child, without being noticed. Kelly was scared, and in desperation placed the child with nuns and fled into the back streets of the East End, falling into a life of drink and prostitution.

Kelly, like so many others in her profession, drank very heavily, and as is often found, the more she drank, the more loose her tongue became. She knew the entire story of Eddy's indiscretion and began spreading it around for the price of another drink. It wasn't long before several of her cronies started pressurising her into blackmailing the government for hush money. These cronies were Polly Nichols, Liz Stride and Annie Chapman.

When Lord Salisbury heard of the threat, he called a meeting with Sir William Gull once again. At that meeting, they decided a fool-proof plan was needed to rid the government and the monarchy of this threat once and for all. Sir William Gull then enlisted the help of John Netley, a coachman who had often ferried Eddy on his forays into the East End. Together they created Jack the Ripper and a Freemason connection. They also enlisted the aid of the Assistant Commissioner to Scotland Yard, Sir Robert Anderson, who was to cover up the crimes and make sure no police officers were about during the murders.

Sickert claimed that the murder of Catherine Eddowes had been a mistake. She often used the name Mary Kelly and the conspirators thought that she was the Mary Kelly they were looking for. When the mistake became apparent, they found the real Mary Kelly and viciously silenced her.

The conspirators did everything in their power to make the murders look as if they were the work of one lone madman, and a scapegoat was chosen to throw to the wolves if ever they felt detectives were getting too close. This is where the barrister Montague Druitt came into the picture. He was chosen to take the blame and possibly, according to Sickert, was murdered for it.

Annie Crook's daughter, Alice Margaret, grew up in the care of the nuns, without knowing who her parents were. In an odd series of events, she later married Walter Sickert and gave birth to their son, Joseph.

It was announced that Sir William Gull had died shortly after the murders, but there were rumours that he had been committed to an insane asylum, where he died several years later. Annie Crook died insane in a workhouse in 1920. John Netley was chased by an angry mob after he unsuccessfully tried to run Alice Margaret over with his cab shortly after the murders. He went to ground shortly after this, and was believed to have drowned in the Thames.

Joseph Sickert said that his father was fascinated with the murders and often spoke of the great guilt he felt over them. Not that Walter Sickert admitted any responsibility for the murders themselves, but his guilt came from the fact that he had been the one who introduced Eddy to Annie and started the whole grisly game. For many years he held his tongue, saying as little as possible about his knowledge of the murders, but he did manage to alleviate his guilt somewhat by painting what many saw as clues into several of his most famous paintings.

There was never any real evidence to link Eddy to Annie Crook, or their supposed love nest in Cleveland Street. Everything was based on rumour and second-hand statements. The royal conspiracy theorists say this lack of evidence proves their theory because all the evidence was destroyed, which sounds like the most preposterous statement as to offering supposed proof of a case.

The theorist, however, wasn't finished yet: Eddy was what Hollywood would today call 'good box office'. Attach his royal name to the story, in any way, and sure enough it would attract attention. The accusations of Eddy actually being the Ripper had been spent and disproved to all reasonable doubt, as too had the Royal Conspiracy Theory.

Eddy's name was next used by Michael Harrison, in his biography of the Prince, entitled *Clarence*, in which he was now relegated to a secondary role in the Ripper case. Harrison used two separate theories, the first involving Eddy's old Cambridge tutor, James K. Stephen. According to this theory, Harrison had looked at Stowell's article in great detail, and had come to the conclusion that the mysterious 'S' who Stowell accuses was not Eddy at all, but James K. Stephen. Harrison claimed that Stephen had committed the murders as some sort of crazed act of revenge on Eddy, whom he alleges had broken off a homosexual relationship between the two men.

In 1883, James Stephen had been Eddy's tutor at Cambridge. His job was to try to bring Eddy's intelligence up to 'acceptable' levels. One former tutor had described Eddy's mind as 'Abnormally dormant'. According to Harrison, it was while Stephen was tutoring Eddy that their sexual relationship began, which Harrison alleges to have resulted in a scandal. As with almost all the other allegations against Eddy, there is absolutely no proof of this. Their relationship supposedly ended when Eddy joined the 10th Hussars on 17 June 1885.

Two years later, Stephen had an accident, when a horse he was riding shied and backed him into the wooden vane of a windmill. The accident was quite serious, causing him considerable damage, but after a long period of medical care and rest, he eventually seemed to make a complete recovery. It was later discovered, however, that his brain had been permanently damaged from the accident and Stephen was slowly going mad.

Stephen's behaviour became more erratic as time went on: he saw himself as a great artist, and even a swordsman; he would rush around town in a hansom cab, brandishing his sword and shouting insanely at passers-by.

In 1887 he became a patient of Sir William Gull, but it seems that even Gull could not do anything for him, as he had begun a rapid mental and physical decline. It was during this period that Stephen opted out of being a famous artist and decided instead that he was now a poet, and wrote two volumes of poetry that included extremely violent images against women. He was eventually committed to a mental hospital in 1891, and died there the following February.

Harrison's theory was that the break up of the homosexual relationship with Eddy, combined with the accident, provoked Stephen to try to avenge himself upon Eddy, but he failed to sufficiently explain why Stephen would have allegedly picked such women as the Ripper murdered, and why he thought that would hurt Eddy in any way. Harrison argued his point in an elaborate and somewhat confusing scheme that included a blood sacrifice, a savage deity named the Great Mother and the Roman god Terminus. Harrison went on to state that the Ripper in fact murdered ten women, including Alice Mackenzie, Frances Coles, Mellett or Davis and Annie Farmer, who was not murdered at all. The ten women theory was important to Harrison, as he believed that Stephen was acting out one of his own poems, 'Air Kaphoozelum', in which the villain kills ten harlots.

Harrison made one last attempt to pinpoint Stephen as the Ripper by assimilating his handwriting with the Ripper letters 'Dear Boss' and 'From Hell'. This attempt at connecting Stephen's handwriting with the Ripper letters was rebutted outright in 1975 by Thomas J. Mann, a handwriting expert, in an article in the *Journal of the World Association of Document Examiners*. Mann stated that only the Lusk letter is likely to be genuine and that the connection between Stephen's handwriting and that letter was minimal. He went on to say that the overwhelming evidence is that the two do not match, and if the author of the Lusk letter was indeed Jack the Ripper, then James K. Stephen was most definitely not that man.

Albert Victor's intellect, sexuality, sanity and murderous intentions, if indeed there were such, have been the subject of much speculation. In fact, it was none other than Inspector Abberline himself who, in July 1889, a year after the Ripper murders had ceased, became the chief investigating officer in a case that became known as the Cleveland Street scandal, involving a homosexual brothel and, believe it or not, Eddy's involvement in this.

The investigation into the Cleveland Street case was long and, at times, very tiresome, with witnesses fleeing the country, and rumour and innuendo being bandied about by all and sundry. Inspector Abberline, however, did not let up, and under his supervision the male prostitutes and pimps started revealing the names of their clients, who included Lord Arthur Somerset, an extra equerry to the Prince of Wales.

Homosexual acts between men were illegal at this time, and those found guilty of such faced social ostracism, prosecution and possibly two years' imprisonment with hard labour. As the Cleveland Street scandal dragged on, it started to implicate other high-ranking figures. Rumours swept the upper echelons of London's society of the involvement of a member of the royal family: Prince Albert Victor. Eddy's name was dragged in even though the defendants in the case had not named him as ever being there. It was suggested that Somerset's solicitor, Arthur Newton, fabricated and spread the rumours to take the heat off his client.

It later came to light that letters exchanged between the Treasury solicitor, Sir Augustus Stephenson, and his assistant, the Hon. Hamilton Cuffe, make coded reference to Newton's threats to implicate Eddy. When the Prince of Wales heard about this, he personally intervened in the investigation, calling for an end to gossip and rumour. In the end none of the clients who had visited the brothel were ever prosecuted and no evidence implicating Eddy in any way was ever offered up.

As seems usual in such cases, and especially those involving Eddy, because there was no conclusive evidence for or against his involvement, or whether he even visited the brothel or not, certain biographers assumed that this lack of evidence must be some sort of cover-up. They also deduced from their 'cover-up' theory that he more than likely did visit the Cleveland Street brothel, and that he was possibly bisexual, not homosexual.

When questioned, Lord Arthur Somerset's sister, Lady Waterford, denied that her brother knew anything at all about Eddy, insisting that as far as she knew, 'The boy is as straight as a line'. She insisted that her brother knew absolutely nothing about how or where Eddy spent his time.

Many years later, when Harold Nicholson, the official biographer of King George V, was researching his book, he spoke to Lord Goddard, who was a 12-year-old schoolboy at the time of the scandal, and Goddard told him that Albert Victor had been involved in a male brothel scene, and that a solicitor had to commit perjury to clear him. The solicitor, he said, was struck off the rolls for his offence, but was later reinstated.

The rumours have unfortunately persisted, and are still damaging to Eddy's reputation to this day. None of the lawyers in the case were convicted of perjury or struck off during the scandal. Somerset's solicitor, Arthur Newton, was convicted of obstruction of justice for helping his clients escape abroad and was sentenced to six weeks in prison.

There is another fact, however, that although doesn't implicate Eddy in any way, still tends to leave one thinking, and that is that Cleveland Street comes up twice in the allegations against him: firstly in the address where Annie Crook was alleged to have worked and later lived, which was 21 Cleveland Street, and secondly in the homosexual brothel scandal, which took place at 19 Cleveland Street. A coincidence? You must judge for yourself!

16

Another Ripper Suspect?

*A*t exactly 3.45 a.m. on 31 August 1888, Robert Paul was on his way to Corbett's Court, Spitalfields, where he worked as a car-man. It was still dark as he turned into Buck's Row, but in the darkness he saw the figure of a man in a slightly crouching position just ahead of him. As he got nearer the figure it straightened up and started to approach him. At this point Paul could see something like a bundle, lying on the floor of a stable yard gateway, just a little way behind the man. His immediate thoughts were of any possible danger to himself, as he had heard of people being attacked and robbed in that vicinity during the hours of darkness. It was then that the man called to him, saying, 'Quick, come over here and look at this, there's a woman lying here'.

The man was Charles Cross, who indicated towards the body of the woman, who was later identified as Polly Nichols. She was lying on her back with her skirt lifted almost to her waist. Cross then lifted one of her hands, and turned again to Paul, saying, 'She's stone cold'. He then looked up at Paul, asking him to feel, but Paul declined. He declined again when Cross said they shouldn't leave the woman lying uncovered like she was, and that they should help to cover her up before anyone else saw her.

Paul didn't want to touch the victim in any way, and suggested that the best thing they could do was to go as quickly as possible to find a constable. Cross agreed and the two men left the scene together. Just minutes after Cross and Paul had left the scene, another constable, PC Neil, happened to enter Buck's Row, completely independently, and saw the bundle lying on the pavement, and so the murder of Polly Nichols, Jack the Ripper's first victim, was reported; within hours Inspector Abberline was seconded from Scotland Yard onto the case.

When the police first interviewed the witnesses, they spoke to both Paul and Cross, but for some reason they did not pay too much attention to Cross. They treated him as just another man on his way to work that morning. When Robert Paul walked into Buck's Row on the morning of 31 August 1888, and saw Charles Cross crouching over the body of Polly Nichols, he may have been the first and only man to have disturbed Jack the Ripper in the course of his ghastly work.

Very little is known of Charles Cross apart from the fact that he lived in Doveton Street, Bethnal Green, and worked at the Pickfords' depot in Broad Street (near Liverpool Street station). In his witness statement to the police, he said he was walking to work that morning, as he always did, which usually took him on average approximately forty minutes. The only other fact that is known about him is that he was the man Robert Paul found by the body of Polly Nichols.

There is no doubt that the wounds inflicted on Polly Nichols were savage and brutal to say the least, but they were far less so in comparison to later murders attributed to the Ripper, which involved even greater mutilation. With this in mind, the question that hangs over this murder is: had her killer completed his work or was he interrupted in the course of doing so? When Robert Paul walked into Buck's Row that morning and saw Charles Cross stooping down by the body of Polly Nichols, had he in fact interrupted the Ripper while conducting his work?

Another side to this question is: if Cross was the Ripper, and had heard footsteps and seen Robert Paul coming towards him just as he was in the midst of slaughtering Polly Nichols, why didn't he flee the scene before Paul got too close and was able to recognise him?

His other options, of course, would have been firstly to attack and maybe even kill Paul, or secondly, to establish an illusion that he was just an innocent, on his way to work, who had the misfortune to discover a corpse in Buck's Row. At the end of the day, Charles Cross was accepted by the police and everyone else at the time as an ordinary car-man on his way to work who had stumbled across the body of Polly Nichols.

What knowledge there is of Charles Cross is very limited. The surviving police records are basic and uninformative, as are the few newspaper articles in which he was briefly mentioned. When *The Times* reported on the inquest on 4 September 1888, they didn't even bother to double check as to Cross' first name, and published it as George.

This misnomer could have been due to the fact that when Charles Cross and Robert Paul went off together to find a police officer, they found and reported it to PC Jonas Mizen, and it was his evidence at the inquest that may have caused the newspaper's confusion over Cross' first name. It was Mizen who referred to the car-man who had spoken to him on the morning in question as George Cross, and *The Times* as well as the *Morning Advertiser* had picked up on that name and used it in their articles.

As unimportant as the newspapers and the police seemed to think Cross was at the time, we should still consider him as a suspect for a number of reasons, not least because he was found at the scene of the crime. There are also some discrepancies regarding the time he left his home in Doveton Street and the information given by the newspapers, which was contradictory.

On 3 September, *The Star* wrote that Cross was employed by Pickfords, that he left home on Friday at 3.20 a.m. and got to Pickfords' yard, Broad Street at 4 a.m. *The Times* confirmed this in their article. Both statements, however, were wrong. Charles Cross was with Robert Paul in Buck's Row at approximately 3.45 a.m. It took the two men approximately five minutes searching the streets before they found PC Mizen. If one allows another five minutes to report to Mizen what they had seen, this would then have meant Cross getting to Pickfords' in Broad Street in just five minutes, which is impossible.

To walk from Doveton Street, where Cross lived, to Broad Street, where he worked for Pickfords', usually took Cross approximately forty minutes. On this particular Friday, however, he said that he was late for work and didn't leave home until 3.30 a.m.; this would have meant arriving in Buck's Row at approximately 3.36 a.m.

Dr Llewellyn, who lived close by, was called by the police within minutes of them arriving at the murder scene. When the *Daily News* and the *Evening News* for 1 September published a statement given to them by the doctor, he allegedly gave them the time of his arrival on the murder scene as about 3.55 a.m. The following day, after giving evidence at the inquest, he told reporters that he was called to Buck's Row at about 4 a.m., which is a lot less precise than his earlier statement. More importantly, perhaps, might be: what time did he actually arrive in Buck's Row?

These might seem like minor points, but if we consider the fact that when Dr Llewellyn first saw Polly Nichols, he stated that, in his opinion, she had not been dead for more than half an hour at the most. In Inspector Abberline's report, which was written after the inquest, he gave the time for Cross' finding of the body at about 3.40 a.m.

At the inquest, Cross gave evidence that he had just arrived by the body of Polly Nichols when he was joined by Paul, but Paul said he had left home, about 3.45 a.m. This would mean that one of the men was not telling the truth. If Cross was lying, and had left his home in Doveton Street at his normal time of 3.20 a.m., he would have had time to meet and kill Polly Nichols. If he had left at 3.30 a.m., he would still have had time to attack her before being interrupted by Paul.

A reporter for the newspaper *Lloyd's Weekly* interviewed Robert Paul on the night of the murder, and the article was published in the paper that Sunday. This was the day before Cross gave evidence at the coroner's court. In the article Robert Paul stated that it was exactly 3.45 a.m. when he walked up Buck's Row, on his way to work, and saw the crouched man. The inquest into the death of Polly Nichols was delayed for two weeks, while further evidence was searched for. When it was resumed, Robert Paul was called to give evidence, and according to *The Times* dated 18 September, he stated that as he passed up Buck's Row he saw a man standing in the roadway. No one bothered to establish the exact distance that Cross was to the body when Paul saw him there that morning. There seemed to be no suspicion whatsoever that Cross was anything other than the harmless witness he appeared. When *The Star* newspaper wrote its piece on the inquest, it did not even bother giving Cross' name, and no one bothered to ask his age, although one newspaper did mention that he had worked for Pickfords' for more than twenty years. He was mentioned as a witness, who happened to be a car-man, and wore a coarse sacking apron.

There is, however, one more very important piece of information that connects Charles Cross with the Ripper murders. His route between his home in Doveton Street and his place of work at Broad Street took him directly through the area in which the Ripper murders took place. Cross had multiple choices he could take, all eventually taking him to his final destination. Whitechapel Road would be the direct route, but one can cut off any number of different streets from there to eventually lead to his destination at Broad Street. He could walk through Osborn Street into Brick Lane, or through Old Montague Street or Wentworth Street. He could head down Hanbury Street or Dorset Street. In the warren of narrow streets and alleys that intertwine this area, all streets lead to Rome as they say, or, in this instance, Ripper Territory.

As already pointed out, Polly Nichols was murdered on Cross' path to work in late August. Annie Chapman was murdered in Hanbury Street, which was another possible route. Mary Kelly was found mutilated in Miller's Court, just off Dorset Street, which again is just off Commercial Street, and most definitely a possible route for Cross. Elizabeth Stride was found dead in Dutfield's Yard, Berner Street, which is a little off the normal Ripper patch, but still only some five minute's walk away. She lived in Flower and Dean Street, which was on Cross' route and could have easily been followed by the murderer from there to her place of death. Lastly, we have Catherine Eddowes, who also lived in Flower and Dean Street, but had been arrested by the police on the night of her death and held for some hours at Bishopsgate police station. This police station is just a few minutes' walk away from Cross' place of work at Broad Street.

If these scenes of murder and mutilation were not enough to make Charles Cross a major suspect, then we need to also consider two more murders, which have been downgraded, so to speak, as 'possible' Ripper murders.

On Tuesday 7 August, the body of Martha Tabram was found in the stairwell of George Yard Buildings, just off Wentworth Street. This would also have fitted in perfectly with the route Cross would have taken on his way to work, and even his timings would have been perfect. Martha Tabram has never been officially recognised as a Ripper victim, only a possibility, but the opportunity and the known timetable of Charles Cross was there.

The final 'coincidence' happened in April 1888, and involved yet another known prostitute named Emma Smith. There is no suggestion whatsoever that Smith was a victim of the Ripper, as she lived long enough to identify her assailants as a gang of ruffians who robbed and assaulted her. She died of her wounds several days later in the London Hospital. She was subjected to the assault at the junction of Osborn Street and Wentworth Street, and was left wounded and bleeding in a shop doorway. The time she was lying there coincided exactly with the time Cross would have been walking to work through Wentworth Street.

There is no suggestion that Cross committed this crime, as Smith had already named the people who committed it as a gang, but the location of her killing occurred on streets he knew well, and there is a strong possibility that he had walked past her body that morning and seen her lying in a pool of blood. The sight of this death may have triggered something off within his subconscious, which later evolved and helped turn his fantasies into reality that autumn.

The evidence against Cross might well be circumstantial, but we need to bear in mind that Cross was seen by most people, the police included, as a poor working man and nobody of any significance. People like Cross were familiar sights on the streets of Whitechapel; they blended in with their surroundings. While the police and the press looked for madmen and strange-looking foreigners carrying packages and lurking in doorways, ordinary-looking working men such as Cross were ignored as they trudged through the darkly lit streets on their way to work. While the police struggled to keep pace with the continuing murders, Cross completely vanished from their investigations. He was just a part of the Nichols murder paperwork, pigeon-holed forever as the car-man witness who discovered her body.

Even today, not many people have shown a great deal of interest in Cross as a likely contender for Jack the Ripper. This might be in part due to the intellectual appeal of the far more complex theories, in stark contrast to Cross, the ordinary man in the street. Cross was not an elegantly dressed gentleman, a Mason or a mad doctor out for revenge. Neither was he an artist or a member of the royal family. If one wanted to sell a story about Jack the Ripper, Cross would probably be the last name on the author's lips, for he was just an unknown local man who had, according to police records, been found beside a dead woman. He is most definitely not the most romantic solution to the Jack the Ripper murders, but he just could be the right one. One day, I am sure, we will hear much more about Charles Cross.

17

Did Abberline Know the Identity of the Ripper?

*A*bberline was not looking for romantic solutions to the murders; he was a genuine pragmatist in his approach to work. Why then did he not take suspects such as Charles Cross seriously? We have to take into account that when Abberline was still working for the police, most if not all of the actual evidence gathered by the Metropolitan Police in the course of the investigation, passed through his hands at some point. In spite of this, however, he was not known to have ever expressed a definite opinion on the Ripper's identity during this period.

In March 1889, Albert Backart, a high-ranking member of the Whitechapel Vigilance Committee, expressed the committee's displeasure that since there had not been any more murders for some months, there seemed to be a great deal of complacency within the force regarding any ongoing investigation into the Ripper case.

It is then alleged that a senior officer contacted Backart and told him that he would explain all if he would agree to swear to secrecy, which he then did. The officer went on to tell him that the Vigilance Committee and its patrols could now be safely disbanded, as the police were quite certain that the Ripper murders were finished. Backart protested and said he needed to know more, to which the officer replied, 'It isn't necessary for you to know any more, the man in question is dead. He was fished out of the Thames two months ago and it would only cause pain to relatives if we said any more than that.'

The man the police were talking about was obviously Montague Druitt, who was found drowned in the Thames on 31 December 1888. Abberline himself didn't acknowledge the fact, as others had done, that the Ripper was known to have been dead soon after the autumn of 1888 – as per his interview with the *Pall Mall Gazette* in 1903, mentioned earlier.

The man Abberline always suspected the most was, of course, Severin Klosowski (aka George Chapman), and in 1903 Klosowski was indeed dead; in fact; he was hanged at Wandsworth prison on 7 April; 1903. When Sergeant George Albert Godley, who was once part of Abberline's team in the hunt for the Ripper, actually arrested Klosowski and charged him with poisoning his wife, Abberline is alleged to have said to him, 'You've caught Jack the Ripper at last!'

It has also been alleged that this remark was actually made after Klosowski was convicted and not when Godley first arrested him. So why did Abberline pick Klosowski?

When Abberline was speaking about the case in 1903, he said that during one of the inquests into the murders, the coroner 'Told the jury a very queer story'. It seemed that the divisional surgeon who made the post-mortem examination spoke of the skill and precision in the way the killer had wielded his knife. He stated that there was overwhelming evidence to show that the killer had mutilated the body in such a way that he could possess himself of one or more of the victim's organs.

When the coroner spoke of his 'very queer story', he went on to say that he had been told by the sub-curator of the pathological museum connected with one of the great medical schools that, a few months earlier, an American had called upon him and asked him to supply him with a number of organ specimens. The American apparently stated that he was willing to pay $100 for each specimen.

The strange American was told in no uncertain terms that his request was impossible to fulfil. Undeterred by this, the American went on to repeat his request at another similar institution in London, where once again he was turned down. In summing up these strange requests, the coroner went on to say:

> Is it not possible that a knowledge of this demand may have inspired some abandoned wretch to possess himself of such specimens? It seems beyond belief that such inhuman wickedness could enter into the mind of any man; but, unfortunately, our criminal annals prove that every crime is possible!

When Abberline made the statement in the 1903 *Pall Mall Gazette*, he also elaborated on his thoughts regarding Severin Klosowski:

I have been so struck with the remarkable coincidences in the two series of murders that I have not been able to think of anything else for several days past – not, in fact, since the Attorney-General made his opening statement at the recent trial, and traced the antecedents of Chapman before he came to this country in 1888. Since then the idea has taken full possession of me, and everything fits in and dovetails so well that I cannot help feeling that this is the man we struggled so hard to capture fifteen years ago.

As I say, there are a score of things which make one believe that Chapman is the man; and you must understand that we have never believed all those stories about Jack the Ripper being dead, or that he was a lunatic, or anything of that kind. For instance, the date of the arrival in England coincides with the beginning of the series of murders in Whitechapel; there is a coincidence also in the fact that the murders ceased in London when Chapman went to America, while similar murders began to be perpetrated in America after he landed there. The fact that he studied medicine and surgery in Russia before he came over here is well established, and it is curious to note that the first series of murders was the work of an expert surgeon, while the recent poisoning cases were proved to be done by a man with more than an elementary knowledge of medicine. The story told by Chapman's wife of the attempt to murder her with a long knife while in America is not to be ignored.

When Frederick George Abberline wrote his memoirs, in the early 1920s, he was totally silent on the subject. However, Abberline was not the only person involved in the Ripper case to voice his opinion or non-opinion, as the case might be, as to the identity of the Ripper.

SIR ROBERT ANDERSON

Sir Robert Anderson had replaced James Monro as the Assistant Commissioner of the CID in August 1888.

Anderson was born in Dublin, Ireland, in 1841. He received a BA from Trinity College Dublin in 1862, and in 1863 was called to the Bar. In 1876 he was brought over to London as part of an intelligence branch to combat Fenianism. The branch was soon closed but Anderson remained in London as a Home Office 'Advisor in matters relating to political crime'. He was also the controller for the spy Thomas Miller Beach, who had penetrated the Fenian movement. In 1886, however, he was relieved of all duties, with the exception of controlling Thomas Beach, after becoming embroiled in a political argument with the Home Secretary Hugh Childers.

As well as being the Assistant Commissioner of the CID, he was also made secretary of the Prison Commissioners in 1887–88. With such a high position in public life and such obviously close connections to what was going on within police circles, Anderson's views, especially on the subject of the Ripper, were particularly sought after. After he retired in 1901, he set about writing his memoirs, entitled, *The Lighter Side of My Official Life*, which were published in 1910. In this book he stated: 'In saying that he was a Polish Jew I am merely stating a definitely ascertained fact.'

His certainty of this statement is reinforced in the *Police Encyclopaedia* (1920), which he wrote the introduction to, saying: 'There was no doubt whatever as to the identity of the criminal.' Anderson is not just saying that he suspected somebody, but that the identity of the killer was known to the police and the investigating team.

SIR CHARLES WARREN

Born in Bangor, North Wales, in 1840, Sir Charles Warren was educated at Cheltenham, and commissioned into the Royal Engineers in 1857. Upon the outbreak of the Kaffir War, he was appointed to command the Diamond Fields Horse Regiment, and was promoted to lieutenant colonel. He went from strength to strength, reaching the position of major general and then colonel.

In 1885 Colonel Sir Charles Warren was appointed to the post of Commissioner of the Metropolitan Police, upon the resignation of Sir E. Henderson. He had, during his three years of rule, many very difficult and complicated problems to solve, among which were the suppression of the Trafalgar Square riots (when troops sent in by Warren to clear the square opened fire on the rioters) and, of course, the Jack the Ripper case.

Warren's biggest difficulty with the Jack the Ripper case was that he was probably unfairly blamed for the failure to track down the killer. He also faced press accusations that were frequently baseless. He was accused of failing to offer a reward for information, although in fact he supported the idea but it was blocked by the Home Office. He was also accused of not putting enough police officers on the ground, whereas in fact Whitechapel was swamped with them.

It was said that he cared more about uniformed policing than detective work, which simply wasn't true, because the course that he did take was to allow his experienced detective officers to conduct their own affairs and he rarely interfered in their operations.

He was quite rightly very angry with these unfounded accusations about him, and responded by writing an article in *Murray's Magazine*, in which he stated that he supported vigilante activity, which the police on the streets didn't agree with at all. He also complained in public about the lack of control he was allowed over the CID. The Home Office was not very pleased at all about his remarks, and officially reprimanded him for discussing his office publicly without permission.

On 9 November 1888, Warren had had enough and resigned. Later that same night, Mary Jane Kelly was found murdered in her room in Spitalfields. Earlier on in the investigations, he had given an order that if another murder occurred nobody was to enter the scene until he arrived to direct the investigation. The police did not enter the murder scene for over three hours because, unaware of his resignation, they were waiting for Warren to arrive.

During the period of his career in the police force, Sir Charles Warren did not profess to have knowledge or private thoughts on the identity of the Ripper. After his resignation, Warren returned to military duties. He died in 1927 at the age of 87.

JOHN GEORGE LITTLECHILD

Born in Royston, Hertfordshire, on 21 December 1847, John George Littlechild joined the Metropolitan Police in 1867. In 1871 he was transferred to Scotland Yard, where later that same year he was promoted to sergeant.

In the next few years he worked on, and solved, several important cases, including the turf fraud scandal and a number of high-profile murder cases. In 1878 he was again promoted, this time to inspector.

In 1882 he was promoted to chief inspector and was involved in the investigation into the Phoenix Park murders. The following year he was made head of the Special Irish Branch. After a further eleven years of hard work, he eventually retired in 1893, possibly due to ill health, but he still continued to work as a private investigator.

On 23 September 1913, he wrote a letter to a journalist, Mr G.R. Sims, in which he named Francis Tumblety as a strong suspect for the Ripper. This was somewhat strange, in the fact that Littlechild had never worked on the Ripper case.

In the letter, Littlechild states that he had never heard of a Dr Druitt, but he goes on to say that Dr Tumblety was to his mind a very likely suspect. He also says that Sir Robert Anderson famously stated that he only thought he knew who the killer was, which undermines the certainty with which Anderson had written his version of events in the first place. Littlechild then seems to undermine himself, as he does not say that Tumblety was the Ripper, only that he could have been. The very words 'could have been' might apply to almost anyone, but he says his views were based on events at the time of the murders and not hindsight, which he claimed were what Abberline's views were based upon. Nobody was looking for Severin Klosowski in 1888, says Littlechild, because Klosowski had not done anything.

MELVILLE LESLIE MACNAGHTEN

Born in 1853, Melville Leslie Macnaghten was the son of the last chairman of the East India Company. He was educated at Eton, and by 1887 had become overseer of the family tea plantations in India.

In 1881 he met James Monro, who was district judge and inspector general of police in Bengal at the time. The two men became good friends. When he returned to England in 1887 he was offered the job of assistant chief constable in the Metropolitan Police by his good friend James Monro. When Commissioner Warren discovered the two men's connections, however, he blocked the appointment, thus causing a rift between Warren and Macnaghten, which lasted for years. Two years later, however, he was appointed assistant chief constable in the CID, and from there promoted to chief constable in the CID the following year.

In 1914, after he had retired, he published his memoirs, *Days of My Years*, in which he devoted a whole chapter to the Ripper murders, and implied that the identity of the killer was known. The description in the chapter points to Druitt. Many years later, Macnaghten's daughter, Lady Christabel Aberconway, made a transcript of the notes that he used to dictate his report to his elder daughter, and in 1959 she showed it to the author Daniel Farson. He later used much of this information in his book about the Ripper.

In Aberconway's version, Macnaghten wrote that he had always held strong opinions regarding Druitt. 'The more I think the matter over,' wrote Macnaghten, 'the stronger do these opinions become.'

In *Days of My Years*, Macnaghten confirmed his suspicions of Druitt, when he wrote, 'Although the Whitechapel murderer, in all probability put an end to himself soon after the Dorset Street affair in November 1888, certain facts, pointing to this conclusion, were not in the possession of the police till some years after I became a detective officer'.

Although Macnaghten did not join the Metropolitan Police until June 1889, he had worked with Monro, Anderson and Swanson and so was very well informed about the case. He was also adamant about the number of victims, stating: 'The Whitechapel murderer had 5 victims, and 5 victims only.'

JAMES MONRO

Born in Scotland in 1838, James Monro spent nearly thirty years in India, where he joined the legal branch of the Indian Civil Service and met Melville Leslie Macnaghten. In 1884, Monro resigned from the Indian Civil Service and returned to Britain, where he was appointed as the first Assistant Commissioner of Crime in London. He succeeded Howard Vincent, whose title had been Director of Criminal Investigation, as head of the Criminal Investigation Department (CID). He resigned as Assistant Commissioner Metropolitan Police (CID) after a breakdown of relationship with Commissioner Warren. The actual date of his resignation was 31 August 1888, which was the day Polly Nichols was murdered, and also the date that Abberline was brought in. Monro resigned and returned to India in 1890 after further arguments. He died in England in 1920 without publishing any memoirs.

When Monro was interviewed in *Cassells Magazine* he said that he had 'Decidedly formed a theory and when I do theorise it is from a practical standpoint and not upon any visionary foundation'. He failed, however, to say exactly who the choice of the subject was in his so-called theory. After his retirement, he was also reported to have said, 'Jack the Ripper should have been caught'. Most people will agree with that statement, but Monro sounded like he was saying more than that. As he worked with all the major players involved in the case, was he then saying that someone, perhaps everyone, knew the identity of the Ripper?

INSPECTOR EDMUND REID

Born in 1846, Edmund Reid joined the Metropolitan Police in 1872 and was transferred to the CID in 1874. He was promoted to sergeant in 1878 and to detective inspector at Scotland Yard in 1884.

Reid was a hard-working and diligent police officer who impressed his superiors. In 1886 he organised J Division, Bethnal Green CID, and was transferred to Whitechapel in 1888, the year the Ripper murders began, as local inspector, head of CID, H Division.

Reid retired in 1896 and gave a number of press interviews. He also wrote about the Ripper in an article he sent to the *Morning Star* in 1903. He held out his beliefs that there were nine Ripper murders, not five as the official line proclaimed. Reid declared that Frances Coles, who was murdered on 13 February 1891, was the last, and that there was no more after her because the killer was himself then dead, although he never published his thoughts as to how or where the Ripper died.

In 1912, Reid published yet more of his reminiscences on the case in *Lloyd's Weekly News*. He said that, 'It still amuses me to read the writings of such men as Dr Anderson, Dr Forbes Winslow, Major Arthur Griffiths, and many others, all holding different theories, but all of them wrong'. Once again Reid was quick to condemn others' theories as wrong, without ever bothering to say why and, if they were wrong, what he considered to be right.

Reid didn't seem to have a particular name in mind when speaking about his opinions on the Ripper. He believed the Ripper to be a man who was in the habit of using a certain public house where prostitutes gathered. The man would probably need to get drunk before plucking up the courage to talk to one of these women and eventually leave with her. According to Reid's theory, the man would then take her to some dark street or alley, where, under the influence of drink, he would go about the ghastly business of murdering her and ripping her up. Having satisfied his maniacal blood lust, he would go away home, and the next day would presumably know nothing about it. Reid's suspect, then, was not an individual, but a theory of the type of person the Ripper was.

SIR HENRY SMITH

Born in 1835, Sir Henry Smith was educated at Edinburgh Academy and Edinburgh University. In 1869 he was commissioned in Suffolk Artillery Militia, and in 1885 he was appointed chief superintendent for City of London Police.

He became Commissioner of City of London Police from 1890 to 1901, and was knighted in 1910. He also published his memoirs, *From Constable to Commissioner*, in that same year. He died in 1920.

In his memoirs Smith admitted that Jack the Ripper had beaten him, as well as every other police officer in London. He claimed to have known more about the Ripper's crimes than anybody else, but as to the identity of the killer, he said he had no more idea about who he was or where he lived than he had twenty years earlier.

At one time, during the Ripper murders, Smith thought he was very close to catching the murderer. This was on the night of the Catherine Eddowes murder, but in reality the Ripper must have long escaped from the immediate scene. If Smith's claim has any element of truth in it, then surely he would have had some idea of who it was that he claimed he was close to catching.

Another contradiction to his statement of having absolutely no knowledge of who the Ripper might be comes a short while after the Eddowes murder, when he stated categorically that he did have a suspect. He then stated that his suspect had been a medical student, had been in a lunatic asylum and had spent a great deal of time with women of loose character. According to Smith, his 'lunatic' suspect also used to swindle these women by passing polished farthings off on them, making them out to be sovereigns.

Smith said that he even sent two men to a house in Rupert Street, Haymarket, after receiving a tip off that his suspect would be there. The suspect did indeed turn out to be there, but he had what Smith described as a perfect alibi, even though he also had a number of polished farthings in his possession. Not much can be gathered from the statements and writings of Smith; he seems to leap backwards and forwards, one minute saying that he had no idea whatsoever as to the Ripper's identity, and the next saying that he was hot on the trail of the killer. At one time he even attacked Sir Robert Anderson for saying that the ripper's identity was known and that he was a Jew.

DONALD SUTHERLAND SWANSON

Born in Thurso, Wick, Scotland, in 1848, Donald Sutherland Swanson joined the Metropolitan Police on 27 April 1868, and by November 1887 had achieved the rank of chief inspector, CID, Scotland Yard.

In 1896 he was promoted to superintendent, and was involved in a crackdown on male prostitution in 1897. He retired from the force in 1903 and died in 1924.

Swanson was a close friend of Robert Anderson. Melville Macnaghten called him a very capable officer. In the famous *Swanson Marginalia*, Swanson wrote that the suspect was sent to Stepney Workhouse and then to Colney Hatch Lunatic Asylum where he died shortly afterwards. Swanson does not say that Kosminski was the killer, only that he was the suspect Anderson was referring to. This shows that Kosminski was a serious suspect and not just a name that Macnaghten had plucked out of the air.

An article in the *Pall Mall Gazette*, dated 7 May 1895, stated that Mr Swanson believed the crimes to be the work of a man who was now dead. It did not name a specific person, but it could well refer to Kosminski, who Swanson said he thought was dead, but it could also refer to Druitt or many others.

POLICE SUPERINTENDENT THOMAS ARNOLD

Born at Weald in Essex on 7 April 1835, Thomas Arnold joined the Metropolitan Police's B Division (Chelsea) on 19 March 1855 and resigned again on 20 September that same year in order to fight in the Crimean War. On

29 September 1856, when the war had ended, he rejoined the police and was attached to K Division (West Ham). He served most of his career in London's East End. He was promoted to inspector on 14 March 1866, and transferred to B Division.

In 1887 Arnold was involved in the Lipski case. Israel Lipski was a Polish Jew, living in the East End of London. On 28 June 1887, police were summoned to 16 Batty Street, where a young woman named Miriam Angel had been murdered after being forced to consume nitric acid. She was six months pregnant at the time. Lipski was found underneath her bed, with acid burns inside his own mouth, and was subsequently arrested. Lipski protested his innocence, claiming that Schmuss and Rosenbloom (two employees of his) were responsible, but he was charged with murder, found guilty and hanged on 21 August 1887 in the yard of Newgate prison

By 1888 Arnold had been made police superintendent of H Division (Whitechapel) at the time of the Whitechapel murders in that district.

In an interview with the *Eastern Post* in February 1893, Arnold stated that not more than four of the Ripper murders were committed by the same person. The four he spoke of were the murders of Annie Chapman in Hanbury Street, Polly Nichols in Buck's Row, Elizabeth Stride in Berner Street and Mary Kelly in Mitre Square. There seemed to be some confusion between Eddowes and Kelly, as he had earlier said that he did not believe the murder of Kelly had been committed by the same person.

WALTER DEW

Born in 1863, Walter Dew joined the Metropolitan Police in 1882 and was posted to X Division (Paddington Green). He was transferred to H Division (Whitechapel) in 1887.

In 1906 he was promoted to chief inspector, and in 1910 he arrested Dr Crippen, after which he resigned from the force and set up as a confidential agent. In 1938 he published his memoirs, *I Caught Crippen*. Dew died in 1947.

In his book, Dew described the sight of Mary Kelly's body in her room as 'The most gruesome memory of the whole of my Police career'. In the same book, he set out that he was of the opinion that Emma Smith was the first victim of Jack the Ripper and 'Someone, somewhere shared Jack the Ripper's guilty secret'. He also dismissed the idea that the Ripper displayed some sort of medical skill.

LEWIS HENRY KEATON

Lewis Henry Keaton was born in 1870, and joined the Metropolitan Police in August 1891. He eventually retired from the force in 1917, having achieved the rank of inspector.

Before he died, aged 100 in 1970, ex-Inspector Lewis Henry Keaton gave a recorded interview, in 1969, in which he proposed the theory that the Ripper was a doctor who was collecting specimens of wombs infected with venereal disease and that he used strychnine. It has been said that he could have been confusing the Ripper with Doctor Thomas Neil Cream, who was a Scottish-born serial killer, also known as the Lambeth Poisoner. We must not forget that Keaton was very old at the time of this interview, and his mind might have been somewhat muddled.

He did try to name the doctor who he claimed was the Ripper, but just as he was about to name his suspect as either Dr Cohn or Koch, or someone else whose name he could not recall, the interviewer spoke over him and drowned out Keaton's words.

Keaton did not, in fact, join the police force until 1891, which was three years after the Ripper murders had ceased, so therefore he had no first-hand knowledge of the Ripper case.

BENJAMIN LEESON

Leeson did not join the police until October 1890 and was not posted to Whitechapel until 1891. This means that he was not a police officer at the time of the Ripper murders, but it does not mean that he knew nothing of them. The best historians and archaeologists in the world were not around when their particular subject was actually being lived out, but they are nevertheless experts on their chosen subjects.

In Leeson's memoirs were *Lost London*, which were published in 1934, Leeson wrote, 'Amongst the police who were most concerned in the case there was a general feeling that a certain doctor, known to me, could have thrown quite a lot of light on the subject.' Some authors have questioned Leeson's reliability, saying that he was often wrong about events revolving around the siege of Sidney Street, even though he was very much involved in them. In spite of his lack of first-hand knowledge into the case, both Leeson's and Keaton's views may reflect a widespread belief amongst the lower ranks of the police that the Ripper was a doctor.

ROBERT SAGAR

Born in 1852, and died in 1924, Robert Sagar became a City of London CID officer, later promoted to inspector. According to the press reports of his retirement, Robert Sagar also represented the City of London Police at Leman Street police station in nightly meetings with the Metropolitan Police during the period of the Whitechapel murders.

Sagar prided himself in his ability to disguise himself and track down suspects. So effectual was his disguise, that on one particular night, when he donned the disguise of a labourer in order to follow a Ripper suspect in Butchers' Row, Aldgate, he was actually tracked himself by two police officers, who thought they had reason to regard him as a suspicious character.

Regarding the murders and the identity of the killer, several of Sagar's opinions are quoted in the reports of his retirement. One such report stated: 'We had good reason to suspect a man who worked in Butchers' Row, Aldgate. There was no doubt that this man was insane, and after a time his friends thought it advisable to have him removed to a private asylum. After he was removed there were no more Ripper atrocities.' This is especially interesting as it sounds very similar to what Swanson wrote about Kosminski. It is strange, however, that Henry Smith made no mention of this suspect since he also knew Sagar, and later wrote, 'A better or more intelligent officer than Robert Sagar I never had under my command'.

FREDERICK PORTER WENSLEY

Wensley joined the Metropolitan Police in January 1888, serving in H Division (Whitechapel), and was therefore directly involved in the investigation of the Ripper murders.

During the time Wensley was with the force, he rose in rank to eventually become chief constable of the CID. He published his memoirs, under the title *Detective Days*, in 1931. The title was later changed to *Forty Years of Scotland Yard*.

In *Detective Days* Wensley wrote, 'Only five, with a possible sixth, murders were officially attributed to Jack the Ripper.'

In the latter edition, *Forty Years of Scotland Yard*, Wensley seemed to play down his role in the investigation, writing in a somewhat light-hearted manner that the only discovery he was privy to was the invention of the rubber-soled boot, which was worn by patrolmen on their beat. From this light-hearted intervention, he then goes on to detail the Frances Coles murder, which happened on Friday 13 February 1891, almost two years after the official five victims were murdered. Was this, then, the sixth murder he spoke of earlier?

IN SUMMING UP THE POLICE AND THEIR SUSPECTS

We need to ask did the police, as a collective body, know who Jack the Ripper was? The above list of policemen and their views shows that they did not have one equally shared view regarding the identity of the Ripper. There is even disagreement among them as to the number of victims, with estimates ranging from four to nine. One thing that they do seem to have in common is that the murderer was dead or in an asylum. If we consider, however, that the majority of their summing up happened quite some time after the events occurred, it doesn't take too much intellectual consideration to assess that the killer would have almost certainly been either dead or in an asylum by this time. In fact, it would have been quite an obvious conclusion.

Henry Smith openly admitted that he didn't have a clue as to who the murderer was. Donald Sutherland Swanson seemed to play a middle-of-the-road card, by not actually saying if he thought Kosminski was guilty or not, only that he was the suspect Sir Robert Anderson was writing about. Melville Leslie Macnaghten professes not to know one way or the other, as does John George Littlechild.

Sir Robert Anderson was the only officer involved in the Ripper case to state that the Ripper's identity was known beyond any doubt. Every other officer talks of 'a very likely suspect' or 'someone they had good reason to suspect'. None of them claim, like Anderson did, that the killer's identity was definitely known.

Donald Sutherland Swanson was almost certainly correct in his assumption that Anderson was writing about Kosminski. Macnaghten mentioned Kosminski along with two other suspects, Ostrog and Druitt. Robert Sagar wrote about somebody with a name that sounded very much like Kosminski.

Inspector Abberline, of course, named one suspect and one only, and that was Severin Klosowski (Chapman), whom he firmly believed to be the killer; but could Abberline, in naming Severin Klosowski, have been referring to the same person as Anderson and Sagar had also named? In other words, a suspect with the same sounding name, beginning with 'K' and ending in 'ski'.

It is very difficult to ascertain a general consensus of opinion among the police officers and their superiors of the day, as so many of their opinions were diverse in a number of areas. There does seem to be, however, one aspect of the case in which they all agreed upon, and that was a general belief that a Polish Jew was in all probability the killer. The general consensus was therefore that, according to the vast number of witness statements, their suspicions were based upon reasonable grounds.

There can be no denying that they were entitled to their suspicions, but as we all now know, these suspicions never accounted for a conviction in this case.

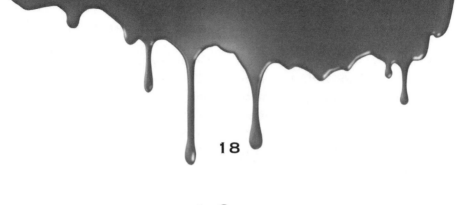

18

Victims

We know of the five women who were brutally murdered in what became known as the Jack the Ripper murders, but there were six other victims as well, who were also brutally murdered in the same manner, who even to this day some say were victims of the Ripper as well. This is a list of all eleven women, in chronological order, who were murdered during the period known as the Whitechapel murders.

EMMA SMITH

Prostitute Emma Elizabeth Smith was assaulted and robbed at the junction of Osborn Street and Brick Lane, Whitechapel, in the early hours of the morning on Tuesday 3 April 1888. She had been severely injured and possibly left for dead by her attackers, but she somehow managed to survive the attack and walk back to her lodging house at 18 George Street, Spitalfields. She told the deputy keeper, Mary Russell, that she had been attacked by three youngish men. Mrs Russell took Smith to the London Hospital, where medical examination revealed that a blunt object had been inserted into her vagina, rupturing her peritoneum. She developed peritonitis and her wounds were unfortunately too severe for her to survive, and she died four days later, having never regained consciousness.

The local inspector of the Metropolitan Police, Edmund Reid of H Division (Whitechapel), investigated the attack, but the culprits were never caught. Detective Constable Walter Dew, stationed with H Division, later wrote that he thought Smith was the first victim of Jack the Ripper, but his colleagues didn't agree with him, saying that it was the work of a criminal gang. Emma

Elizabeth Smith failed to describe her attackers; this was either because of her poor condition at the time or because she was scared of recriminations. There were known gangs around at the time, who lived off the earnings of the prostitutes, and this particular group could well have been one such gang, who had decided to punish Smith for maybe not paying them or disobeying them in some way. It is widely accepted that Smith's murder was unlikely to be connected with the Ripper killings.

MARTHA TABRAM

On Tuesday 7 August 1888, a second prostitute, Martha Tabram, was murdered at about 2.30 a.m. Her body was found in a stairwell at George Yard Buildings, George Yard, Whitechapel. She had been stabbed thirty-nine times with a short-bladed weapon. On the basis of statements from a fellow prostitute, and PC Thomas Barrett who was patrolling nearby, Inspector Reid put soldiers at the Tower of London and Wellington Barracks on an identification parade, but without positive results. The police did not connect the murder with Smith's, but they did connect her death with the later murders. Most experts today do not connect this murder with the other killings, as Tabram was stabbed whereas the later victims were slashed; but a connection cannot be ruled out.

The following five women have already been extensively covered in this book, and are recognised as victims of Jack the Ripper:

Mary Ann Nichols 31 August 1888

Annie Chapman 8 September 1888

Elizabeth Stride and **Catherine Eddowes** 30 September 1888

Mary Kelly 9 November 1888

The final four women on our list have never been accepted widely as Ripper victims. They are, nevertheless, still classed as victims of the Whitechapel murders.

ROSE MYLETT

The body of 29-year-old prostitute Rose Mylett (also known as Catherine Millett and Lizzie Davis) was discovered by a police officer on Thursday

20 December 1888, in Clarke's Yard, just off Poplar High Street, East London; she had been strangled.

Rose Mylett had lodged at 18 George Street, which was the same lodging house that Emma Smith, our first victim, had lodged in. A total of four doctors examined the body of Rose Mylett, and all agreed that she had been murdered. Sir Robert Anderson, on the other hand, thought she had accidentally hanged herself on the collar of her dress while in a drunken stupor. Anderson had no specific medical knowledge, as he was trained in law, so why his reasoning on this should have even been considered is beyond comprehension. Anderson requested another doctor, Dr Bond, to give his verdict on the case, which he did, agreeing with Anderson. Wynne Baxter, the coroner in the case, told the inquest jury: 'There is no evidence to show that death was the result of violence.' The jury nevertheless returned a verdict of 'wilful murder by some person or persons unknown' and the case was added to the Whitechapel file.

ALICE MCKENZIE

At around 12.40 a.m. on Wednesday 17 July 1889, Alice McKenzie was found murdered in Castle Alley, Whitechapel. Her left carotid artery was severed from left to right and there were wounds on her abdomen. It is not known for certain, but McKenzie was thought to be a prostitute, as all the Ripper victims had been.

Her injuries were very similar to those of the Ripper victims, apart from the fact that they were not as deep as in the earlier murders, and a shorter blade had been used. Police Commissioner James Monro was adamant that McKenzie was a victim of Jack the Ripper, as too was one of the pathologists who examined the body. Sir Robert Anderson disagreed with this, as did Inspector Abberline and another of the pathologists.

Throughout the years there has been much conjecture on this murder; some state that it was definitely a Ripper murder, and others say that the unknown murderer tried to make it look like a Ripper killing to deflect suspicion from himself. At the inquest, Coroner Wynne Edwin Baxter acknowledged both possibilities, and concluded: 'There is great similarity between this and the other class of cases, which have happened in this neighbourhood, and if the same person has not committed this crime, it is clearly an imitation of the other cases.'

PINCHIN STREET TORSO

At 5.15 a.m. on Tuesday 10 September 1889, the grisly remains of a woman's torso were discovered by PC William Pennett, under a railway arch in Pinchin Street, Whitechapel. PC Pennett was first alerted to a horrible stench that was emanating from what he thought was a package of some type, covered over with an old chemise. What he saw when he removed the covering made him reel back in horror, for the headless and legless body was already in an advanced state of decomposition.

An immediate search of the area was organised, but no other body parts were found, and neither the victim nor the culprit were ever identified. The pathologists noted that the general lack of blood of the tissues and vessels indicated that haemorrhage was the cause of death. Newspapers vied with each other to be the first to publish the victim's identity. The first name to be exposed was Lydia Hart, who had disappeared some days earlier. This was refuted, however, when she was found recovering in hospital after what she described as 'a bit of a spree'. Another claim that the victim was a missing girl called Emily Barker was also refuted, as the torso was from an older and considerably taller woman. The age of the victim was estimated to be between 30 and 40 years old.

Donald Sutherland Swanson did not consider this to be a Ripper case. He suggested it could possibly be linked to similar dismembered body cases in Rainham and Chelsea, as well as the 'Whitehall Mystery'. The case that became known as the Whitehall Mystery took place on 2 October 1888, during construction of Scotland Yard's new headquarters on the Victoria Embankment near Whitehall, Westminster. A worker found a parcel in part of the old cellar which contained a female torso. It had been placed there at some point between 29 September, when one of the workmen had last been inside the unlocked vault, and 2 October, when it was discovered. The body had been wrapped in cloth, possibly a black petticoat, and tied with string.

There was indeed much similarity in the two cases, and James Monro agreed with Swanson's assessment. These three murders and the Pinchin Street case were suggested by both men to be the work of a serial killer, nicknamed the 'Torso Killer', who was thought to be either Jack the Ripper himself or a separate killer of similar persuasions. Most Ripper experts today discount any connection between the Torso and Ripper killings on the basis of their different modus operandi.

FRANCES COLES

Friday the 13th has always been associated with bad luck in one way or another. In prostitute Frances Coles' case it was very bad luck indeed, for it was on this date in February 1891 that her body was found at Swallow Gardens, a passageway under a railway arch between Chamber Street and Royal Mint Street, Whitechapel.

Her body was found by PC Ernest Thompson only moments after the attack at 2.15 a.m. She had minor wounds on the back of her head, suggesting that she had been thrown violently to the ground before her throat was cut at least twice, from left to right and then back again. There were no mutilations to her body, but this could have been due to the fact that the killer was disturbed by PC Thompson before he could complete his work.

Superintendent Arnold and Inspector Reid arrived soon afterwards from Leman Street police station, which was very close to the murder scene. Chief Inspectors Donald Swanson and Henry Moore, who had been involved in the previous murder investigations, arrived by 5 a.m. Investigation into this case started immediately, and within hours the police had the name of a suspect who had been seen with Coles earlier that night. The man was James Sadler, who was tracked down and arrested by the police and charged with her murder.

Swanson and Moore proceeded with a high-profile investigation into Sadler's past history and his whereabouts at the time of the previous Whitechapel murders. After two weeks of non-stop intensive police work, on 3 March Sadler was released due to lack of evidence.

This was the last case in the series of murders which became known as the Whitechapel murders.

19

An Inspector Calls

*I*n February 1889 Inspector Abberline was called upon again, this time by the Dundee Police to investigate the case of William Henry Bury.

It seems that Bury had walked into the Dundee police station and claimed that his wife had been murdered by a burglar. When the police went to his basement flat, he showed them her body, which, according to Bury, had been placed in a trunk by the burglar, but not before she had been strangled and mutilated, with her abdomen sliced open and intestines removed.

The Dundee Police were naturally very suspicious and thought the crime was so similar to the Whitechapel murders that there was every possibility Bury might just be Jack the Ripper. They made a quick call to Scotland Yard and asked if they had any information on this man. Scotland Yard took their enquiry very seriously and immediately drafted Inspector Abberline onto the case. Abberline set forth for Dundee and interviewed Bury without delay. After listening to his side of the story for a very short while, Abberline came to the conclusion that Bury was what he described as 'demented'.

As Abberline delved deeper into Bury's background, facts started to appear, which reiterated his belief that Bury was demented, to say the least.

William Henry Bury was born on 25 May 1859 in Stourbridge, Worcestershire. He came from an ordinary working-class family, his father being a fishmonger. Bury had a normal schooling without any problems, and by the age of 14 went to work in a local horse butcher's shop. The wages and the small town way of life, however, didn't appeal to Bury, and he soon moved to a nearby town. It was, however, London that he had heard so much of and wanted to go to, so in November 1887, at the age of 28 he finally packed his bags and moved to Whitechapel, where he had been told his skills with a knife would pay him handsome dividends.

Whitechapel, however, wasn't quite the place he thought it would be, and most butcher's shops were run and staffed by either Jewish or Polish immigrants. Bury would have to bide his time before he could put his skills with the knife to good use.

It didn't take long for Bury's meagre savings to run out, and so when he was offered a job as a sawdust collector by a man named James Martin, whom he had met in a pub, Bury jumped at the chance, especially as Martin had also offered him a room in his house in Quickset Street.

What Martin had failed to tell Bury was that he also ran a brothel at his house, employing several prostitutes. When Bury found this out, far from fazing him, he quite liked the idea, and within a few weeks he had befriended Ellen Elliot, one of the prostitutes. As unlikely a liaison as it might have seemed, the couple were soon married and moved out of the brothel and into their own lodgings, courtesy of a small inheritance from Ellen's parents.

Ellen was happy for the first few weeks of her marriage, thinking that her squalid life was now behind her and she could settle into a new life of domestic bliss. This, however, was not to happen, for she soon found out that Bury was a drunkard and a thief. What little money she did have, Bury soon stole and used it on alcohol and prostitutes. In February 1888 Bury accosted 38-year-old Annie Millwood, in Spitalfields, and asked her to have sex with him, but when she asked him for money, which he didn't have, he suddenly became very violent and attacked her with a knife. Bury slashed at Annie Millwood's legs and genitals, and it was a miracle that she survived. By the time the police arrived on the scene, Bury had long gone, and it wasn't until much later that she identified him as the man that had attacked her that night.

A few weeks later, on 28 March, a penniless Bury went out looking for someone to rob. He had heard that Ada Wilson, an elderly seamstress who lived nearby, was supposed to have a hidden stash of money at her house. Bury forced his way into Ada Wilson's home, attacked her, and forced her to hand her money over to him. The money, however, was nothing like as much as he had expected, and in a mad rage he then stabbed her twice in the throat. Fortunately for her, as with his first victim, she survived and gave the police a good description of him.

Bury's wife, meanwhile, was going through quite a disturbing period, for not only was her husband staying out until the early hours of the morning, she had also heard that he was stealing and still going with prostitutes; if that wasn't bad enough, she then discovered that he was sleeping with a knife under his pillow. On the night of 7 April, he came home drunk as usual, and when she tried to remonstrate with him, he took the knife out of his pocket and attempted to cut her throat. Luckily for her, he was so drunk that she managed to fight him off.

Despite this attack on his wife, and the attacks on the other women, Bury still somehow managed to evade arrest. He was still having sex with prostitutes and had now contracted syphilis, which in turn he had passed on to his wife Ellen.

Whether it was the syphilis that was now affecting his mind, or whether it was his madness getting worse, he was becoming more violent and unpredictable by the day. On 20 December 1888, Bury approached Rose Mylett, who was yet another prostitute, and after being turned down by her – which he saw as a huge insult to him – he strangled her and left her body in Clarke's Yard.

Bury thought that someone had seen him commit this murder, and he was also aware that the police were looking for someone of his description in regard to the other attacks on prostitutes. He realised that he had to get as far away from London's East End as he could, before the police put two and two together and arrested him. He told his wife that he had been offered a job in Dundee, and had to move there immediately. For some reason, which seems incomprehensible, Ellen decided to go with him, even though she knew he was a liar and a thief, and had tried to slit her throat.

In January 1889, Bury and his wife travelled to Dundee on the London packet steamer *Cambria*. Just a couple of weeks later, on 5 February, Bury strangled Ellen in their basement flat in the city. He then mutilated her body, slicing open her abdomen and removing her intestines. He then placed her body in a trunk.

This is when Bury decided to go to the police and make up his preposterous story about the burglar breaking in and murdering his wife. This was also when the Dundee Police decided to call Inspector Abberline in.

Abberline was astounded by the facts that Bury related to him, and began to believe that he might indeed be the elusive Jack the Ripper. Abberline obviously had a better method of coaxing information out of suspects than the Dundee Police did, for not only had Bury admitted to attacking women in London, but he also changed his story regarding his wife and her death in Dundee.

Bury now changed his original story, which he had recounted to the police, and now told Abberline that he had awoken from a drunken stupor to find his wife had been strangled. On an inexplicable mad impulse he took a large knife and plunged it into her abdomen several times. He couldn't explain to Abberline why he had done it, but he said that he thought he might be suspected of being Jack the Ripper, so he put the body in a large box and kept it there for several days before going to the police with his invented story.

Bury's trial was short and, after listening to Abberline's evidence, the jury found Bury guilty of the murder of his wife, and on 24 April 1889 he was sentenced to death and hanged a few days later. Bury showed no contrition for his crimes. In perhaps the most feeble gallows speech on record, he eschewed the traditional plea for forgiveness or rant of defiant innocence, merely sneering at the hangman and saying, 'I suppose you think you are clever to hang me'.

In 1889 the *New York Times* cited William Henry Bury as the Whitechapel murderer, Jack the Ripper. Although two messages referring to Jack the Ripper were chalked on a door to Bury's house, it was presumed by both Abberline and Scotland Yard in general that Bury had put them there himself. The Metropolitan Police did not see Bury as a serious suspect, and the British press appeared to agree with them, and took little notice of the *New York Times*' opinion

In summing up the case for William Henry Bury being Jack the Ripper, there are certainly a great deal of similarities between his modus operandi and that of the Ripper. There was also the fact that he had lived briefly in the East End of London. The Ripper murders had started shortly after he arrived, possibly with the death of Martha Tabram, and they ended with the death of Mary Kelly shortly before Bury left for Scotland. Those are the main facts which link Bury's name to Jack the Ripper.

The facts against him being the Ripper are, firstly, that Inspector Abberline certainly didn't think he was, and neither did Scotland Yard. On the whole it seems rather unlikely that the killer who had so confounded the Metropolitan Police during the autumn of 1888 would have then committed such a ham-fisted crime as the Dundee murder only a few short months later.

As a postscript to the many and varied Ripper suspects that have been mentioned in this book, I did say that I was a little surprised that no one had, as yet, come up with the rather absurd theory that Inspector Abberline himself could be the Ripper.

Today, as I write this (November 2011), that absurdity has actually happened. An 84-year-old Spanish writer, Jose Luis Abad, has claimed in his book *Jack the Ripper: The Most Intelligent Murderer in History*, which has been published in Spain, that Inspector Abberline was the killer.

It seems that Jose Luis Abad is a handwriting expert and has compared Abberline's writing with that in the Ripper's diary, which surfaced in Liverpool in 1992. The diary was attributed to a Liverpool cotton dealer called James Maybrick, who many still believe to be the murderer, while other experts say the diary is a hoax. Jose Abad, however, is adamant that the diary is real, but he claims that the author was Abberline, and not Maybrick. Jose Abad says: 'I have no doubt Abberline was the Ripper. Handwriting does not lie.'

One can only wonder what the future will unearth regarding this latest accusation!

20

Retirement Beckons

With the Ripper case coming to an unsuccessful ending, and the investigation into a homosexual brothel in Cleveland Street, which became known as the Cleveland Street scandal, becoming politically sensitive, Abberline was starting to feel very low in regard to his career. It had been discovered that Queen Victoria's grandson, Prince Albert Victor, the second in line to the throne, was a frequent client at the Cleveland Street brothel, and in order to prevent a scandal the investigation was hushed up and the proprietor of the brothel allowed to leave the country.

There were suggestions that Abberline publicly voiced his misgivings about the way the cover-up was handled and that this may have upset his superiors. Whatever the truth, the Cleveland Street scandal was the last significant case Abberline investigated for the Metropolitan Police. Although still only 46 years old, Abberline began to feel the strain of police work that was seemingly going nowhere. His wife Emma, fearing for his health, began badgering him either to apply for a steady desk job or, failing that, to consider a change of career altogether, as he continued to work sometimes into the early hours of the morning. A significant part of Emma's wish came true, for Abberline was promoted to chief inspector at the Criminal Investigation Department at Scotland Yard, and given a desk job there.

Desk work, however, might have been what Emma wanted for her husband, but it certainly wasn't what he wished for. He was a man of the streets, and always had been. Maybe it was in deference to his wife's wishes that he stayed and endured the course for another two years, before announcing his retirement from the force in January 1892.

Abberline actually retired from the Metropolitan Police on 8 February 1892. He retired on a full pension, after twenty-nine years' service. During the course of his police career he had received eighty-four commendations and awards. He was 49 years old.

On Saturday 8 May 1892, the following article was published in *Cassell's Saturday Journal*:

There had lately retired from New Scotland Yard on a liberal pension, and much to the regret of his Chief, Dr. Anderson and his colleagues, a Chief Inspector of the Criminal Investigations Department, Mr. F.G. Abberline. No man in the Police Service now alive – except, perhaps Mr. Shore has a greater claim to speak of the changes, which have come about in the force of all departments. During the past thirty years Mr. Abberline has in his career had much experience in uniform and out of it, and his name has been prominently before the public with cases of more than ordinary interest. His all round success is certainly an instance of experience on the beat and at the station desk as a preliminary training to the detective who discharges his duties in civilian, or as the police call them 'plain clothes'. A man of such intimate acquaintance with the East End as Mr. Abberline naturally found himself recalled to the scene of his former labours when the series of Whitechapel Murders horrified all the world. His knowledge of crime and the people who commit it, is extensive and peculiar. There is no exaggeration in the statement that whenever a robbery or offence against the law has been committed in the district the detective knew where to find his man and, the missing property too. His friendly relations with the shady folk who crowd into the common lodging houses enable him to pursue his investigations connected with the murders with the greatest of certainty, and the facilities afforded him make it clear to his mind that the miscreant was not to be found lurking in a 'dossers' kitchen.

On 8 June 1892 Abberline was once again recalled by Scotland Yard. This time it was not to undertake more excruciating detective work, but to invite him to a retirement dinner and presentation on his behalf. The dinner was held at the Three Nuns Hotel on Aldgate High Street. This ceremony was so popular that a large public crowd stood outside the hotel during the ceremony, hoping, perhaps, to get a glimpse of the great detective. The Three Nuns Hotel is also significant because it featured in several incidents related to the Whitechapel murders. The ceremony created so much interest that the *East London Observer* carried an article entitled, 'Presentation To A Well-Known Detective'. The subheading read: 'Chief Inspector Abberline Retires from the Service and is the Recipient of a Presentation.'

Sitting at home and pruning the roses in his garden didn't exactly appeal to Abberline's temperament, and within a few months he was eagerly looking for fresh employment. He didn't have to wait too long, for none other than John George Littlechild, who Abberline knew from the Ripper case and now represented the Pinkerton Detective Agency in London, offered Abberline a job in Monte Carlo on behalf of Pinkerton's/Littlechild.

The casinos in Monte Carlo were experiencing something of a bad patch, with cheating and stealing on a huge scale. There was pressure from outside interests to close the casinos down, but Monte Carlo had some very rich and powerful friends, including Pope Leo XIII, who called for outside help in cleaning up the casinos' images.

The Pinkerton Agency was brought in with Abberline at the helm, who in turn hired a group of plain-clothed men to infiltrate the customers at the casinos. These men were experts in their field, and could spot card cheats and frauds a mile off. They also watched the staff and made arrests where necessary. Within the first year of Abberline arriving there, the casinos saved enormous amounts of money, which in today's terms would probably equal between £10 and £20 million a year.

The casinos' image was also suffering from over 2,000 suicides and murders during a three-year period. Abberline couldn't personally come up with a remedy to prevent this, but he did suggest an idea which the casinos took up. This was for them to hire a team of men who would be paid to help dispose of the bodies of the dead losers. The casinos took to this idea and corpses were taken to a secret morgue, where they were stored until a sufficient number were in place, and then a steamer would slip into a small harbour nearby and spirit them away to a secret location, where they would be weighted down and dumped at sea. It was estimated that more than 50 per cent of the deaths in Monte Carlo were never heard about by the general public, and that only the staff at the casinos knew the truth.

Although neither Abberline or Littlechild were personally involved in this operation, they did very well for themselves from cleaning up the casinos in general during their three seasons in Monte Carlo; and probably enjoyed vastly enhanced and comfortable retirements from their efforts there.

Abberline only enjoyed three terms in Monte Carlo, but he continued to work for Pinkerton's for twelve years, taking on various tasks, mostly in England, which earned him an even more considerable reputation than he already had from his years in the police force.

Frederick George Abberline retired again for the final time in 1904 at the age of 61, and bought a house with his wife at 195 Holdenhurst Road in the seaside town of Bournemouth, where he actually did tend the roses and the lawn. Retirement had finally caught up with the ex-chief inspector.

Frederick George Abberline died in his Bournemouth house on 10 December 1929, at the age of 86. He was buried in an unmarked grave at

Wimbourne cemetery, which was the same cemetery where the Ripper suspect Montague Druitt was buried. Abberline's wife survived him by one year.

Abberline is today commemorated by a blue plaque, which was unveiled on Saturday 29 September 2001, by John Grieve, the Deputy Assistant Commissioner of the Metropolitan Police. The plaque is on the house in Bournemouth where Abberline spent his final years. The plaque was unveiled in the presence of His Worship, the Mayor of Bournemouth.

Index